AN INTRODUCTION TO BUSINESS PLANNING

Reproduced by permission of Wight, Collins, Rutherford Scott Limited

AN INTRODUCTION TO BUSINESS PLANNING

Kevan Scholes
Director, Sheffield Business School

and

Mary Klemm
Senior Lecturer in Business Policy,
Sheffield Hallam University

First published 1987 by
MACMILLAN PRESS LTD
Houndmills, Basingstoke, Hampshire RG21 6XS
and London
Companies and representatives
throughout the world

ISBN 0–333–41435–7 hardcover
ISBN 0–333–41436–5 paperback

A catalogue record for this book is available
from the British Library.

This book is printed on paper suitable for recycling and
made from fully managed and sustained forest sources.

8   7   6
06 05 04 03 02 01 00

Printed in Great Britain by
Antony Rowe Ltd
Chippenham, Wiltshire.

To our students

Acknowledgements

The authors and publishers wish to thank the following who have kindly given permission for the use of copyright material: H. Igor Ansoff for material from *Corporate Strategy*, Penguin, 1968; The Free Press, a Division of Macmillan, Inc., for material from *Competitive Strategy: Techniques for Analyzing Industries and Competitors* by Michael E. Porter. Copyright © 1980 by The Free Press; Peter Jennings for material on Supergrip Tools; Peter H. Jones for material on Doman Synthetic Fibres; Lonrho for material from their annual report and for reproduction of their logo; *Management Today* for relevant material; Marks & Spencer plc for material used in Case Study 19; Midland Bank plc for material used in Case Study 29; Glyn Owen for material on Lord Rotherson's newspapers; Margareto Pagano for material on 'Next' written for the *Guardian*; Prentice-Hall International for material from *Exploring Corporate Strategy* by Johnson and Scholes; Radio Hallam for material reproduced in Chapter 7; Times Newspapers Ltd for an extract from 'How they sold their soul to St Michael' from *The Sunday Times*; Western Jean Company Ltd for relevant material; Wight Collins Rutherford Scott Ltd for the adapted Midland Bank 'Graph' advertisement.

Every effort has been made to trace all the copyright-holders, but if any have been inadvertently overlooked the publishers will be pleased to make the necessary arrangement at the first opportunity.

Contents

List of illustrations

List of figures

List of tables

Preface

At a course review meeting, one staff member reflecting on the performance of their students on the Business Planning Module remarked that the students could jump through all the hoops but didn't seem to know what the hoops were for! It is this experience and others related to us by colleagues in many institutions which have prompted us to write this book. The text is appropriate for introductory courses in business planning in a wide range of further and higher education programmes in business and management requiring a practical and vocational approach.

Like many of our colleagues we have struggled hard to design and run useful and interesting programmes on business planning for students many of whom have little experience of business and may feel that the early parts of their careers will give them little opportunity to be involved in business planning. This book has evolved from this practical experience of course design and operation linked to our own direct work with a wide variety of companies and public service organisations. We have tried to reflect the realities of business planning, with all its warts, whilst providing an approach with which students will feel comfortable and find interesting.

It is worth saying at the outset that we do *not* share the view that business planning skills are of too high a level to be of value to students in their first employment. However, we do feel that the style and content of business planning courses does need to be carefully considered to suit the personal and career needs of students. This book has been written to provide readers with:

- An *understanding* of how business planning is undertaken in a wide variety of work organisations from multinationals to small co-operatives in the public and private sectors.

- An *appreciation* of the different types of planning – for example, strategic and operational planning – and the way in which they relate to each other.
- The development of a variety of *skills* in a practical context. The student tasks are realistic problem solving and planning exercises ranging from planning a student disco to devising a production planning schedule for an engineering company. There is also an emphasis on presentation skills where exercises require students to adopt a role or to make an oral or written presentation for a specific audience. Some of the exercises are designed for group work and role-playing.
- An appreciation of the practical *difficulties* of implementing plans and how people within organisations can cope with these short-comings.

Unlike some other books on business planning this is *not* a book about decision-making techniques, managerial economics or corporate strategy although clearly each of these has a place *within* the book. Equally the book does not attempt to provide a précis of planning in each of the functions of a business organisation (finance, marketing, etc.). Instead we have chosen to develop readers' understanding and skills in business planning in the following way:

- By structuring the book around the **major planning tasks** which organisations need to undertake. We hope that this will reinforce the integrative purpose of the book since each major theme includes discussion and examples from the different functional areas of an organisation (for example, scheduling is a planning task found in all parts of an organisation to help plan a variety of specific tasks.)
- By recognising that most business planning students will have **parallel** or **preceding** studies concerned with the major business functions. This book tries to link with/build on those studies rather than attempting to repeat them.
- By emphasising the key **business themes** of people, money, numeracy, communication and technology. All of these are critically important ingredients of business planning and the book is designed to make readers familiar with their role within planning.

It is important that both students and teachers are aware of how the book has been styled to help fulfil the aims outlined above. This is not an academic book in the traditional sense – it has been deliberately designed to help readers learn from examples and through their own work. It should become apparent to readers that the following are important to this process:

- There are **exercises** relating to each of the major sections of the chapters. Whereas the text can be read without undertaking these exercises we would encourage readers to do as many exercises as possible. They have been designed to consolidate the learning in that section and to develop communication and presentation skills. They should be useful to set as student assignments.
- Many of the exercises are related to the fifty or so **illustrations** which allow readers to think about the planning problems in a real context and to undertake tasks as though they were working in that organisation.
- Each chapter is concluded by a list of **key readings**. These are designed for those readers who would like to know more about particular aspects of planning discussed in the chapter.

One of the problems of textbook authors is choosing words to describe various aspects of the subject without slipping into too much jargon, being unduly verbose, or boringly repetitive. We have tried to write this book in an easy and interesting style and as a result have needed to take some licence in the use of particular words. For example, we have tended to use the words 'organisation', 'company', 'firm' as largely interchangeable and to refer to work organisations of all types, large and small, and both public and private sector. We know that strictly speaking this is bad practice but we hope it makes the book more readable and that we are forgiven for that reason!

We have already mentioned that the book is structured around the **major planning tasks** of organisations. A few more words about this might be useful. Following the opening chapter readers are introduced to the way in which business planning is organised in different organisations as a useful background against which later discussions and exercises can be put. Chapters 3 to 6 form the core of the book addressing the major planning tasks of **thinking ahead**, **making decisions**, **completing jobs on time**, and implementing plans respectively. Given our emphasis on integration the final chapter is devoted to a case study of one organisation (Radio Hallam) and how it deals with all the aspects of business planning discussed in previous chapters. We hope that readers will find this a good way of consolidating their learning.

Although books are written by authors they are very dependent on the help and goodwill of many people and we would wish to acknowledge them here. First, our colleagues at Sheffield City Polytechnic – in particular Bill Richardson, Peter Jennings, Liz Rick, Rod Apps and

Maurice Brown – who have helped with comments, ideas and some examples. More importantly they have used our earlier drafts in their teaching and reported on the shortcomings. Second, the BTEC students at Sheffield, particularly the 1985–6 groups who were guinea-pigs with much of the text and exercises and who have proved invaluable in the redrafting and improvement of both of these. Thanks are also due to those colleagues who have given permission to use material for illustrations and they are acknowledged separately in each case.

We are particularly indebted to Bill MacDonald and the staff at Radio Hallam for their help and support in preparing Chapter 7. We appreciate their willingness to speak frankly about business planning within their organisation and the time they have given in ensuring the accuracy and quality of text in that chapter.

A special thank you to Jenny Scholes who has undertaken the preparation of the manuscript (with its endless changes!) whilst learning the blessings (and shortcomings) of a word-processing, spreadsheet and database system. At least we have attempted to practice what we preach.

We hope you enjoy the book and find it useful – we would love to hear any comments you may have for improvements.

KEVAN SCHOLES
MARY KLEMM

January 1987

CHAPTER 1

Introduction

In early 1985 the UK home computer market looked a good deal less rosy than the heady days of the previous two years when companies such as Sinclair, Commodore, and Acorn had seen their sales grow at a phenomenal rate. For Acorn in particular, this period following disappointing sales at Christmas 1984 was to prove a most difficult time for the company. Planning the establishment and growth of Acorn had been no mean task but in many ways Chris Curry and Hermann Hauser, the founders of Acorn, faced many more planning problems in 1985 than they had done before.

Illustration 1.1 details many of the problems which the company faced. Not only were there doubts about the adequacy of the company's product range – in particular the over-reliance on the BBC microcomputer but new competition, in the shape of Apple, was threatened. The internal strains of this situation were also showing, financial restructuring of the company was urgently needed, the founders were apparently feeling the stress, and there were major worries about high stocks of unsold computers.

All these factors had shaken the City's confidence in Acorn (and home computers generally) forcing the company to think about possible diversification. Through this crisis, however, they were able to protect their major asset, namely their people, in the hope that they would ride out the storm. Eventually the company's position was rescued by Olivetti, the Italian computer and office-equipment manufacturers who bought 49 per cent of the shares in the company at the end of January 1985.

Fortunately, business life does not proceed like this all the time – the particular circumstances of the home-computer market at the time led to high levels of uncertainty and change for all those involved in the industry. Nevertheless the example acts as a sharp reminder that a key feature of business organisations is that their circumstances *do* change

ILLUSTRATION 1.1   Acorn Computers: need for planning

In February 1985 one of the UK's most successful computer companies, Acorn Computers, announced a sales loss of £11m on its BBC micro- and Electron computers for the previous half year. Its shares had already been suspended on the Stock Exchange. Acorn's dynamic co-founders, Chris Curry and Herman Hauser, were desperately looking for financial backing to save the company and resist a possible take-over by Thorn EMI.

Why had things gone wrong? Acorn had many of the ingredients of a successful business: a good product, a secure foothold in the expanding market for educational computers and software (it claimed that 74 per cent of British schools had a BBC microcomputer), a dynamic and innovative management team who still owned 85 per cent of the business and had a reputation as tough negotiators. In the words of Bob Gilkes of Cambridge Venture Management:

> When a company is controlled by two people it makes it very difficult for other managers to make their opinions felt. Acorn needs to put together a **business plan** emphasising the future rather than the past, with a new management team and future product range.

Some of Acorn's problems could have been avoided by planning ahead. For example, the launch of the Electron computer in 1983 failed because the company was unable to get stocks of the Electron into the shops for Christmas. By the time the computers were available in large quantities, increased competition had forced the price down and by 1985 there were £30m worth of unsold stocks. Ruthless pricing policies by Apple, one of Acorn's major rivals, had forced Acorn out of the US market, and there were unsuccessful ventures into the educational computer market in Ireland and West Germany. Another of Acorn's problems was that it was a one product company in an industry where the life cycle of the product was becoming shorter and shorter. By the time Acorn realised the need to diversify, the share price had fallen so that it was impossible to raise the money needed to do so.

At the end of February 1985 Olivetti, the Italian-based multinational business systems and computer company, negotiated a merger with Acorn. Under the terms of the agreement Acorn was to be split into four divisions covering its activities in the consumer, business, education and scientific markets. Each division was to operate as an individual profit centre. The company was to pull out of the lower end of the home computer markets and Curry and Hauser, though they lost control of the company, remained as deputy chairmen in charge of product development.

and that a failure to recognise that fact is likely to lead organisations into significant difficulties. Ironically it is often successful companies who fail to take adequate steps to secure their future. It is quite sobering to reflect on how rapidly a company's fortunes can change. Only 10 per cent of the *Management Today* top fifty companies for 1970 (in terms of annual growth) appeared in the same list in 1985.

Clearly the reasons for the rise or decline of organisations during this, (or any other) period are many and varied. The relative economic performance of the UK and her major trading partners, the rise of new competition, the run-down of a company's equipment, failure to train and develop people or the advent of new technologies may all play a part. However, whatever the detailed reasons the **business planning efforts** within organisations must be regarded as being central to the performance of companies. This book is concerned with introducing readers to the many different business-planning activities which typically occur within organisations. It is hoped that the discussions and examples in the text will allow readers to:

- Understand the extent to which business planning helps to maintain an organisation's **performance** at a satisfactory level as circumstances within and around the organisation change.
- Appreciate the **variety** of planning tasks which are undertaken within organisations.
- Understand **how** business planning is carried out in a variety of different types of organisation.
- Use planning techniques as a means of addressing a selection of planning problems identified in the text.

In order to prepare readers for a more detailed discussion of these issues this opening chapter is devoted to introducing business planning and explaining the scope and variety of business planning activities within companies. Specifically the following issues will be discussed:

- What is planning?
- Different 'levels' of planning in companies.
- Different approaches to planning.

1.1 What is business planning?

A **plan** has been defined as 'an indication of the times, places, etc. of intended proceeding, etc.' **or** 'a way of proceeding' **or** 'arrangements beforehand' **or** 'an attempt to decide how best to respond to change'.

Although such broad definitions are of little practical value to a detailed discussion of business planning they do provide a useful starting-point. In particular they identify two key features of planning which will receive considerable discussion in this book, namely:

1. **Plans** are prepared **before actions** are undertaken, and serve to indicate what those actions should be. For example, one of the worries for Acorn (as shown in Illustration 1.1) was the **intention** of Apple to gain 25 per cent of the schools market during the first part of 1985. At the time this threat had not arrived and yet Acorn already needed to lay plans on how to counter such an attack.
2. Plans must incorporate a **variety** of different factors as can be seen at Acorn:

   (a) It was necessary to plan **how** the company's resources should be used – for example, too much money was being tied up in stock of Electron computers.
   (b) Planning **when** various tasks should be carried out – for example, the need to launch new products before others made too much impact in the market.
   (c) Planning **who** would be responsible for the various tasks needed to make the plans successful – for example, whether the selling job would be undertaken by Acorn's salesforce or through distributors.

These issues will be discussed more fully later in the chapter.

It has been shown in the preceding discussions that **changing circumstances** are perhaps the main reason why business planning is so important to companies. However, this should not be taken to mean that planning has no place in organisations which are changing only slowly. Planning is also an important means of ensuring the **efficient operation** of an organisation's activities on a day-to-day basis. Many business-planning activities such as stock control, credit control, planning sales calls, etc., are essential to an organisation's success irrespective of the rate of change which is occurring around the company.

It is also important to establish that planning is not normally a discrete and separate activity within organisations. Nor is planning usually the province of planning 'experts' – more commonly planning is undertaken by a large number of people throughout an organisation. For example, the production departments will be planning how and when the various orders are to be completed, the personnel function may be planning recruitment, training or redundancy; the marketing team may be planning their next advertising campaign whilst the financial function will be planning how to pay for all of these things!

There are obvious dangers if business planning is too fragmented – namely, these various functional plans (production, personnel, etc.) may be inconsistent with each other. For example, Acorn's decision to diversify into business machines was unlikely to prove successful unless the appropriate marketing skills and support services could be properly planned and executed by the company. Hence, business planning must be seen as something more than the collection of planning activities within the separate business functions, important as these are. The way in which planning is organised within companies will be discussed more fully in Chapter 2.

It should be noted that the discussions in this book about business planning are not intended to conjure up the idea of 'glossy booklets' entitled 'Company Plans 1987–1990'. Whether plans are held in people's heads, committed to paper, or even stored as complex models on a computer is to some extent incidental to understanding the need for planning. The form in which plans exist within companies will be dictated by the type of organisation and the extent to which plans need to be **communicated** between various individuals or different parts of the organisation. So, for example, it would be inappropriate for a small family company to prepare its plans in the same way as might Esso, or British Telecom or Birmingham City Council. However, all these organisations are engaged in business planning in many different ways and the discussions in this book are of relevance to *all* of them irrespective of whether they have 'glossy books' or not.

Finally, it should be appreciated that 'business planning' as described in this book is equally relevant to non-business organisations, such as public services or voluntary organisations. Although the objectives of these organisations are often different from a typical business organisation the planning problems are largely similar. So, for example, the Recreation Department in a major city has to plan and organise a wide variety of amenities – from parkland to sports centres. Equally, they need to plan and budget, recruit and train people, and deal with large

TABLE 1.1   Some important features of planning

1. Plans must **precede** actions – they are a statement of what future actions should be taken
2. Plans must cover many **different** aspects such as what should be done, when and by whom
3. Plans are necessary to **maintain** company **performance** as circumstances change. They are also needed to maintain the efficient operation of a company's day-to-day activities
4. Planning is normally to be found **throughout** an organisation
5. Plans may take **various forms** – they need not be 'glossy books'

numbers of 'customers' in just the same way that business organisations do. Throughout this book 'business planning' will be taken to include planning in non-business organisations and there will be many examples from that sector. Table 1.1 summarises some of the main features of planning discussed in this section.

1.2 Different levels of planning

Already it should be clear to readers that the word 'planning' is used to encompass a wide variety of activities within an organisation. In order to gain a clearer understanding of the various types of business planning it is helpful to identify different levels of planning which typically occur within organisations. Figure 1.1 shows these levels of planning. Although the boundaries between levels are often blurred, the distinctions are useful:

- *Strategic planning* is concerned with the broader issues about an organisation's future and the way in which the organisation will cope with change. For example:

  — the company size
  — the range of products/services
  — which markets to serve
  — the financial structure of the company
  — how best to exploit the special skills of employees
  — the types of production technology

- *Management planning* centres on the need to make strategy work in practice. It is often concerned with the reallocation and rescheduling of resources in order to facilitate company strategy. For example, a company which had chosen to diversify would need to

FIGURE 1.1   Three levels of business planning

plan how to develop new business through building up contacts with new outlets, rearranging the sales-force, training, organising new production and delivery procedures, changing quality controls, etc.

● *Operational planning* is the most detailed level of planning within organisations. It focuses mainly on the smooth running of the day-to-day activities of the organisation. Operational plans will be needed in all functions of the organisation. For example, jobs need to be planned for the production or work schedule; payments to suppliers and receipts from customers form a central part of cast planning; stock levels need to be planned and maintained; recruitment and training are needed to meet any seasonal peaks in demand.

EXERCISE 1.1

Read Illustration 1.1, Acorn Computers. You are a business planner at Olivetti in February 1985, and have been asked for a brief analysis of the following issues:

1. Why did Olivetti buy a major share in Acorn?
2. List the major issues which you think the company's **strategic plans** for Acorn should address.

3. Identify the **management plans** and **operational plans** which will be necessary to carry out your strategic plans over the next three years.

There has been a tendency amongst some authors to identify business planning too closely with strategic planning to the exclusion of the other levels of planning. It is the intention in this book to give proper attention to all of these levels of planning within organisations.

It is important at this stage for readers to consider some of the important differences in the types of planning which will occur at these different levels. Some of these differences are summarised in Table 1.2 and arise for a number of reasons:

- Strategic planning is concerned with the broad, longer-term future of an organisation. As a result it is subjected to far greater uncertainties, must necessarily avoid too much detail, and it is more difficult to assess its value to the organisation than is the case with management or operational planning.
- In contrast operational plans tend to be confined to one specific aspect of a company's operations, such as production planning, and often lend themselves to programmed systems (often computerised). It should be noted, however, that there are still relatively few areas of operational planning where a programmed system would be allowed to operate without human intervention. This would only occur in some of the detailed **parts** of a production system – such as the operation of an automatic machine (for example, the preparation of rate demands by a local authority). Even there the machine operations are normally taking place **within** the confines of a human-designed plan (the production system).

It is useful to note that the balance of planning tasks will be very different at the different levels of planning. Since this book has been structured around these major planning tasks the consideration of the different planning levels will necessarily occur unevenly through the book. So, for example, Chapters 3 and 4 which are concerned with how organisations **think** about their future and **decide** what actions need to be taken will be weighted towards a consideration of strategic and management planning (although not exclusively so). In contrast Chapters 5 and 6 will be more concerned with management and operational planning – planning **how** and **when** actions should be undertaken, although discussions will take place within the framework which strategic planning would typically provide. A fuller discussion of these various planning tasks will be given in the final section of this chapter.

TABLE 1.2   Differences between the levels of planning

	Strategic planning	*Management planning*	*Operational planning*
Time horizon	Long (often years)	Medium (1 year?)	Short (daily, weekly, etc.)
Major purpose	To map out future directions	To plan how strategy will be implemented	Plan the day-to-day company operations
Uncertainty	Very high	Medium	Least
Level of detail	Broad issues only	More detailed	Very detailed
Breadth of coverage	Very broad	Confined to details of given strategies	Very specific
Planning methods	Often unstructured	More structured	Highly structured (often programmed systems)
Assessing value of plans	Very difficult	Whether strategy is operationalised	Often easy to assess and amend

1.3 Types of planning

It has already been mentioned that there are dangers in believing that business planning refers to 'glossy books'. Equally important is to dispel the myth that there is a universally correct way to plan which should be adopted by all organisations. Often students of business, and even business managers, fail to appreciate this point and are constantly in search of the 'Holy Grail' – a planning system which will remove all their problems for ever! Such a system does not exist – nor is it ever likely to exist – and it is against the reality of this situation that a variety of different types of business planning need to be reviewed. It is particularly important that the appropriateness of each type of planning should be related to the circumstances in which any one organisation finds itself – this will be the aim of the discussions in this section. This latter issue will be discussed in greater detail in Chapter 2.

In order to illustrate why different types of planning might be needed it is useful to consider the factors which describe the *type* of planning being undertaken by a company (see Figure 1.2):

● The **flexibility or rigidity** of the plan. At one extreme a blueprint plan would be regarded as completely rigid – to be implemented in

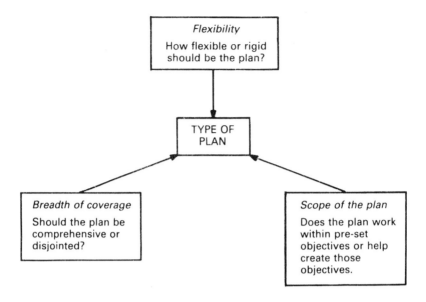

FIGURE 1.2   Factors which describe the type of planning in an organisation

Note: Any organisation will have a variety of planning activities which will need to differ in type (as described by this diagram).

every last detail. This might be appropriate where the situation is understood in some detail and there is little uncertainty surrounding the major aspects of the plan. Many of the technical aspects of a business plan might lend themselves to such a rigid process – for example, the design of a new piece of production equipment or the statutory health regulations being imposed by an Environmental Health Department. In contrast there are many aspects of planning which are subject to high levels of uncertainty and require a far more flexible approach to planning – where the plan is changed and adapted as more information becomes available. Good **strategic** planning should normally show such flexibility. It is fair to say that early attempts to produce corporate plans in many organisations (including local authorities in the mid-1970s) were discredited because they failed to be flexible enough in the light of significant uncertainties surrounding the organisation. As a broad generalisation rigidity is likely to be less appropriate in strategic planning than for operational planning.

● The **breadth of coverage** of a plan. Whether the plan is regarded as a comprehensive plan for the organisation as a whole or whether it addresses just one part (or aspect) of the company's activities. Clearly, strategic planning is more comprehensive than either management or operational planning. However, even within strategic planning there are choices of approach. Formalised corporate planning has usually been associated with a desire to have a comprehensive organisation-wide plan which encompasses all the organisation's activities. Whereas the motives for such an approach are easily understood – the desire to improve efficiency by getting all parts of the organisation to pull in one direction – the reality of trying to achieve such comprehensive planning has proved very difficult. Some companies have disbanded large planning departments to dispel the idea that planning is the province of experts. More emphasis is being placed on devolving strategic planning down to smaller units of the organisation – whether it be separate businesses, divisions or even different business functions (marketing, finance, etc.). In many cases the losses in terms of less co-ordination of corporate efforts would appear to be outweighed by a clearer picture of the direction in which these separate parts are moving.

Similarly many of the larger public authorities are placing more emphasis on improving the quality of strategic planning within the various parts of the organisation and confining centralised strategic planning to a broad overview of the whole authority. So, for example, the centralised planning might be limited to the allocation of budgets to the various service areas (housing, education, etc.) and intervening only where significant overlap and/or co-operation between service areas is needed. Perhaps the most important contribution from the centre is in determining the overall style and philosophy of the organisation and endorsing (or otherwise) the plans of each service area. This provides some degree of commonality across the whole authority. So the housing policies tend to be consistent with provision of recreational amenities, social services, etc., without the need for a highly bureaucratic and centralised planning system.

In these circumstances it is important that the planning at the centre of organisations has a sensible relationship with the more detailed (yet nevertheless strategic) planning within the various parts (such as divisions). This matter will be discussed more fully in Chapter 2.

● The **scope** of the plan. In particular whether the plan is concerned with spelling out how detailed pre-set objectives will be achieved or whether the plan forms part of the process of setting objectives or targets. Operational planning is normally of the former type. For example, the weekly planning of the nursing duties within a hospital are determined by the number of patients, and the level of care they will need. Whether or not these factors are regarded as desirable is not questioned within operational planning which is confined to working within the current situation and objectives.

In contrast a great deal of strategic planning is undertaken against a background of uncertainty as to what the organisation's objectives or targets ought to be. Some readers may be surprised to read this – perhaps there is a feeling that strategic planning should be confined to achieving pre-set organisational objectives – certainly the corporate planning of the 1960s was apparently aimed at such an ideal. However, not only is it often impractical to plan in such a neat and tidy way, it could well be highly undesirable in the sense that rigidly pre-set objectives can preclude a rethink of a company's direction and many opportunities may be lost as a result.

EXERCISE 1.2

Re-read Illustration 1.1, Acorn Computers. You have been asked by Olivetti to advise on the type of business planning which will be necessary to run Acorn successfully **within** Olivetti. Write a briefing paper which outlines:

1. Which choices are available in terms of the **flexibility, breadth** and **scope** of the planning.
2. Your advice on the type of planning to be adopted and why your feel it fits the company's circumstances at the time.

Common approaches to business planning

Within the three factors of **flexibility, breadth** and **scope** of plans there is an almost infinite variety of plans within business organisations. Any one organisation will need to have many different types of plans as has been illustrated in the previous section. However, it is interesting to observe that there are some common stereotypes in terms of how organisations approach business planning as a whole. Although stereotyping can be dangerous it is also felt to be useful in helping readers to understand the different **attitudes** to business planning which exist. Three commonly occurring approaches are:

1. An **entrepreneurial** approach to planning where the organisation (usually through its leader) has a clear vision of where the organisation should be going – all planning efforts are geared towards achieving this vision – in some instances even when it proves impractical. Planning tends not to be detailed or co-ordinated and often occurs in fits and starts. Nevertheless the successful entrepreneur often knows when to shift direction and in that sense the planning is highly flexible.

2. A **reactive** approach where changes tend not to occur until they are forced upon the organisation. Planning is more associated with fire-fighting rather than the considered judgement of a company's future. The dangers of reactive planning are obvious – namely that the organisation reacts too late. However, there are circumstances where reactive planning may prove to be very valuable if adopted for positive reasons. For example, many retail companies have such a variety of products which they could stock in their shops that the final decision on which product lines should be dropped and which added, in the short term, may be left to the discretion of the individual store manager (within guidelines). In this way a large company is able to respond better to local conditions and also may gain useful ideas from one branch which could be tried elsewhere. The organisation's overall planning is strongly influenced by this constant 'testing of the water' at branch level. This is **incremental planning** because the organisation moves forward in a series of small increments rather than through any obviously dramatic shifts in its plans. Nevertheless the sum total of all these small changes can be significant over time.

3. A **formalised** approach to planning which comes closest to the traditional view of planning in the minds of many people. Here planning tends to be very visible within the organisation – planning systems exist at all the levels discussed earlier. There is often a planning timetable to which people must conform in order to ensure that company plans can be produced 'on time'. Within public service organisations a great deal of this formalised planning is centred on the annual process of setting revenue and capital **budgets**. However, it would be wrong to conclude that this is the only planning within the organisation, or that planning is a one-off event each February.

   The most intelligent use of formalised planning is to view it as a 'snap-shot' of the organisation at a given time where planning continues as an ongoing process. The danger is that formal planning can reduce the real level of useful planning if people feel it only needs to happen once a year.

TABLE 1.3   **Some common approaches to planning**

	Characteristics of approach	*Plans tend to be:*
Entrepreneurial approach	Clear vision of direction, all planning geared to this	Reasonably flexible. Disjointed. Limited in scope
Reactive approach	Responding to events	Very flexible; very fragmented (although perhaps within a clear frame) Scope potentially wide (within the frame)
Formalised approach	Formal, visible planning *systems*	Often rigid; tends to be comprehensive Often scope carefully prescribed

Table 1.3 summarises the most important features of these three approaches to planning and will be discussed more fully in Chapter 2.

EXERCISE 1.3

Read Illustration 1.2, Approaches to Planning.

1. Describe the approach to planning in each of the four organisations in the Illustration.
2. Explain why you feel they had adopted that approach at the time.
3. Would you recommend any changes in approach? Why?

1.5 The major planning tasks

This final section of the chapter will be devoted to a discussion of the major planning tasks which organisations undertake. This is especially important since it is these planning tasks which form the framework around which the remainder of the book is structured. Before these tasks are discussed in detail there are a number of observations which readers should bear in mind:

1. These planning tasks will be found at the various levels of planning previously discussed in Section 1.2. However, some tasks will

ILLUSTRATION 1.2   Different approaches to planning

The four companies detailed below had different approaches to business planning.

IBM Europe.
IBM was an American-based computer company with subsidiaries world-wide. In Europe alone IBM employed over 100,000 people in 1983. The company made a sizeable effort to plan their product strategies for thirteen business areas. They used all the knowledge they could find from inside and outside the company to make reliable forecasts. Consequently the five-year strategic plan was a systematic, disciplined and quantified process checked across countries for consistency in technology, manufacturing capacity and marketing resources. The company had a ten-year time horizon for certain key parameters but the ten-year plan was not a detailed one.

Smiths Industries
In the 1980s this company was changing from its traditional dependence on the motor industry by acquiring companies in developing markets, which often had an entrepreneurial style of management. However, it was hard for the large company to accommodate the entrepreneur. There was a cultural conflict between the loyal company men content with a good salary and security and the less-manageable maverick entrepreneurs. The conflict was emphasised when the entrepreneurs bought out by Smiths Industries became rich through freelance work. Smiths Industries made great efforts to arrange things so that both types of executive could work together. The key was decentralisation – the granting of much more autonomy to individual subsidiaries and divisions.

Shell
For Shell in 1983 the planning approach was based upon the identification of a consistent pattern of social, economic, political and technological developments. These were then incorporated into two sharply-contrasting scenarios (as planners jargon has it, a 'best' and 'worst' situation). Operational managers were then asked to produce a set of plans for their divisions to fit each of the extremes. The logic behind this was that if the

---

ILLUSTRATION 1.2   *continued*

eventual outcome is somewhere between the two extremes,
then the alternative plans, taken together should be able to deal
with any variation when it arises.

Fichter & Sachs
This West German engineering company described its planning
system in 1983 as one which must 'allow external signals to be
picked up quickly and ensure that those signals are incorporated
into management decision-making'.

Source: Authors and *Management Today*, September 1985.

---

    occur more frequently in strategic planning and others in opera-
tional planning.

2. Whatever the *approach* to planning (within the variety of approaches discussed in Section 1.4.) these planning tasks will need
   to be undertaken in one way or another.
3. Many readers may be used to thinking about business planning as
   a collection of functional plans such as financial planning, manpower planning, etc. However, the nature of many planning problems tends to transcend the business functions. For example,
   planning a sales calling-route has much in common with production planning or even cash planning. In all cases there are common
   problems in the area of scheduling of tasks and probably important
   issues of allocating priorities.
4. This book is quite deliberately structured around these planning
   tasks (rather than around functional plans – production, finance,
   etc.) in order to allow readers to understand these issues of commonality. By using a wide variety of examples from the different
   business functions of organisations it is hoped that the links between functional planning and the overall planning efforts of an
   organisation will become much clearer. This should allow readers
   to avoid one of the most common pitfalls in business planning –
   namely, viewing company planning as simply a collection of the
   separate plans of the business functions.

Figure 1.3 is a representation of the major planning tasks which organisations need to undertake and also provides a framework for this book:

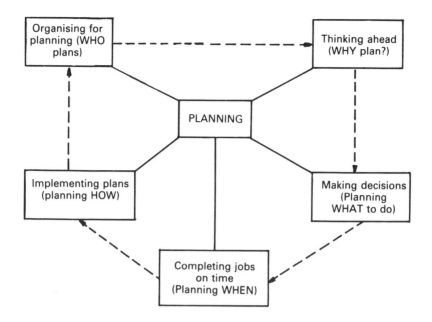

FIGURE 1.3   The major planning tasks

- *Thinking ahead* is an essential planning task – it is the way in which a company explores the changes which are likely to occur within and around the organisation and the broad ways in which the company might need to change. This is largely the province of **strategic planning** and provides the framework within which management planning and operational planning have a purpose. For this latter reason this planning task helps to establish WHY other planning activities need to be undertaken within the company. In the case of Acorn (Illustration 1.1) thinking ahead would be concerned with identifying the significant trends in the computer industry, the rise of competition and the ability of Acorn to prosper in these changing circumstance. 'Thinking ahead' is the subject of Chapter 3.
- *Making decisions* is also a central part of planning which occurs at all the levels previously identified. So at a strategic level Acorn needed to decide whether to enter new market sectors, or perhaps have a fuller involvement in distribution. Decisions would also be part of the management planning – if the business market was to be entered by Acorn, important decisions were needed about which companies would be targeted, what products would be

offered, and payment terms to be operated (and many other issues too). Planning as a means of deciding what should be done is also an important part of operational planning. For example, a computer company like Acorn which was buying many components and assembling them into finished machines would probably try to plan its purchasing and component-stocking policies to minimise the cost of stockholding without risk of a 'stock out' of any key component. Collectively the contribution of planning to decision-making is most simply understood as the task of planning WHAT should be done, and is discussed in Chapter 4.

● *Planning the timing* of a company's actions is a key planning task. Planning has to recognise that the success of a company is not only dependent on its ability to undertake the right tasks but also to undertake those tasks at the right time. This is particularly important within business organisations since it is not usually possible to obtain new resources without some delays. In addition most business activities consist of a complex web of smaller tasks and the sequencing and scheduling of these tasks needs careful planning. At Acorn, for example, computer assembly needs to occur in a given **sequence** – some components need to be assembled before others. Equally important is the need to have computers available **on time** particularly in such a seasonal market as home computers where missing the Christmas boom would be disastrous. It is essential to adhere to the schedule of tasks. All these various aspects of timing are concerned with planning WHEN tasks should be undertaken, and are discussed in Chapter 5.

● *Implementing* plans is also part of planning in so far as the problems of making plans work in practice should be a key consideration during the planning process. For example, Acorn may have decided to enter the business computer market in Spring 1985 but how would they ensure success? This would involve planning how to motivate and reward people (both employees and distributors), and the kind of information and control systems which would be needed to monitor performance in relation to plans. These planning tasks are concerned with HOW the plans will be made to work in practice. Chapter 6 looks at these issues in more detail.

● Lastly there are important decisions to be made concerning WHO should be responsible for planning. There is clearly not a simple answer to this question since it is likely that different groups and individuals will be responsible for different plans. The way in which planning is **organised** will also be influenced by the structure of the company. If Acorn set up a European subsidiary in

Germany they would need to decide how the planning responsibilities would be split between the UK and Germany. For example, it may be that all important strategic planning and the majority of management planning would occur in the UK and the subsidiary would then be given a detailed set of targets to achieve and its planning confined to a largely operational role. In contrast the German subsidiary could be given a simple annual profit target and the freedom to forge its own strategy to achieve this target – this would leave much of the detailed strategic planning in the hands of the subsidiary and the planning within the UK would be confined to planning the flow of funds between the parent and the subsidiary.

EXERCISE 1.4

Read Illustration 1.3, Adlington Building Society. Using the housing market in your own locality as a reference point:

1. List the **major** items which Don Taylor's plan must address under each of the planning tasks outlined in the text above.
2. Which of these tasks will be critically important to the success of the new total house purchase service?

1.6 The relationship between planning tasks

It should be noted that the relationship between these various planning tasks depicted in Figure 1.3 needs to be properly understood. In particular:

● Whereas business planning involves a variety of tasks (as shown in the figure) there is no one right sequence in which these tasks should be undertaken. Whereas, logically it might be expected that there should be a neat sequence of tasks beginning with thinking ahead and concluding with the organisational issues, this is rarely the case in practice. This logical view tends to assume that an organisation stands still while planning takes place and is only put back into action once all the details of the plans are properly finished. This is obviously not the case in practice and so planning needs to be a far more **dynamic** and **responsive** process than this logical view might imply.

In practice the circle of tasks shown in Figure 1.3 might be entered at any point. For example, problems with making plans

---

ILLUSTRATION 1.3   Adlington Building Society: planning for change

In 1985 the Adlington was a major building society with around 1000 branches throughout the UK. The Sheffield office of the society employed a staff of seventy under the District Manager, Don Taylor. The work of the branch office consisted mainly of attracting people's savings and the granting of mortgages. The society had for several years been moving towards competition with the High Street banks by providing a current-account service and loans on the security of mortgagees' property. However, further major changes were imminent: first the change in the legal status of building societies, allowing them to lend money unsecured by property, just like banks. The second was the anticipated removal of the solicitors' monopoly on conveyancing which had failed to get through parliament in 1985, but was anticipated in the next few years.

The head office of the Adlington in 1986 declared an expansion of the society to provide a total house-purchase service, expanding into the market formerly reserved by solicitors and estate agents. Although the launch and advertising of the new service would be handled by head office, the local managers (like Don Taylor) were asked to draw up a five-year plan for the marketing, staffing and operation of the new services at local level. Don voiced some of his difficulties in drawing up the plan:

> 'We have two major problems. The first is getting the staff with the right skills in the legal, property valuation and marketing fields. The society has a tradition of internal promotion for all senior posts, but I see no alternative to bringing in outsiders if we are going to get these skills in time. The second problem is our relationship with local solicitors and estate agents with whom we have always worked very closely. It's all very well for head office to see this as a lucrative market, but the operational difficulties at local level will be enormous. I may have to resign from the golf club!'

---

work might trigger off the need to reassign responsibilities for certain aspects of the plans or even to rethink the wisdom of the company's plans. In other circumstances a company might find difficulties in keeping to its production schedules and conclude that it would be desirable to seek out new market-segments which would not require such tight schedules.

● Many people mistakenly hold the belief that planning can be a 'once and for all exercise' – in terms of Figure 1.3 this would mean that having successfully undertaken all of the planning tasks the process is completed. Again this fails to take account of the dynamic nature of planning. Planning should never end within an organisation. Whereas the time and effort being spent on any one planning task will almost certainly change with time, the **process** should not end, as the company has a constant need to adjust to ¢hanging circumstances and to run its activities efficiently.

1.7 Summary

This opening chapter has been concerned with introducing readers to the idea that business planning takes on many different forms within organisations. There is no one right approach to business planning and the organisation's circumstances must dictate the type of planning which is needed. The chapter concluded by identifying the most important planning tasks which need to be undertaken by organisations (Figure 1.3). There is a danger that a textbook on business planning will give the impression that planning is easy, neat and tidy and not subject to difficulties and pitfalls. Readers should follow the discussion of the following chapters in the knowledge that business planning is difficult – often subject to problems, mistakes, and power struggles between various factions leading to criticism within the organisation. Indeed a central aim of this book is to dispel the myth that business planning is a bag of magic tricks and to make readers more familiar with the realities of business planning. One of the major difficulties in business planning is to strike an intelligent balance between having a properly co-ordinated approach to planning (both between the different parts of the organisation and between the different levels of planning) and the need to avoid an unnecessarily bureaucratic system of planning.

It is particularly important to understand the role that people within and outside an organisation might play in business planning. For this reason the more detailed discussion begins (in Chapter 2) with this theme of organising the planning effort which is felt to be an essential background to understanding later chapters. A final word of warning! Whereas it is necessary to divide the book into chapters on particular topics in order to allow readers to develop a better in-depth knowledge –

the overall aim of the book is that readers should improve their understanding of business planning as a whole – which involves understanding the relationships between the various planning tasks (and therefore,
the chapters of this book).

Recommended key readings

John Argenti, *Practical Corporate Planning* (Allen & Unwin, 1980), is a useful
and readable text about systematic approaches to planning.

David Hussey, *Corporate Planning: Theory and Practice* (Pergamon, 1982, 2nd
edn) is a comprehensive book about corporate planning. Readers should find
Chapters 1, 2 and 3 useful.

Michael Nash, *Managing Organizational Performance* (Jossey Bass, 1983).
Chapter 1 is a useful introduction to planning issues.

Robert Appleby, *Modern Business Administration* (Pitman, 1981, 3rd edn).
Chapter 2 looks at the scope of planning within businesses.

Martin van Mesdag, 'Planning's New Purpose' (*Management Today*, September
1983) takes a practical look at how planning has changed over the past twenty
years.

Rudi Rozman, 'Developing a Practical Planning System' (*Long Range Planning*,
April 1986, p. 90) is useful reading.

Organising for planning

The previous chapter outlined the various types of planning which occur within organisations. One of the most difficult problems is deciding on how to organise these various activities. Deciding WHO should be involved in and responsible for the different planning efforts of an organisation is just as important as the content of the plans. It is for this reason that these issues are raised at this early stage in the book before a more detailed consideration of the content of business plans. If companies do not organise their planning properly it can result in wasted effort, poor quality plans, and a lack of commitment within the organisation to make the plans work.

This chapter begins by looking at the people and groups who are likely to be involved in business planning. This is followed by a discussion of how an organisation's circumstances such as size, diversity of activities or production technology are likely to influence the approach to business planning. It will then concentrate on the key organisational issues which will affect the quality of business planning in practice. The organisational difficulties are most easily understood by looking at the problem of dividing responsibility for planning within organisations. Figure 2.1 describes this in terms of the **two opposing forces**:

- On the one hand there are strong arguments for planning responsibility to be **divided** so that more people are involved in planning with the obvious advantages of spreading the work-load and making people feel more committed to making the company's plans work.
- However, division of responsibility brings problems. In particular there is a need to have some reliable means of **co-ordinating** the various planning efforts of the company to make sure that they make sense as a whole.

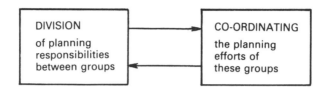

FIGURE 2.1   Organising for planning: the two opposing forces

Successful planning manages to balance these two opposing forces. The chapter concludes by looking at some of the most commonly used planning systems in different types of organisation and the way in which they attempt to cope with this dilemma of *division versus coordination* of planning effort.

2.1 Who is involved in planning?

There is no one system of planning which is appropriate for all types of organisation. Each organisation's circumstances, such as its size, the nature of its business, and the attitudes of the people within it should all have a significant effect on the way in which planning is organised. Notwithstanding this it is still useful to see who are likely to be involved in business planning within organisations, and the type of involvement they might typically have. Figure 2.2 shows some of the most important groups of people who may be involved in planning and the typical roles which they play will now be discussed more fully.

These groups are often referred to as *stakeholders* since they all have a 'stake' in what the company does. The figure is deliberately drawn with **managers** as the central focus of business planning since this is most commonly (although not universally) the case. Other groups are divided into 'Insiders' and 'Outsiders' although it needs to be recognised that in some circumstances a group may be both (for example, a parent-company who trades with a subsidiary may be an owner, a supplier, and a customer at the same time).

2.1.1. Owners

It might be expected that the owners of a company would have a key involvement in planning. Certainly when businesses are set-up it is likely that the planning at all levels (strategic, management, operational) will be carried out by the founders as they struggle to establish the

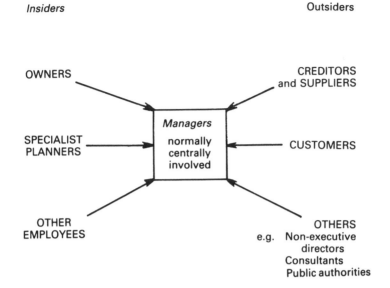

Insiders   Outsiders

OWNERS   CREDITORS
                                      and SUPPLIERS

                        Managers
SPECIALIST   normally
PLANNERS   centrally   CUSTOMERS
                        involved

OTHER   OTHERS
EMPLOYEES   e.g. Non-executive
                                      directors
                                   Consultants
                                   Public authorities

FIGURE 2.2   The people who might be involved in business
                      planning (stakeholders)

organisation. However, as the organisation develops and grows it is
almost certain that responsibility for planning is gradually handed over
to other employees. This would normally begin with the **operational
planning**, such as production planning, which might be taken over by a
foreman. At some stage the owners will need to employ **managers**,
usually to look after specialist parts of the business such as marketing or
finance – gradually the **management planning** in those functions will be
taken over by these professional managers. In a company of this type it
is quite likely that the owners will continue to have a dominant role in
strategic planning – often excluding everyone else from that process –
even the managers they have employed.

However, this is not typical of the role of owners in larger organisations – particularly once the organisation becomes public through a
share issue. It is rare for shareholders of public companies to have much
involvement in planning of any type within the organisation – unless
they are also directors of the company and sit on the board. Some
readers may be surprised that shareholders have such little involvement
in the strategic planning of the company which they partly own. They
do, of course, have opportunities to register their lack of approval of
company plans, through voting at AGMs or, of course, by selling their
shareholding. Large institutional shareholders, such as insurance com-

panies, do from time to time make their views clear to the Board of Directors but their main concern is to ensure that the company produces a return on their investment.

In public-sector organisations, such as nationalised industries and public services, the 'owners' are supposedly the citizens represented by the Government (nationally) or the local council (regionally). It is interesting to note how attitudes have changed regarding the involvement of government (national or local) in the planning activities of public-sector organisations. Theoretically it has always been the view that the **elected representatives** (government, local councillors) were responsible for defining the **objectives and strategy** of each public-sector organisation – whilst the professional **managers** (civil servants, nationalised industry chairmen, local government officers) were responsible for carrying out these policies. In terms of the framework of this book this would seem to be a clear-cut division between owners' responsibility for strategic planning and managers' responsible for management and operational planning.

In practice the situation is very much more complex than this (as was illustrated in the BBC series of *Yes Minister*). At both national and local levels there has been an increasing tendency through the 1980s for politicians to seek a more direct influence over the planning and decision-making within public-sector organisations. In certain instances this has led to considerable friction between politicians and the managers of these organisations.

EXERCISE 2.1

Imagine yourself as the owner of your own business organisation. Decide on a specific type of business and its size (for example, a travel agency with forty employees).

List the advantages and disadvantages you would see from being in *direct* control of the following planning activities:

- deciding on new products/services
- setting departmental budgets
- scheduling orders
- allocating duties to staff
- planning sales-call routes

2.1.2. Managers

As a broad generalisation it is true to say that business planning within organisations is dominated by the managers of the organisations. In many ways this might be regarded as a proper state of affairs – after all, why have managers at all if they do not take responsibility for planning? However, this dominance by managers at all the levels of planning does raise some uncomfortable questions about the way in which companies are run and the kind of business plans which they are following:

● If managers are dominating strategic planning they are most likely to push for plans which best suit their own personal objectives. This is why **growth** tends to be a more commonly pursued objective than profit maximisation. Growth is favoured by many managers as it enhances their status and provides better career opportunities.

● The most 'legitimate' planning role for managers, as the term would suggest, is that of **management planning** (making strategy work). However, as will be seen later in the book unless managers are prepared to recognise the need to motivate people to carry out business plans they are likely to encounter difficulties. Too many managers view management planning as something which they do by themselves with the expectation that everyone else in the organisation will be willing to implement business plans under their guidance.

● Ironically another criticism of many managers is that they are excessively involved in **operational planning**. This is a particular problem for managers who have been promoted 'from the ranks' – they find it difficult to devolve responsibility for operational planning to subordinates. For example, the production manager may not be content to set up a system for monitoring overdue orders but may constantly interfere by rescheduling certain orders without consulting the foreman who is supposedly responsible for day-to-day order scheduling.

Although this section has tended to be critical of the role of some managers in business planning it needs to be recognised that managers **must** play a central role in planning – it is the question of the boundaries of their responsibilities which tends to prove difficult.

2.1.3. Specialist planners

Although business planning is a very important part of a manager's job it is not normally possible nor desirable for managers to undertake all of the planning activities within a company. As a result there are certain planning tasks which might be so important that they are given over to specialist planners who will be responsible for advising management on the company's business plans. This can occur at all levels of planning:

● *Corporate planning teams* became very fashionable in the late 1960s in many of the larger companies and the practice was followed by many local authorities after local government reorganisation in the mid-1970s. The motives behind this idea of specialist strategic planners seemed quite sensible:

   (a) managers were often too busy with their day-to-day responsibilities to have enough time to 'think ahead'. Specialist planners who were not burdened with other duties would be able to perform this role.
   (b) since most managers represented particular functions of the company (personnel, sales, etc.) they may not have been able or willing to think broadly about the company's overall strategic problems.

Although in many organisations corporate planners have made significant contributions to strategic planning it has also become apparent that there are potential dangers in using specialist corporate planning teams:

● the 'thinking' and 'doing' aspects of business planning can become separated. Managers can feel that it is not their job to think about the future of the company, whilst planners run the risk of not appreciating the practical difficulties of implementing plans. Such a division of attitude would defeat the purpose of having corporate planners – to complement and improve management thinking rather than replace it.
● although corporate planners are meant to transcend the politics and vested interests within the organisation this has proved to be an unrealistic expectation. Some planning teams have become regarded as the henchmen of certain senior managers and viewed with great suspicion by others. Again this frustrates the ability of a planning team to act as a unifying and co-ordinating force when formulating strategic plans.

As a result of these problems some organisations have opted for what would be regarded as a sensible compromise. Corporate planning specialists do exist but the teams are very small and tend to be made up (at least partially) of line managers seconded from their normal duties for a period of one to three years. This is an attempt to prevent the rift between the 'thinkers' and the 'doers'.

ILLUSTRATION 2.1   Planning in ICI

ICI have always regarded planning as a major activity. In the 1980s they had planning departments in each of the divisions as well as a central planning organisation. In the 1970s ICI planned for, and built, a new chemical plant at Wilhelmshaven in West Germany. However, by 1982 changes in the exchange rate resulted in the plant only operating at only half its capacity. Why did the planners fail to realise that an exchange rate change would result in a 20 per cent cut in profitability? Were they so bogged down in detailed planning of construction and production schedules that they failed to see this as a possible threat? Surely planners consider the impact of changes in the economic environment? The Head of Central Planning for ICI in 1982 claimed that this scenario was considered, but the Directors and line managers were already committed to the project, so the message about possible threats did not get across. A common reaction from those managers who had invested a great deal in getting the plan accepted was to reject the unacceptable scenario as unlikely (changes in the macro-environment being notoriously difficult to predict) and to say that in any case the new plant would enable them to increase market share. Once building had started everyone had to be committed to making it work, even if doing so meant digging their heads further into the sand. The 'judgement effect' meant that the planners' job was to produce the budgets, schedules and action plans necessary to implement the decision to build the plant – not to cast doubt on the original decision.

Other large organisations with planning departments have found themselves resisting rather than responding to external environmental changes. General Motors was widely criticised for failing to react fast enough to the effects of rising oil prices and Japanese competition; IBM for a long while allowed newcomers to dominate the microcomputer market; BP continued too long with the assumption that oil prices would continue to rise.

Source: *Management Today*, June 1982.

EXERCISE 2.2

Read Illustration 2.1, Planning in ICI:

1. Why was the West German plant built?
2. What role did the following play in the decision:
   - planners?
   - managers?
3. Would a better decision have been made if planning had been organised differently in ICI?

● *Operational planning specialists* exist in most organisations and range from the production planner of a manufacturing company, to a wide range of administrative posts within most organisations. For example, within a local authority department such as housing, there are administrative officers responsible for planning the utilisation of most of the department's resources. There are planners concerned with equipment utilisation, building maintenance and cleaning, routine purchasing, etc. The intelligent use of these specialist operational planners is clearly essential in organisations of any size or complexity and helps to avoid the problem of managers being too involved in detailed planning. However, there are potential dangers very similar to those which exist with corporate planning teams:

    (a) friction between the planners and other staff who may not fully appreciate each other's problems or planning objectives. For example, the allocation of bus crews to routes may result in an increase in customer complaints about the service which the depot manager could have avoided with more careful planning.

    (b) planners are used politically by the more astute staff at the expense of others. For example, some sales managers will pressurise the production planners to reschedule their customers' orders ahead of others in the queue.

The overall conclusion is that specialist planners can make very valuable contributions to business planning and in large organisations are probably essential. However, it is important that their efforts are not seen as separate from the mainstream activities of the company (the 'ivory tower' syndrome) and that they play a largely **advisory** role rather than creating vast empires of their own.

EXERCISE 2.3

You are an administrative assistant in a large college responsible for planning the booking of rooms for teaching purposes.

1. Why might your room allocations be criticised by the lec-
   turers in the college?
2. In what ways would you try to ensure that these complaints
   were:
   (a) minimised
   (b) capable of a quick solution if justified

2.1.4. Creditors/suppliers

Most organisations have a considerable number of creditors – people to
whom they owe money – who fall into two broad categories:

● *Suppliers* of materials and services who are normally owed
  money for short periods of time up to 3 months.
● *Lenders* of money such as banks who may be owed money in the
  form of loans for periods of several years.

In many situations it would not be anticipated that creditors would have
any major involvement in a company's business planning. However,
this is not always the case and readers need to be aware of several
situations where an involvement *would* be expected:

● The provision of major loans to organisations would not normally be made without some scrutiny of the strategic plans of the
  company. It is quite common for banks to lay down conditions
  regarding the types of plans for which the loan can be used. For
  example, they may be willing to fund new buildings and equipment but not increases in stock. The major banks have specialists
  to deal with certain planning problems like exporting.
● Suppliers of goods into the retail trade have a major interest in
  the way the retail outlets will market their goods, for example,
  whether they will be guaranteed prominent display, whether
  completing lines will be stocked etc. A great deal of effort is put
  into trying to influence the business plans of retail outlets. Many
  manufacturing organisations now employ teams of specialist
  merchandisers who are responsible for ensuring the best possible efforts from their retail outlets and providing support to retailers (for example, promotional materials, etc.) This, of course,

represents a direct involvement in the operational planning by suppliers.

● When companies get into financial difficulties the major creditors will appoint a receiver who will take over responsibility for all planning activities in the company on behalf of the creditors. They will decide whether the company should be wound-up (liquidated) or sold off, or simply restructured to be more viable.

EXERCISE 2.4

You are the manager of a kitchen centre selling kitchen units and domestic appliances to the public. You have six major suppliers of kitchen units – Hygena, Grovewood, Eastham, Gower, Crosby and Limited Edition. Hygena have offered you an attractive package of support including local advertising, in-store demonstrators and special give-aways to consumers. In return they want to plan the store-display with you and to have exclusive rights to the advertising in the store entrance.

1. List the advantages and disadvantages of this arrangement in terms of your business plan.
2. What arrangements, (financial or otherwise) might be acceptable to both parties?

2.1.5. Customers

There are parallel arguments in the case of customers. Whereas many organisations would not expect customers to have any direct involvement in their business planning this *does* occur quite frequently:

● Major retail organisations, like Marks & Spencer, or major industrial purchasers, like Ford, have a very close relationship with their suppliers and strongly influence the way in which they in turn plan and organise **their** business. On occasions these large companies have been criticised for **too** much involvement in the planning activities of their suppliers.
● Some organisations in the service sector pride themselves on allowing customers to comment on their business plans and performance. Some local radio-stations have listeners represented at their programme-planning meetings.
● State-owned monopolies, such as Gas, Electricity and Railways have statutory consultative committees which represent the views of customers.
● In principle all local authority services are subjected to criticism

by 'customers' through the process of democratic local elections. It must be realised that this type of customer involvement in the planning of local authorities can only be regarded as very remote. It is simply a 'mandate' for general policy rather than any kind of detailed involvement or influence on the planning process. As a result of this, users of public services will often try to influence operational plans by more **direct action**, such as petitions or the use of the media.

EXERCISE 2.5

Read Illustration 2.2, and complete the following exercise:

You are a management trainee in a medium-sized (200 employees) garment manufacturer. The company has been offered a contract with Marks & Spencer for 10,000 blouses which means that the whole production team will have to be switched to get the order delivered on time. The works manager is against accepting the order, but the finance director is in favour of it, especially since the bank are unhappy about the company's overdraft. The Managing Director has asked you to present a briefing paper to the Board weighing up the pros and cons of being a Marks & Spencer supplier.

2.1.6. Other outsiders

It is often forgotten that the majority of organisations will, from time to time, use other outsiders to help them with their business planning. Some common examples are:

- *Non-executive directors* can perform a useful role, particularly in advising on strategic planning – they are often able to give a more balanced view because of their wider experience and detachment from internal politics.
- *Consultants* are often used to help with business planning at all levels. Sometimes they advise on overall strategic planning, at other times on planning within a particular business function. They are often used because they have detailed knowledge which the company lacks on important operational matters as design, taxation or legal matters.
- *Public planning authorities and agencies* will be of great importance at certain times in a company's development. For example, all major building works will be subject to agreement with local authorities, expansion plans may be partially funded by government and other

ILLUSTRATION 2.2   Mark & Spencer: relationship with suppliers

Until the early 1980s Marks & Spencer were known for the close relationship they developed with their suppliers as described in the following newspaper article in 1983:

'Marks and Spencer keeps its suppliers in a state of 'pleasant imprisonment' which enabled firms like Corah of Leicester and Dewhirst of Leeds to survive the slump of 1980–81 in the clothing industry. This means helping them to develop new products and advising on sources of raw materials. This 'help' ranges from sorting out financial problems to ensuring that the lavatories are brought up to Marks & Spencer standards. Being part of the Marks & Spencer family confers an aura which opens many doors, particularly that of the bank manager. Above all, Marks & Spencer pays promptly. However, suppliers are required to call frequently at Head Office and to give the free run of their factories to St Michael inspectors. They may also be required to switch production runs at a moment's notice if a line is not selling fast enough. St Michael agrees a detailed written specification with the manufacturer for each garment, right down to the number of stitches per inch and precise width of cuff, belt or hem. When production begins, two perfect specimens are removed and sealed in bags. One stays with the maker and the other goes to Marks & Spencer. The slightest deviation from these perfect examples is rated as a reject. Marks & Spencer show its understanding of suppliers' problems by allowing them to sell the rejects.'

Source: William Kay, 'How they sold their soul to St Michael', *The Sunday Times*, 19 June 1983.

agencies (such as New Town Development Corporations, Regional Development Agencies, etc.). Companies planning overseas expansion may seek help and advice from the British Overseas Trading Board (BOTB) and expect their plans to be scrutinised accordingly. Small companies can gain help and assistance in business planning under schemes such as the Business Improvement Services (DTI/EEC).

EXERCISE 2.6

Imagine yourself as the owner of a small company which manu-
factures eldectronic ignition systems for motor-bikes. You are
considering the possibility of extending your premises with the
aim of expanding production some 60 per cent and making a
concerted effort to sell into mainland Europe.

1. To what extent would you wish, and/or need, to use any of
   the outside agencies mentioned in the previous three sections of the text?
2. What would you see as the potential dangers of involving
   them in your planning?

2.1.7. Employees

A traditional view of business planning might suggest that employees
(other than managers) are not involved in the planning process but
simply carry out the tasks prescribed by the management. This is
certainly not in tune with the reality in many organisations. The following should give a better picture:

● It is quite normal for employees to be given some discretion on
  how they perform their duties. Although this varies considerably
  from the production-line worker (with little discretion) to the
  designer or research worker (with a lot of discretion) it is still an
  important way in which employees are involved in the operational
  planning of the organisation. So a social worker will be allocated a
  number of duties and cases but within that constraint may have a
  great deal of freedom on how to handle individual cases. Allowing
  employees the right amount of discretion is one of the important
  skills of management in many organizations. Too much discretion
  can be abused or disorientating, too little discretion can be unduly
  constraining.
● Many public service organisations will have formal decision-
  making procedures whereby employees are properly represented.
  For example, in colleges and universities employees will be represented (by election) on a whole series of committees such as
  Faculty Boards, Course Committees, Academic Board, etc. The
  work of these committees is largely concerned with management
  planning and strategic planning (that is, agreeing policies and
  planning systems). The parallel in the private sector might be
  Works Councils although experience suggests that these latter
  bodies tend to spend the majority of their time on operational
  matters – often welfare and safety issues.

● After the publication of the Bullock Report in 1977 it was expected that some noticeable changes might occur in the UK leading
towards a greater degree of industrial democracy. Bullock recommended that some of the power in planning and policy-making
should be shifted away from management towards trade unions
through the appointment of worker directors – a system which has
been operating in other countries (notably West Germany) for
many years. This has not yet happened – the pressures of high
levels of unemployment during the 1980s relegated the issue of
industrial democracy in the minds of many trade unionists below
that of jobs and pay.

● *Co-operatives* are interesting examples of organisations where the
employees own the organisation and share responsibility for all
aspects of business planning. Readers should recognise that much
of the writing about co-operatives had tended to concern **small**
organisations in low technology industries. In these circumstances
consensus decision-making and sharing of planning responsibilities is very much easier than in larger, more technologically
complex organisations where **specialist** knowledge and skills are
needed to run the organisation successfully.

A useful general conclusion for this section as a whole is that business
plans are likely to be built from a better base of information if more
people are able to contribute to the process. However, there is a price to
pay for this wider involvement. The decision-making processes become
a bargaining process between the various stakeholder groups. The irony
of this is that the quality of the business plans may suffer as the
organisation has to settle for an acceptable plan which may well be the
lowest common denominator. Democratic planning processes have their
advantages but they also have their costs – in particular 'difficult' or
'tough' decisions can be hard to get adopted.

EXERCISE 2.7

Suppose you were one of the members of the Down-to-Earth
Co-operative described in Illustration 2.3:

1. How and why might your attitude towards the following
   aspects of your business planning differ from a normal
   commercial organisation:

   (a) The involvement of members in decision-making.
   (b) The relationship with customers.
   (c) The financial objectives of the company.

ILLUSTRATION 2.3   Down-to-Earth: planning in a co-operative

In 1978 the Down-to-Earth co-operative was running a very successful whole-food shop in a busy suburban shopping centre in Sheffield. The shop had an annual turnover in excess of £45,000 from the sale of more than 150 types of beans, grain, flour, dried fruits, herbs, etc. The co-operative consisted of five ex-students in their early twenties who had strong views on how the co-operative should plan and manage its affairs as the following comments indicate:

'Co-operative working does not begin and end with running the shop but extends into our personal lives. The dividing line between work and non-work is not well defined.'

'The working situation must allow members to experience personal growth, skill-sharing and group support. We are all expected to understand and participate in **all** aspects of the business. We rotate jobs rather than individuals specialising in just one area.'

'Policy decisions are made by consensus rather than by imposing the will of the majority on a reluctant minority.'

'We believe that wage differentials beyond a basic rate should be related to individual **needs** and not to the tasks performed.'

'We try to break down the traditional barrier between workers and customers by encouraging customers to become involved in shop-work.'

'We are worried about our attitude to part-time staff. We feel they should be fully involved in decision-making but we have found it difficult to do so.'

'We look at advertising as providing useful information to our customers rather than whether it will simply generate more income.'

'We feel that the **way** in which the co-operative's activities are planned and undertaken is as important as the financial "results" of our efforts.'

Source: Down-to-Earth Case Study 1978 by Kevan Scholes. Case Clearing House, Cranfield.

2. Do you think they will make better decisions than a commercial organisation?
3. Will their planning be as efficient as a commercial organisation?

2.2 Influences on the choice of planning systems

The planning systems of an organisation are likely to be influenced by
the special circumstances in which that organisation is operating, for
example, its size, the nature of its business, etc. (see Table 2.1). Before
looking in more detail at common organisational problems it is useful to
see how a company's circumstances might influence the general approach to organising the planning effort. This should also be a useful
initial glimpse at some of the planning issues which will be discussed
more fully in later chapters.

2.2.1 Size and diversity

In small organisations many planning tasks have to be grouped together
in order to operate efficiently. For example, production scheduling,
stock control and quality control are all likely to be planned within the
production function whereas in larger companies they may be separate
functions in their own right. So it is in larger organisations that the need
to co-ordinate the planning efforts of many specialist departments tends
to arise.

The extent to which the organisation's activities are diversified (for
example, many different products/markets) will also influence the approach to business planning. Most large organisations will cope with
diversity by dividing responsibility for planning into smaller units (for
example, Product Divisions). Those at the centre of the organisation
have a key co-ordinating role to ensure that the plans of the various
divisions can be achieved within the resources available overall.

2.2.2 Nature of the environment

If organisations are operating in a relatively certain business environment it is quite possible to develop formalised business-planning systems which will be quite detailed and analytical, and will be geared
towards achieving the maximum possible operational efficiency. For
example, elaborate centralised production-planning systems will normally be set up to cope with a predictable demand situation.

TABLE 2.1   Factors influencing the way that planning is organised

Factor	*Reason for importance*
1. Size and diversity	Less co-ordination needed in small, single product organisations
2. Business environment	Uncertainty makes detailed planning difficult and inappropriate
3. Products/technology	Product/process technology will dictate the complexity of planning
4. Ownership	Some owners wish a fuller involvement in planning than others
5. Organisational culture	Some people can cope with bureaucracies others cannot

In contrast many organisations face very uncertain environments where it is very difficult to lay detailed plans too far in advance. In these circumstances it is essential that the business planning is as **flexible** as possible. This is usually achieved by devolving responsibility for planning to smaller units, who will plan in a less detailed fashion than would occur in the first case. This issue is considered in detail in Chapter 3.

2.2.3 Products and technology

In discussing business planning in general terms it is easy to forget that an organisation's products and production technology are likely strongly to influence the type of planning systems needed. A motor manufacturer using production-line assembly of cars containing several hundred 'bought-in' components quite clearly has a need for properly **integrated** planning procedures linking component purchasing, stocking, production scheduling, and shipments to dealers. Without such a system the company would very quickly degenerate into chaos.

On the other hand many service organisations do not have the constraints which producers of physical products have. So in an insurance office it would be quite possible for one group of staff to be given responsibility for certain accounts and to plan their activities relatively independently of other groups. Although co-ordination of planning may be desirable it is not as critically important in the short term as it is for a motor manufacturer.

EXERCISE 2.8

You work in a branch of a major distributor of electrical appliances, such as Comet or Trident. The company has recently introduced a computerised stock control system which allows each store to see whether a particular item is in stock elsewhere.

1. How will this change in technology alter the way in which stock levels are planned at your store?
2. Will the customer get a better or worse service?
3. Will any new planning procedures be needed to ensure that the system works?

2.2.4 Ownership

Section 2.1.1 discussed the type of involvement that owners of organisations are likely to have in business planning. It should be clear from that discussion that there are many different attitudes amongst owners regarding their degree of involvement in business planning. Owner/managers are likely to have a closer involvement than owners who are simply holding shares as an investment.

Centralised business planning is likely to occur where the owners wish to keep a direct involvement in business planning – for example, in family businesses. This can continue even when the business is quite large and publicly owned (for example, Habitat, Mothercare, Tesco). This centralised approach will also tend to occur where **public accountability** is a key issue as in nationalised industries and public services. Public scrutiny is more easily achieved if business planning (at least at the strategic level) is centralised. The price which is paid for this is the detailed central bureaucracy which many employees of public service organisations find so tiresome.

2.2.5 Organisational culture

It would be wrong to leave this section without recognising that the **culture** of an organisation is quite critical in determining the approach to business planning. Some organisations are very much more cautious and bureaucratic than others even when they are operating in the same industry. This may be due to history but is also often a result of the personality of the leaders in the organisation. Organisations with entrepreneurial-type leaders are clearly less likely to have detailed, highly-integrated business-planning systems. Some organisations, such as voluntary organisations, will tend to attract people who have very strong values about 'caring' and may see over-bureaucratic planning systems as frustrating rather than helping the organisation in carrying out its duties.

Media organisations, such as newspapers, radio and television, are very interesting in this respect since there tend to be two quite opposed cultures sitting alongside each other. There are the **creative** culture of the programming/editorial staff and the **business** culture of those who are selling advertising time/space. The senior managers of these organisations need considerable skill in designing business planning systems which will suit both cultures (as shown in Chapter 7).

EXERCISE 2.9

Read Illustration 2.4, Norchester City Council.

1. Was Norchester's existing debt collection plan effective?
2. To what extent was the situation affected by the culture of the organisation?
3. How would *you* plan a debt collection system for the city?

2.3 Dividing responsibility for planning

Since business planning involves a complex set of tasks it is almost inevitable that responsibility for planning will have to be divided in some way. There are two related issues which will have a major influence on this division of planning responsibilities, as shown in Figure 2.3:

● The structure of the organisation will have a strong influence on the division of planning responsibilities. So divisionalised companies will tend to divide planning responsibilities somewhat differently from organisations which are structured by business function (see Section 2.3.1).
● Within any structure there are still choices on the extent to which responsibility (and freedom) in business planning is held at the centre of the organisation as against being devolved to the various parts. Identifying the types of **responsibility centres** which exist within an organisation is very useful in understanding this issue.

2.3.1 Some different organisational structures

For the purposes of this discussion it is useful to review some different types of organisational structure to illustrate how planning responsibilities might be related to those structures. This is not intended to be a comprehensive discussion of organisational structural types but is

ILLUSTRATION 2.4   Norchester City Coucil: effect of organisation culture on planning

The problem of devising a system to collect overdue fees and payments is one faced by planners in many organisations, public and private. To collect these payments Norchester City Council had a department of five employees, three collectors 'on the road' and two supervisors in the office. It had been found from experience that many types of debt required personal collection. In Norchester these were unpaid fees for college courses, planning applications, drain cleaning, overdue library books and fines, rent from market-stall holders and numerous other miscellaneous payments. The total amount collected was in the region of £50,000 a year.

Each week the payments collectors covered about 100 miles, paid for by the council at 19p a mile. Unfortunately half the debtors were out during the day, so the collectors left a card saying they would call later. Of those who were in only about 10 per cent were able to make payments on the spot. However a further 80 per cent of those contacted paid their debts soon after the visit. It was the department's view that the personal visit was far more effective than using the post and persisted with the system even though some debts were small. The payments collectors earned a salary of £6,000 a year, and the supervisors £9,000 p.a.

Some of the younger collectors wanted to work in the evenings, when debtors were likely to be at home, but this raised various problems:

(a) The council could not afford overtime rates, once granted for one group of workers, others would demand it.

(b) Negotiation of flexitime, so that payments collectors could include some evening work within the standard working week, would involve lengthy bargaining with unions over contracts.

(c) There were some legal difficulties in collecting money after dark, but exemptions were possible.

(d) The major stumbling-block was that implementation of such a change would require a radical change in the daily work-routine in the office. The system in operation involved a computer check on payments to date each morning. Evening visits would mean that the check had to be made manually.

These working practices had been developed over many years. Management of this department were mainly older people promoted from the ranks. They were sceptical about suggestions from junior staff, claiming they lacked the necessary experience, and were mainly interested in the overtime pay.

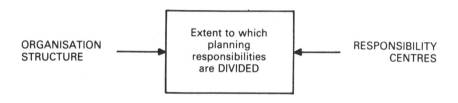

FIGURE 2.3   Dividing responsibility for planning: the two major influences

necessary to provide sufficient background against which the organisational issues of business planning can be discussed. Five commonly used structures are shown in Figure 2.4

1. In the **simple structure**, often found in small owner/manager businesses, the owner/manager will tend to take direct responsibility for most aspects of business planning. This is the entrepreneurial approach to planning discussed in Chapter 1 (see Table 1.3.). Even where operational planning has been made the responsibility of other people the owner/manager may interfere and over-ride decisions fairly frequently.
2. In the **functional structure** the organisation is divided into specialist functional areas – each one being headed by a senior manager. In a company these functions would be production, finance, marketing, etc. In public service organisations they might be somewhat different, for example, personnel, administration, computer services, etc. The strength of such a structure is that these senior managers

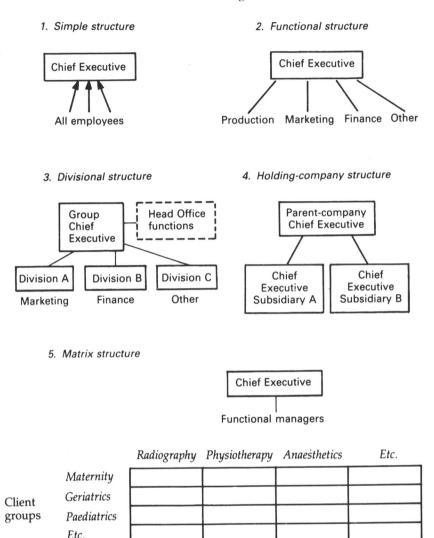

FIGURE 2.4   Five common types of organisational structure

tend to have a good specialist knowledge of their function and are therefore good at overseeing all the planning activities within their functions. The weakness is that strategic planning tends to be neglected or weak. The functional managers tend to view organisational problems in terms of their own function rather than of the organisation as a whole. So the senior manager of the computer services department in a bank who insists on regular maintenance each weekend may fail to understand the impact of this on customer service, and ultimately the company's competitive position. Some of the ways of overcoming this problem will be discussed in Section 2.4 below.

3. In the **divisional structure** quite the opposite situation tends to occur. The divisional management may have a good vision of where the division as a whole is going (strategic planning) but may be rather thin on the specialist knowledge needed to manage the business planning at the management and operational levels. In larger organisations, of course, each division would have a functional structure within it which would alleviate this latter problem.
   ' Another dilemma which often arises in divisionalised companies is the extent to which strategic planning is devolved to divisions rather than held at the centre. There are different approaches to this. In some companies divisions are only responsible for management and operational planning – all strategic planning is done at the centre (although the senior managers of divisions are probably involved in this strategic planning). In other cases strategic planning goes on at both the centre and the divisions, but concentrates on different issues. Central planning is concerned with the broad issues about the company's balance of activities whilst divisional planning concentrates on the detailed aspects of that division's activities. This matter will be discussed more fully in Chapter 3.

4. In a **holding company** structure the responsibilities at the centre are even less detailed than this. Here subsidiary companies are largely viewed as assets to be bought or sold depending on their financial performance rather than whether they fit into the 'strategic logic' of the company as a whole. In this situation the subsidiary companies need to be virtually self-sufficient in their business planning.

5. In many organisations there is more than one way to divide responsibility and often a **matrix structure** is adopted. For example, in a hospital there is a need to emphasise both the separate user-groups (maternity, geriatics, children, etc.) and the specialist skills/technology needed for patient-care (for example, radiography, physiotherapy, anaesthetics, etc.). As a result there are specialists and departments for both these types of activities. In order to treat any individual patient the various departments will have to work together. So a sick child will need the services of the anaesthetist, etc., whilst being under the care of a specialist paediatrician. Many organisations find it necessary to operate a mixed structure of this type, with the result that planning and co-ordination become critically important. For example, the anaesthetist's work-schedule must be harmonised with the patient-care

TABLE 2.2   Types of responsibility centre

Type	Responsibility	Typical extent of business planning	Examples
Cost centre	Cost against budget	Operational planning	Production departments
Revenue centres	Revenue against target	Operational planning	Sales departments
Expense centres	Spending against budget	Operational/ management planning	Public services research departments
Profit centres	Profit against targets	Operational/ management and some strategic	Product divisions
Investment centres	Return on investment	All aspects	Subsidiary companies

plans of each unit to ensure that he is in the right place at the right time.

EXERCISE 2.10

You have just moved from a job as a marketing executive for a medium-sized firm of sweet manufacturers who are structured in a functional way (see Figure 2.4). You have been appointed as divisional manager of the relatively-small boiled-sweets division of a major confectionery company.

1. How might your involvement in strategic planning change?
2. Would your previous experience be valuable in organising the operational planning at your new company?
3. What help and support might you expect on this latter issue?

2.3.2 Responsibility centres

Having looked briefly at some organisational structures it should be apparent that there are many different ways in which responsibility for business planning can be divided. A useful way of understanding how these responsibilities fit together within any one organisation is by identifying **responsibility centres** within the organisation.

A responsibility centre is a part of an organisation (usually a department) which is given a defined responsibility for its activities and performance. The importance of this to the current discussion is that the greater the scope of this responsibility the more freedom there is for business planning in that particular part of the organisation. So responsibility centres with little freedom (see below) are likely to have their business planning confined to operational planning. In contrast, other responsibility centres will have greater freedom and be more involved in strategic and management planning. The following types of responsibility centre are commonly found in organisations and represent an increasing degree of responsibility (and planning freedom) (see Table 2.2):

- *Cost centres* – are held responsible for the costs they incur usually through an ágreed budget related to the level of output. Most production departments in manufacturing companies are cost centres – they are allowed to use certain amounts of labour, materials and services for each unit produced. Their business planning must be geared toward achieving these cost targets.
- *Revenue centres* – are responsible for meeting revenue targets within a fixed expense budget. Sales departments are commonly operated in this way. The planning within the department must work within these revenue targets.
- *Expense centres* – if there is not a clear relationship between expenditure and the revenue or other benefits of that expenditure then the expense centre is expected to produce the best possible service within its budget. Most local authority service departments have to develop their plans in this situation.
- *Profit centres* – are given responsibility to plan the best combination of both costs and revenue (and hence, profit). Profit centres are quite common in divisionalised companies and represent considerable freedom within which to plan.
- *Investment centres* – have more responsibility than profit centres in so far as they are able to make decisions on how money should be reinvested in the business. Subsidiary companies may have this degree of autonomy.

In large organisations there will be a whole variety of responsibility centres – which will have varying responsibilities for the different levels of planning (strategic, management, operational). At the top of organisations are usually investment or profit centres. So the company as a whole is responsible to its shareholders for return on their investment. Lower down in the organisation, responsibilities will be more closely prescribed (as either revenue or cost centres) and in consequence the responsibility for business planning is confined to management and operational planning. For example, if the production departments are cost centres they are only able to plan within an overall strategic plan since their responsibility is to produce goods to a plan and within agreed costs. In contrast a profit centre is more able to plan strategically since it has responsibility for many more factors and is therefore able to put together plans which are relatively complete in their own right. This is also true of many **expense centres** in local authorities. The Recreation department may be allowed to launch some of its own new initiatives providing the total budget is not exceeded.

It is interesting to note that apparently similar organisations choose to divide planning responsibilities quite differently. For example, Marks & Spencers had traditionally operated their stores as cost centres with centralisation of purchasing, pricing, etc. This is in contrast to other retailers who operate their stores much closer to profit centres with more autonomy for store managers.

EXERCISE 2.11

Read Illustration 2.5, Bolton Motors.

1. Why did Mr Bolton change departments from being cost or revenue centres to profit centres?
2. Why was there so much disagreement over the particular car in the case?
3. How much profit would the **whole company** make on the complete deal?
4. How much profit does each department feel that *they* should make?
5. How would you change the system for the better?

2.4 Co-ordinating planning effort

Having spent some time reviewing various ways in which responsibilities for business planning may need to be divided it is now necessary to look at the reverse side of the coin. The danger of dividing responsibilities is that the various planning activities within a company are totally disjointed and lack any kind of co-ordination. Co-ordination will normally be required in two ways (see Figure 2.5.):

● *Vertical co-ordination* between the various levels of planning. Ensuring that operational plans are consistent with the management and strategic planning.
● *Horizontal co-ordination* between the separate business functions (or divisions). Making sure that these separate plans make sense as a whole.

ILLUSTRATION 2.5 Bolton Motors: responsibility centres

William Bolton, part-owner and managing director of a new and used-car dealership, felt the problems associated with the recent rapid growth of his business were becoming too great for him to handle alone. Accordingly he divided up the business into three departments: a new car sales department, a used-car sales department, and the service department. Each of the managers was told to run his department as if it were an independent business. In order to give the new managers an incentive, their pay was calculated as a straight percentage of their department's gross profit.

Soon after these new arrangements came into operation there was a major disagreement among the three departments. The new sales department had sold a new car to a customer at the list price of £7,200 and offered him £2,400 allowance for trade-in of his used car. Since the new car cost the department £5,000 they calculated their margin at £2,200 and passed over the trade-in to the used-car department.

The used-car department were furious at being charged £2,400 since they argued that the **wholesale** value of the car was only £1,800 and in addition it needed some £700 spent on repairs before it could be sold (at a retail price of £2,100).

To make matters worse the repair department wanted their normal 36 per cent mark-up on repair work making the repair bill £950. They were not prepared to subsidise 'internal' work.

William Bolton was very confused by these arguments. He had assumed that his new arrangements would give each department more incentive to do well. Instead it appeared that he had only succeeded in causing more trouble.

2.4.1 Co-ordination between the levels of planning

This is one of the biggest headaches in most organisations – attempting to ensure that the planning efforts at the operational and management level are actually consistent with the strategic plans of the organisation – and vice versa.

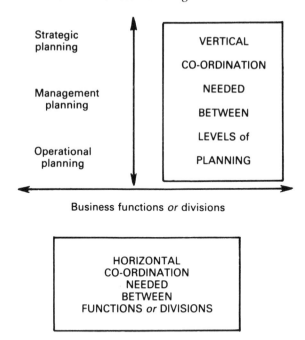

Business functions *or* divisions

FIGURE 2.5   Co-ordination of business plans is needed in two directions

● In the early 1970s 'Management by Objectives' (MBO) was regarded as a solution to this problem. MBO is a system whereby the over-all strategic plan is divided into a **pyramid** of more detailed objectives and plans for each part of the organisation right down to the detailed operational plans of each small section. The aim is to ensure that everyone in the organisation is working towards the same overall goal. In practice MBO has proved difficult to operate since it assumes a degree of stability and level of knowledge which can rarely be achieved within business planning. Equally it assumes that all groups will actually follow these objectives blindly and without question – which is very unlikely, as will be discussed in Chapter 6.

● Other organisations have chosen to take a radically different view on how co-ordination between levels of planning might be achieved. They have started from the premise that complicated systems of co-ordination (like MBO) should be avoided and the organisation should have a much more limited and flexible view of business planning. Here the parts of the organisation are given much more freedom and responsibility for their own strategic planning within centrally-set guidelines and targets. This is much closer to the reactive or incremental approach to planning described in Chapter 1, and requires that the parts of the organisation (such as departments) are given more responsibility for their own planning and, in turn, are more accountable for their performance.

● Often there is difficulty in co-ordinating operational and strategic plans because the timescales for these two types of planning are very different. There is often conflict between the short-term pressures and the need not to compromise the longer term aspirations of the company.

EXERCISE 2.12

Read Illustration 2.6, Austin Rover.

1. To what extent would you view the agreement with Honda as a matter of short-term expediency or part of a longer term strategy?
2. Does the agreement help or compromise the company's strategic plan?
3. Had they any other short-term options which you feel would have been better?

2.4.2 Co-ordination between functions or divisions

Much of the frustration and friction which occurs in business planning results from efforts to co-ordinate the plans of the various functions and/or divisions of the organisation. This is a continuing problem that occurs at all levels of planning as the following examples will show:

● In **strategic planning** this is a particular problem. A publishing company may wish to launch a new magazine into the market. To do this successfully it needs to ensure that each of the business functions plans its activities to be consistent with the others. For example, there is no point running the television advertising campaign until the production departments are ready with their print run. In turn they are unable to print final copies until all editorial work is complete and advertising material has been typeset.

● In **management planning** co-ordination can also be vital. For example, a multi-divisional company may be relying on its European division to market the products of the UK factories. Designing and operating reliable systems for shipping the goods, and

ILLUSTRATION 2.6   Austin Rover: integration of short- and long-term planning

In 1985 Austin Rover faced the problem that sales were not meeting the financial targets necessary to carry out the long term company plan. This five-year plan required investment in a new model range by the end of the decade. Another immediate problem was that current sales were not enough to keep the two main assembly plants at Longbridge and Cowley fully occupied. The company had already taken painful measures to cut costs, by closing factories, shedding labour, raising productivity and investing in flexible manufacturing systems. They had also mounted a 'biggest ever' sales campaign costing £5m.*

Enter the Japanese company, Honda. Austin Rover made agreements with Honda to help to meet their long-term targets in the following ways:

- To save on development costs by jointly developing and manufacturing a new middle-range car.
- In the meantime Austin Rover would assemble Honda cars on a sub-contract basis. This should provide enough throughput to keep the British plants busy.

However there was a danger that these short-term solutions may damage the long-term strategy of Austin Rover. In agreeing to the partnership, they were increasing competition for their own cars in the UK and the EEC. It had been suggested that the long-term Japanese strategy was to use the agreement with Austin Rover to gain a foothold in the EEC where they faced import quotas. Honda had already acquired a 330-acre estate near Swindon which would be ideally suited to a car-assembly plant.* The agreement with Austin Rover meant that for no capital outlay it had a means of assembling its cars and assessing their market potential.

The government was also involved in this dilemma – on the one hand it had a political stake in the continuation of Austin Rover as a 'British flagship' but on the more practical side it was aware that the merger would have a beneficial effect on the UK components industry which provided so many jobs. Austin

Rover, in their negotiations with Honda had to ensure that the agreement reached helped to solve their short-term problem without damaging their long-term strategy.

* *The Financial Times*, 19 June 1985.

providing proper documentation in both directions requires a high degree of co-operation between the two divisions.

● Co-ordination at the **operational planning** level is also essential. For example the operation of a stock control system may require co-operation between salespeople (whose sales are diminishing the stock), production and purchasing staff (who are replenishing the stock) and the finance department (who are attempting to control the amount of cash tied up in stock).

EXERCISE 2.13

Read Illustration 2.7, Next. The three ingredients of success are identified as financial skills, selling instinct and product innovation.

1. Using these three headings list what *you* would regard as the key aspects of the Next plan. (e.g. under 'selling instinct' you could list – medium price, short life-cycle, etc.).
2. Who would you make responsible for ensuring co-ordination of each of these factors when launching a range of clothing for a new season.

2.4.3 Co-ordination procedures

It is usually necessary to have agreed procedures to ensure that co-ordination does occur in business planning:

● Sometimes problems are relatively infrequent and in these circumstances it may be left to the Chief Executive to sort out problems of co-ordination as they arise. They are able to resolve difficulties quickly because of their senior position in the company. For example, the Chief Executive of a local authority might instruct the Chief Officers for Recreation and Education to work out sensible arrangements for out-of-hours use of school sports facilities.

● If too many difficulties are arising it may be necessary to lay down new procedures to ensure that co-ordination occurs. Network analysis may be used to define precisely when various

ILLUSTRATION 2.7   Next: exploiting a gap in the market

The success of 'Next' in the early 1980s showed that even in fiercely competitive markets, it was possible by effective planning to find and exploit a gap.

George Davies joined Hepworth in 1981, and revitalised the company with the launch of the 'Next' chain of women's clothing shops. Next was a retailing phenomenon and in three years 200 shops opened country-wide. 'Next Man' was successfully launched in 1983.

The phenomenal growth of the 300 'Next' shops lay in the way three essential ingredients had been brought together: financial skills, the selling instinct and excellent product innovation. Davies described it as a 'carefully planned exercise in marketing and merchandising stemming from intuition and experience'. He based his strategy on a glaring gap in the 25 to 40 year-old women's fashion market which he believed wanted classless, styled but fashionable clothes at the right price. And, crucially, the 'right aspirational image'.

At the top end he saw Jaeger and pricy exclusive European labels. At the bottom a mass of rather shoddy, badly-made high-fashion clothes. His small design team, working from the Leicester head office, brought out five high season collections with a short life-span. As soon as a new season was welcomed in, the old was ushered out. Clothes were sold off via a handful of 'sale' shops.

All these basic principles had also been applied to 'Next Man' and worked successfully: proving that 'Next' was not a flash in the pan. Where possible 'Next' women and men were put together in the old Hepworth stores which were slowly closed down. Davies was only too aware that 70 per cent of women influence the clothes their male partners/husbands buy. Women actually buy about 30 per cent of all menswear. As he put it, 'In every Next woman there is a Next husband or son'.

In 1982 the profits of the Hepworth Group slumped to £3.9m. By August 1984 profits had soared to £13.6m.

Source: The *Guardian*, 25 March 1985.

TABLE 2.3   Co-ordinating plans: some different approaches

Method of co-ordination	Attempts to:	Examples
VERTICAL		
Management by Objectives (MBO)	Co-ordinate all levels of planning through detailed objectives	Many organisations in 1970s
Central guidelines and targets	Allows flexibility whilst still defining overall strategy.	Many organisations in 1980s
More involvement of people	Improve co-ordination by allowing more people to be involved in strategic planning.	Industrial democracy
HORIZONTAL		
Authority	Chief executive sorts out problems by use of authority.	Small companies
Procedures	Rules about how activities should be planned.	Bureaucracies
Committees	Involve people in joint discussions	Public-sector organisations
Co-ordinating roles	People with sole responsibility for co-ordination.	Project leaders Product managers

functional tasks need to be performed (see Chapter 5) which would be particularly useful when planning big events such as an annual open-day where many departments are involved.

● A number of individuals from the various functions/divisions may be given temporary or permanent responsibility to ensure that co-ordination occurs. This may be done in several ways. It may be through a **committee** of representatives of the functions, or through a **task-force** or **project-team**.

● In some organisations permanent **co-ordinating roles** are created. Product managers are a good example – they are responsible for ensuring that all functional efforts are properly co-ordinated in producing and marketing a particular range of products. Within the public services the parallel might be a **project leader** with similar responsibilities.

Table 2.3 summarises some of the commonly adopted approaches to co-ordinating planning discussed in the previous sections.

EXERCISE 2.14

You work for a major manufacturer of fridges and freezers. The company has just completed some market research and decided to add washing machines to their product range. The Managing Director has asked you to advise on how the production and launch should be planned and co-ordinated.

1. Outline the various alternative procedures which could be used to ensure that the production and launch are properly co-ordinated.
2. Write down the major advantages and disadvantages of each of these.
3. What do you feel they should do?

2.5　Summary

This chapter has been concerned with an aspect of business planning which is often neglected by students. Business planning will only work in organisations if it is organised in a way which fits the circumstances of the organisation. There are a wide variety of different people who could legitimately be involved in some or all of an organisation's business planning. The difficulty is in weighing the obvious advantages of wide involvement with the problems which it brings in terms of creating over-bureaucratic planning systems. The key to organising effective planning lies in the way in which the responsibility for planning is divided whilst providing sufficient co-ordination between the various planning efforts within the organisation.

The discussion in this chapter has introduced readers to a very wide variety of planning issues and problems. The next four chapters are concerned with a detailed consideration of how these issues are tackled within organisations.

Recommended key readings

R. Edward Frieman, *Strategic Management, A Stakeholder Approach* (Pitman, 1984), provides a good discussion of the concept of stakeholders.

John Argenti, *Practical Corporate Planning* (George Allen & Unwin, 1980). Chapter 1 reviews some of the organisational issues in business planning.

J. C. Higgins, *Strategic and Operational Planning Systems* (Prentice-Hall, 1980), is useful to those readers who have a particular interest in formal planning systems.

John Fawn and Bernard Cox (eds), *Corporate Planning in Practice* (ICMA, 1985). Chapter 6 looks at the organisation of a formal planning system.

Roy Amara and Andrew Lipinski, *Business Planning for an Uncertain Future* (Pergamon Press, 2nd edn, 1984). Chapter 10 is concerned with the politics of planning.

CHAPTER 3

Strategic planning – thinking ahead

3.1 Introduction

The previous chapters have stressed the importance of business planning as a means of ensuring that an organisation remains successful over time. **Strategic planning** is particularly concerned with the **longer-term** health of an organisation and identifying the changes which may be necessary in order to secure a successful future.

It is easy for companies to be so busy with the day-to-day operations of the business that little time remains for thinking ahead. Companies riding on the wave of their current success may forget that circumstances around the company will inevitably change and that continued success will require changes to the company's activities. Strategic planning is concerned with understanding the major factors which dictate the long-term success or failure of a company, and with helping the company to make sensible choices about its future activities.

It is helpful to look at strategic planning under three headings (see Figure 3.1):

1. A company's strategic plans are strongly influenced by the **objectives** of the organisation. It should be remembered from the discussions in Chapter 2 that there are many different groups of people (stakeholders) who might wish to influence the organisation's objectives through their involvement in business planning.
2. The organisation's **environment** is constantly changing, creating new opportunities and threats for the company. Monitoring and

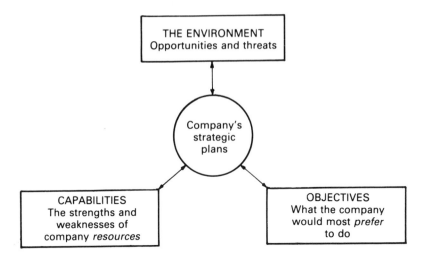

FIGURE 3.1   Major factors influencing strategic change

analysing the key factors in the business environment is a most
important part of strategic planning.

3. Gaining a proper and realistic understanding of a company's **capabilities** is essential when decisions about future activities are to be
made (discussed in Chapter 4). Many organisations find themselves in 'dead-end' markets where their capabilities are under-
exploited. Others come unstuck by undertaking tasks which are
beyond their capabilities. The company may not have the necessary
skills, or money, or perhaps its plant and equipment is inadequate
to perform the necessary tasks.

Traditionally it has been popular to analyse a company's strategic
position by using an SWOT analysis (Strengths, Weaknesses, Opportunities and Threats). In terms of the discussions which will follow it
should be clear that a SWOT analysis could form a useful summary of
the major factors in a company's environment and capabilities. However, it does *not* give consideration to an organisation's objectives. Care
needs to be taken not to assume that objectives are a predetermined and
unchangeable aspect of planning – they too may need to change.

EXERCISE 3.1

Read Illustration 3.1, North Country Breweries.

1. Identify the key issues in the organisation's objectives, environment and resources which shaped the changes between 1970 and 1985.
2. What would have happened if these changes had not been made?

In this chapter each of these three themes of **objectives**, **environment**, and **capabilities** will be discussed as separate influences on strategic planning. However, it should be remembered that it is their **combined** effect which is crucial in shaping the company's future (see Figure 3.1.).

In addition to analysing these various influences on an organisation's current activities, strategic planning is also concerned with identifying the various **development options** open to the organisation in the future. These various options will be discussed in the latter part of this chapter.

3.2 Organisational objectives

Much of the writing about business planning starts from the premise that business planning is concerned with a detailed assessment of how an organisation's objectives will be achieved. Some go so far as to suggest that the only important objectives concern the maximisation of the financial return to shareholders.

Before commencing the discussion in this section readers should be clear that this is **not** the view taken in this book. Whereas, objectives are regarded as being extremely important their role in business planning is seen differently from that described above as follows:

● Objectives are regarded as an important indication of what individuals or groups would prefer the organisation to do.
● However, these preferences will need to be tempered by the realities of the environment and the company's capabilities as discussed below. Therefore, objectives can and should be challenged during planning rather than being regarded as an unchangeable element within planning (see Chapter 1).
● There are many different groups of people who may wish to influence the policies which a company pursues in addition to the shareholders. These include management, unions, customers, suppliers, etc., (see Chapter 2). These stakeholders are unlikely to agree with each other in detail about the objectives which the company should follow.

ILLUSTRATION 3.1 North Country Breweries: response to changing environment

In the early 1970s North Country Breweries (NCB) was a small regional brewery based in Hull. It owned aroud fifty managed houses in the Humberside area, but supplied beer to over 300 outlets nationwide. The brewery had a traditional image, and concentrated on a single product, beer. In 1972 it was taken over by the much larger Northern Foods group. In 1976 the brewing industry predicted that spending on all types of beer would at best increase by 2 per cent over the next few years. This pessimistic forecast, together with the threat that bad summers could cause a 30 per cent reduction in sales led NCB to look for more stable and expanding business ventures. The company decided to expand into the catering and leisure market in the following ways:

1. By providing a meal service in all the managed-house pubs. This would provide an outlet for some of the food products of the group.
2. By becoming involved in large-scale high-class catering. In July 1984 a new banqueting suite was opened at a cost of £250,000.
3. By acquiring profitable managed houses in the more-heavily populated areas of Yorkshire at a rate of three or four a year. This also increased the asset base of the company.
4. By providing a wider choice of beer. They filled a gap in the market place in 1984 by introducing Riding Bitter, a real ale which was available in selected outlets.
5. In October 1984 Brewery Bitter was made available in 2-litre plastic bottles for supermarkets and off-licences. It was planned to extend this to other products if successful.
6. It was acknowledged that the company did not have a distinctive image compared with its competitors. They embarked on a campaign of image building in the 1980s by sponsorship of Hull's three professional sporting teams, race meetings, cricket matches, and competitions in the local press.

ILLUSTRATION 3.1 *continued*

This diversification programme required a large investment in building conversions, new staff and equipment, promotion and training and the introduction of a profit-sharing scheme in 1985.

By 1984 the company profile had changed dramatically from a traditional, one-product organisation to one whose activities were more broadly based in an expanding industry.

Source: BTEC student assignment, Sheffield City Polytechnic, 1985.

● The objectives actually being pursued by an organisation will be the result of a political process between the various stakeholder groups. For example, one group, (usually management) may impose their objectives on others, or perhaps objectives are a compromise between the wishes of various groups arrived at through bargaining.

● Publicly-stated objectives (for example in a company's annual report) are likely to be unreliable or of little practical value in working through detailed plans. It is more accurate to infer the objectives from the company's past decisions and actions.

It is against this background that organisational objectives as a part of business planning will be discussed.

3.2.1 Levels of objectives

Often objectives are discussed as though they were a single statement of intent which provided detailed guidance to all parts of an organisation. This is not the case in practice. Objectives tend to exist at different levels and in different forms as shown in Figure 3.2:

● The **mission** of the organisation is the broadest way in which the objectives can be expressed. It is normally a statement about the underlying purposes of the organisation. Mission is normally expressed in a generalised way and, as such, tends not to change too much over time. For example, Rolls Royce might have a mission of 'being the best in precision engineering'.

● The **organisational objectives** tend to be rather more specific and

FIGURE 3.2   The levels of objectives

are statements of intent concerning the organisation as a whole.
For example, the Rolls Royce mission might lead to an organisational objective of 'retaining a major market share in world-wide
aero-engine sales'.

● In large organisations it is quite common for parts of the organisation to have their own objectives – often called **unit objectives**.
Within Rolls Royce the Development unit may have an objective
'to develop a new aero-engine every ten years'.

Chapter 2 discussed the difficulties which companies can face in
ensuring that the various planning efforts are properly co-ordinated.
One of the important tasks of business planning is to assess the extent to
which these various levels of objectives are consistent with each other.
In addition the objectives being pursued by the various parts of the
organisation (unit objectives) will also need some proper harmonisation.
For example, the owners of a chain of restaurants might regard their
mission as being the 'best in town'. This may not be consistent with the
objectives being pursued in the individual restaurants. Perhaps one
restaurant manager has decided to introduce some cheaper dishes on
the menu to reverse a decline in customers. Even within that one
restaurant there may be inconsistencies where the chef (whose objective
is to enhance his reputation) continues to stress quality and all the extra
costs which that incurs whilst the reduced price menu requires some
cost-savings.

It was mentioned in Chapter 2 that some organisations try to improve
this co-ordination between the various objectives through a system of
'management by objectives' (MBO). Readers are referred back to this
discussion in Chapter 2 and reminded of some of the difficulties of
making MBO work in practice.

EXERCISE 3.2

Read Illustration 3.2, Alcan.

1. What is the relationship between the purpose, objectives and policies in this company statement?
2. Are there any conflicts between these three levels?
3. Most of the policies are concerned with particular functions of the business, for example, marketing, finance, personnel, etc. Are there any possible inconsistencies between these various functional policies?

It would be wrong to assume that the relationship between the various levels of objectives is one-way traffic, with the higher levels dictating the more detailed objectives which are being pursued lower down in the organisation. Indeed this is one of the complaints about MBO systems.

In particular the encouragement of information and ideas flowing *up* through the organisation is important. In general it is people lower down in organisations – those who carry out the operational tasks (production, marketing, etc.) who are most in touch with the reality of the company's position. The problem is that by the nature of their job such people will only be expected to have a partial view of the company's activities and plans, and may be unable to see their own efforts and activities in this wider corporate setting. The most successful companies would encourage ideas and information from lower down the organisation and allow the organisational objectives to be challenged (and amended if necessary) in the light of this information. The role of senior managers within such a system is to be sensitive to the messages coming from below and to use their judgement to shape and amend objectives and performance targets accordingly.

3.2.2. Conflicting objectives

There are many practical difficulties which will be encountered in trying to plan in the flexible way proposed in the previous section. The major problem is that the information and ideas being fed up through the organisation are likely to be inconsistent with each other. Inevitably the process will be used politically by the various parts of the organisation and external stakeholders (such as suppliers, customers, banks, etc.) to further the objectives they would most like the organisation to pursue. The likely consequence of this process is conflict and senior managers are responsible for containing and managing these potential conflicts.

ILLUSTRATION 3.2 Alcan: levels of objectives

In 1978 Alcan Aluminium was an international mining and refining company based in Canada. Over the preceding fifty years Alcan had evolved into an extensive network of subsidiaries in thirty-three countries. Much of this activity was in developing nations like Jamaica whose attitude to Western-based mining companies became more critical in the 1970s. The company's stated objectives in 1978 were summarised as follows:

Purpose

To utilise profitably the risk capital voluntarily invested by the shareholders.

Objectives

- To operate at a level of profitability which will ensure long-term economic viability... and which compares favourably with other similar industries.
- To maintain an organisation of able and committed individuals and provide opportunities for growth both nationally and internationally.
- To strive for a level of operating, technical and marketing excellence which will ensure a strong competitive position.
- To seek to balance the interests of shareholders, employees, customers, suppliers and governments. Also to take into account the differing social, economic and environmental aspirations of the countries and communities in which we operate.
- To conduct all business with integrity.

Policies

- To promote employees' understanding of the company's work, and to be alert to their needs and attitudes.
- Where possible to employ and develop the nationals of the countries in which the company operates.
- To pay fair and competitive wages.

ILLUSTRATION 3.2 *continued*
- To promote high standards of safety and appropriate standards of quality.
- To publish clear information on company activities and accounts.
- To refrain from offering improper payments by ensuring that all financial transactions are recorded.
- To require that all employees disclose commitments which might involve a conflict of interest.
- To improve our competitive position by supporting research, innovation and relevant technology in the countries in which we operate.
- To take all practical steps to prevent pollution and conserve resources.
- To respect human rights and individual freedoms; not to discriminate or become involved in political activities.

Source: Abridged from company statement 1978.

Decisions tend to be made through a process of continual bargaining between stakeholder groups.

Table 3.1 shows some common conflicts over organisational objectives. In practice most conflicts are resolvable even if this results in an uneasy peace. This is because there are certain objectives, such as survival, about which all stakeholders are agreed. It is often the case with newly-formed companies that there is a high level of co-operation during the early months or years when the objective is clear and simple – becoming established. Once this has been achieved conflicts tend to become more frequent as different groups try to push the organisation's plans in different directions.

EXERCISE 3.3

Choose an organisation public or private and:

1. Identify the stakeholder groups.
2. Identify **specific** examples of each of the conflicts outlined in Table 3.1.
3. What would be the attitude of each major stakeholder to each conflict (that is, what objectives would they *prefer*?).
4. How would each conflict be resolved (that is, which objectives would the organisation tend to follow?) Why?

TABLE 3.1 Some common conflicts of objectives

1. In order to grow, short-term profitability and cash-flow and pays levels may need to be sacrified

2. When family businesses grow, the owners may lose control if they need to appoint professional managers

3. New developments may require additional funding through share issue or loans. In either case financial independence may be sacrificed

4. Public ownership of shares will require more openness and accountability from the management

5. Cost-efficiency through capital investment can mean job-losses

6. Extending into mass-markets may require decline in quality standards

7. In public services a common conflict is between mass provision and specialist services (e.g. preventive dentistry or heart transplant

3.2.3 Use of objectives in planning

It should be clear from the discussion that objectives are a very important part of business planning and are used in a variety of different ways:

- It is very valuable to look at the dominant objectives in understanding the historical performance of an organisation. For example, a company may have been stuck in declining markets because its owners had a reluctance to change the organisation's products in any way. This in turn will indicate some of the difficulties to be faced if performance is to be improved in the future.
- It is important to remember that organisational objectives are the outcome of the various objectives of different stakeholder groups and the extent to which they are able to influence the business plans of the organisation. Business planning must reflect this political reality, that is, be clear on **who** is driving the plans and policies of the company.
- Since objectives should not be regarded as unchangeable in the planning process they will need to be consistent with the realities of the organisation's environment and resource capabilities. In other words objectives may well be the consequence of these other pressures rather than necessarily leading the business planning.
- Later sections of the book will discuss the way in which objectives (for example targets) will be used to monitor and control the performance of an organisation during the process of implementing

plans. Budgets are a commonly-used method of translating objectives into performance targets.

EXERCISE 3.4

Referring back to Illustration 3.2, Alcan, explain how you might use the various objectives to achieve the purposes outlined in this section:

1. Do these objectives give any clues about the type of business Alcan was in 1978?
2. Can you identify the way in which various stakeholders might have influenced these objectives?
3. Which objectives would you regard as resulting from the reality of Alcan's environment and resources?
4. Which could be used to develop performance targets?

3.3 The business environment and forecasting

3.3.1 Environmental influences

In discussing the business environment it is *not* intended to review in detail all the various aspects of an organisation's environment and the way in which they impact on a company. Such a detailed treatment can be found in specialist texts about the business environment and it will be assumed that readers have some background knowledge of this type of environmental analysis.

Most organisations' environments are very complex because of the wide variety of potential influences on the organisation. Not only is a company subjected to the effect of changes occurring in its immediate environment such as its customers, or labour unions or suppliers, it must also be mindful of the more general influences which can affect the viability of the business. So changes occurring in the legal, political, economic, social or technological environment are likely to have an influence on a company's position. Often these broader environmental influences are difficult to predict and it is especially difficult to understand the **specific** impact on any one company. For example, considerable vision would have been needed in the early 1950s to predict, in detail, the extent to which the wider availability of the motor-car would change shopping patterns and the structure of retail distribution (particularly in groceries through the advent of supermarkets). Similarly new cheap information technology (microcomputers and telecommunications) will bring further changes in shopping patterns in many industries and impact significantly on service industries.

Most companies' plans are affected by the economic climate, but not always in the same way. Whereas perhaps the majority of companies feel that a growing economy best suits their purpose this is not universally true. A buoyant economy may lead to considerable 'trading-up' in purchasing patterns – for example, the DIY enthusiast buys power-tools instead of hand-tools; food consumption moves away from basics such as bread to more sophisticated tastes; preferences within leisure and entertainment also change – away from watching league football to newer sports or more family weekends away from home.

Social changes are also easy to miss – or rather, it is easy to fail to understand their impact on a company's future. The advent of the teenage consumer in the late 1960s created significant opportunities for a new wave of entrepreneurs in the pop-music industry and clothing boutiques. Many well-established companies failed to respond to this change – it took the best part of a decade for the traditional clothing retail chains to address the 15–24 year-old market in any serious way.

Sometimes social and legal changes can have a combined impact on companies. During the 1970s there was a great deal of legislation concerned with various aspects of 'socially responsible' behaviour. Health and Safety and Work legislation; racial and sex discrimination in employment; and pollution control are prominent examples. All of these significantly influenced the circumstances within which companies were able to plan their activities. This legislation captured the prevailing mood of the time – namely that perhaps economic growth had been pursued at the expense of other issues and that legislation was needed to force companies into line with the social values of that time.

EXERCISE 3.5

Read Illustration 3.3, The Business Environment. Imagine that you are a business planner in each of the organisations mentioned in the Illustration and (in each case):

1. Would you regard the change in the environment as an opportunity or a threat (or perhaps both)?
2. What specific changes might need to be considered in the organisation's business plans as a result of these environmental influences?

ILLUSTRATION 3.3   The business environment

There are many different ways in which changes in the business environment could influence an organisation's business planning, in addition to the immediate pressures from suppliers, competitors and customers

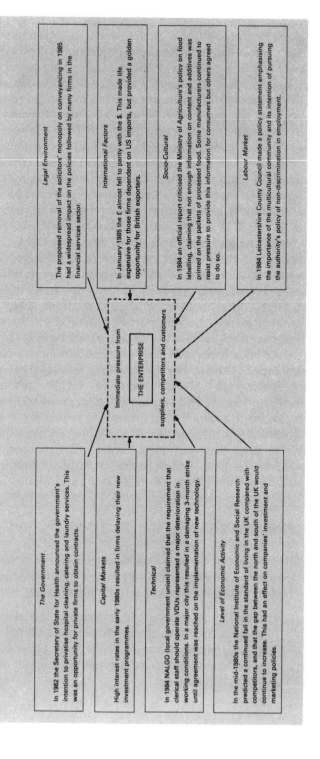

Legal Environment

The proposed removal of the solicitors' monopoly on conveyancing in 1985 had a widespread impact on the policies followed by many firms in the financial services sector.

International Factors

In January 1985 the £ almost fell to parity with the $. This made life expensive for those firms dependent on US imports, but provided a golden opportunity for British exporters.

Socio-Cultural

In 1984 an official report criticised the Ministry of Agriculture's policy on food labelling, claiming that not enough information on content and additives was printed on the packets of processed food. Some manufacturers continued to resist pressure to provide this information for consumers but others agreed to do so.

Labour Market

In 1984 Leicestershire County Council made a policy statement emphasising the importance of the multicultural community and its intention of pursuing the authority's policy of non-discrimination in employment.

The Government

In 1982 the Secretary of State for Health announced the government's intention to privatise hospital cleaning, catering and laundry services. This was an opportunity for private firms to obtain contracts.

Capital Markets

High interest rates in the early 1980s resulted in firms delaying their new investment programmes.

Technical

In 1984 NALGO (local government union) claimed that the requirement that clerical staff should operate VDUs represented a major deterioration in working conditions. In a major city this resulted in a damaging 3-month strike until agreement was reached on the implementation of new technology.

Level of Economic Activity

In the mid-1980s the National Institute of Economic and Social Research predicted a continued fall in the standard of living in the UK compared with competitors, and that the gap between the north and south of the UK would continue to increase. This had an effect on companies' investment and marketing policies.

Immediate pressure from

THE ENTERPRISE

suppliers, competitors and customers

The emphasis in the discussion which follows is the way in which the business environment influences strategic planning and some of the ways in which the business environment can be analysed and understood **for this purpose**. This discussion will be divided into two major topics:

1. **Analysing** a company's **competitive** position – particularly through the use of **structural analysis**. This helps in identifying the most important opportunities and threats in the environment.
2. **Forecasting** methods which help to predict how the various parts of the environment are likely to change in the future.

It is the **combination** of this broader framework (structural analysis) and the more detailed investigation of particular aspects of the environment which provides a useful analysis of a company's situation.

One of the difficulties with environmental analysis is that there are so many factors which could theoretically affect a company's success in the future. It is easy to create long lists of these factors, such as exchange rate shifts, changing consumer preferences, more militant unions, new government regulations, etc. However, the really important skill in environmental analysis is the ability to sort out the **key issues**. These key issues should then be summarised as the major **opportunities** and **threats** which the organisation must take into account when thinking ahead. Clearly plans which avoid major threats and seize opportunities are likely to be the most successful. The purpose of the analytical techniques which will now be discussed is to help companies to identify these major opportunities and threats in a systematic way.

3.3.2 Analysing the competitive environment

One of the mistakes which companies often make when thinking about their future is to take too narrow a view of the competition which they face. If asked to list competitors most companies would identify other organisations which are involved in the same line of business. So the Ford Motor Company would rightly see British Leyland, Renault, Vauxhall, Toyota, etc., as their competitors. However, whereas the company's competitive position is affected by the activities of these other motor companies it is influenced by many other factors too. It may well be that one or more of these other factors will be more important than the activities of Renault or Toyota.

A useful approach to identifying and analysing the various factors which influence a company's competitive position is shown in Figure 3.3, and will be used as a framework for the discussion in this section.

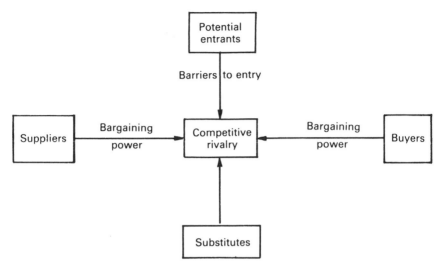

FIGURE 3.3   A model for structural analysis (Porter)

Source: Reprinted with permission of the Free Press, a division of Macmillan, Inc. from *Competitive Strategy: Techniques for Analyzing Industries and Competitors* by Michael E. Porter. Copyright © 1980 by the Free Press.

This approach is often referred to as a **structural analysis** of the competitive environment. The analysis is concerned with establishing the following:

● The extent to which the business is threatened by the possibility of new organisations entering the 'industry' or genuine substitutes being offered to replace the company's products or services.
● The way in which the relative power of the various organisations involved in the 'industry' is likely to shift. This involves a consideration of the changing role of suppliers (of materials, equipment and money), organised labour, manufacturers, distributors and consumers.
● The competitive rivalry within the industry – this is the head-on competition between similar companies already mentioned (for example, Ford and British Leyland).

Of course, each of these factors is influenced by the others. For example, the entry of new companies may upset the *status quo* and trigger off competitive battles between established companies which in turn may weaken their position *vis-à-vis* consumers in the market place. Bearing this in mind these factors will now be discussed in more detail.

TABLE 3.2   **Some common barriers to entry or substitution**

Barrier	*Reasons*	*Examples*
Economies of scale	Fixed costs are high favouring companies who have high volume output	Process industries – chemicals, steel, etc.
Capital investment needed	product/service requires expensive equipment or facilities	Football League Clubs
Experience	Cost-efficient operations may take time to learn, favouring established companies	High-technology industries
Distinctive image and customer loyalty	Customers have no good reasons to change	Heavily branded goods (e.g. chocolates and sweets)
Business contacts	Established companies have high degree of loyalty from suppliers or outlets. In some cases suppliers or outlets are owned	Tied houses in the brewing trade
Legal or government action	Regulations restrict competition and protect established companies	State monopolies, e.g. railways, postal services

THREAT OF NEW ENTRANTS OR SUBSTITUTES

A useful way of thinking about the likelihood of a company's competitive position being upset by new entrants or substitutes is to consider the extent to which **barriers** to entry or substitution exist. There are many different reasons why entry or substitution might prove difficult. These are summarised in Table 3.2, with some examples. Many of the barriers to entry which could protect the company from new entrants may well not be present in the case of substitutes, for example:

● Whereas the skill and experience of the Swiss watch-makers was of central importance to the dominant position they held in the world markets for many decades it proved of little value and relevance when micro-electronic technology (digital watches) replaced the precision-mechanical technology of traditional watches.
● The traditional strength of many British manufacturers of electrical goods (cookers, washing-machines, etc.) was the loyalty of

their customers, mainly wholesalers and electrical showrooms. However, the advent of new outlets during the 1970s – distributors like Comet, Trident, Bridgers etc. – allowed easier entry of foreign competitors often offering substitute products (such as split-level, microwave and dual-fuel cooking).

● Sometimes substitute products are unexpected. This is particularly true with consumer goods and services. Companies supplying videos, home computers, holidays and kitchen furniture are competing with each other for the disposable income of consumers. Sometimes the efforts of one of these industries is able to claim a disproportionate share of consumer spending than had hitherto been the case. For example, consumer spending on kitchen furniture rose from a mere £3m in 1963 to almost £200m by the late 1970s because of the efforts of a few go-ahead companies like Hygena.

Whereas the discussion in this section has tended to take the viewpoint of an established company identifying the competitive **threats** which it faces, the same analysis would be used to spot **opportunities** where a company might be considering entering new industries or new lines of business.

POWER OF SUPPLIERS AND BUYERS

The balance of power between the various sectors of an industry is a very delicate matter and significant shifts tend to occur over time. For example, in both the Do-it-Yourself (DIY) and grocery industries there has been a significant shift of power away from manufacturers towards the larger distribution companies (superstores) over the past few years. Similarly if organised labour is regarded as a key supplier within an industry its power has waxed and waned as the fortunes of various industries have changed.

Table 3.3 summarises some of the issues which may affect these changes in power, with examples. The importance of understanding the changes which are occurring within any industry is that they affect the likely attractiveness of business ventures in any one sector of an industry. For example, a manufacturing company which is simultaneously subjected to increasingly strong suppliers of raw materials, more militant unions, and larger/stronger distributive outlets may have considerable difficulty in protecting the profitability (or even viability) of its business in the future. Such a combination of events would be regarded as significantly threatening and undoubtedly result in a search for other opportunities into which the business might develop.

TABLE 3.3 **Factors governing the power of suppliers and buyers**

Factor	Reason	Examples
1. Number and size of companies	In general suppliers and buyers are weaker if they are fragmented (many small companies) as against concentrated (fewer larger companies)	Growing power of supermarkets, DIY superstores, etc.
2. Specialisation or dependency	Where it is difficult or costly to change suppliers or customers, this becomes a source of power for those companies	Companies manufacturing aerospace components cannot easily be 'dropped' once they become a recognised supplier
3. Relative importance of item being traded	Many items may be a small part of a company's cost or sales and therefore relatively unimportant	Companies hiring outside consultants for training programmes – where quality of input outweighs the cost. The major items of training cost lie in the overheads and the participant's time
4. Threat of vertical integration	If barriers to entry are low between the various parts of an industry companies may be tempted to take on more than one role by vertical integration.	In the motor industry the number of components made 'in-house' as against sub-contracted is consistently open to review.

EXERCISE 3.6

You are the assistant to the owner/manager of 'Second City Timber', a Birmingham-based manufacturer of wooden doors and window-frames. The company's turnover is £1.5m; about 50 per cent from direct sales to building companies and 50 per cent through DIY outlets. Using the list in Table 3.3 together with your general knowledge of the building and DIY industry:

1. Make an assessment of the power of the suppliers to, and buyers from, your company.

TABLE 3.4   **Reasons for competitive rivalry**

Competitive rivalry is often high if:	Reason	Example
Companies are of similar size	No one company dominates the industry. There are constant worries about this competitive balance becoming upset	UK chocolate confectionery industry. Rowntrees, Cadburys and Mars are all of similar size
Market growth slows down or declines	During growth individual companies can grow without gaining market share. This is not possible without market growth	Periodic price-cutting wars between petrol companies
Fixed costs are high	Companies need to maintain volume of output even at the expense of margins	Car manufacturers like Ford, Vauxhall and British Leyland who have invested heavily in automated production lines
Little difference between products	Customers are able to switch and choose often playing off companies against each other	Most commodity markets, particularly when supply exceeds demand
It is difficult to leave the industry	If costs of exit are very high, e.g. expensive fixed assets may have no other use	Chains of cinemas are stuck with property which is difficult to use for other purposes without considerable investment

2. Suggest ways in which the company's plans might be changed to strengthen its position *vis-à-vis* its buyers and suppliers.

COMPETITIVE RIVALRY

It is important to predict whether the head-on competition between the established companies in an industry is likely to increase or decrease. There are a variety of reasons why this competitive rivalry might change as outlined in Table 3.4. Such an analysis should help both in identifying possible threats within the company's current industry, and also in assessing the extent to which any business ventures being planned in new industries are likely to meet resistance.

EXERCISE 3.7

Read Illustration 3.4, Wispa. Imagine you are part of the product team planning the launch of Wispa.

1. Use the list provided in Table 3.4 to make your assessment of the difficulties which would be faced in launching Wispa.
2. How would this assessment influence your plans?

Whereas a structural analysis will help a company identify many of the opportunities and threats it is very likely that the precise impact of many of the factors considered will need more detailed consideration. Business forecasting is an important way in which this is done.

3.3.3 Forecasting for business planning

Business forecasting is a major topic in its own right and it is not the purpose of this section to provide a definitive account of forecasting methods. Instead the discussion will focus on the ways in which forecasting contributes to business planning. First, it should be recognised that forecasting is likely to be most valuable when the environment has some degree of stability or is changing in a way which can be understood. Often a company's environment is either extremely complex or changing rapidly or unpredictably and in these circumstances traditional forecasting methods are of less value. In such situations other ways of coping with this uncertainty will be needed and these are discussed in Chapter 4.

In order to make the discussion as clear as possible, it will be assumed that *demand forecasting* is being undertaken, however, the methods are appropriate to forecasting any aspect of interest to the planner, for example, cost, price, etc. There are three broad categories of forecasting method:

1. *Time-series* or *projection* methods which assume that the future is a direct reflection of the past, and therefore concentrate on identifying past trends as a basis for predicting the future.
2. *Cause and effect* methods, such as multiple regression, which analyse the past to establish which factors most strongly influenced demand and then use this knowledge to forecast the future.

ILLUSTRATION 3.4   Wispa: competitive rivalry

Cadbury's 'Wispa' chocolate bar was launched in 1983 backed by a £6m advertising campaign. It proved successful in halting 20 years' declining market share for Cadbury's and the excess production capacity which resulted. The table below shows how Rowntrees 'Kit Kat' and the 'Mars Bar' dominated the market in the early 1980s. The £12m dedicated to a new manufacturing plant was a sign of the importance of the brand to Cadbury in this fiercely competitive market.

Top-selling confectionery products

	Cadbury	Rowntree	Mars	Others
£100m+		Kit Kat	Mars Bar	
£80m+	Dairy Milk			
£30m+	Flake Milk Tray Roses	Quality Street Yorkie Aero	Twix Bounty	
£20m+	Creme eggs Crunchie Double-decker	Smarties After Eight Polo Mints	Milky Way Galaxy Marathon Maltesers	
£15m+	Wholenut Fruit and Nut Fudge	Black Magic Pastilles Rolo	Opal Fruits	Extra Strong Mints All Gold
£10m+	Caramel Buttons Chocolate cream Turkish delight Chocolate Eclairs	Lion Bar Dairy Box Glacier Mints Fruit Gums	Topic Treets Tunes	Toblerone Spearmint Allsorts Milky Bar

Data Source: Cadbury
Note: By 1985 sales of Cadbury's Wispa exceeded £70m,
gaining the position of third largest brand in the confectionery
market.

3. *Other* methods such as scenarios which are needed when the future is expected to be very different from the past, as might be the case when launching a new product.

Illustration 3.5, 'Super Bolts', shows how a combination of these methods is needed to forecast demand and is used as the basis of the discussion which follows.

TIME SERIES

Time-series methods use information about the past to *describe* what has happened (e.g. to demand) without explaining why. The most valuable analytical techniques are extrapolation, moving averages, or least-squares regression. Often these methods can best be shown graphically. Whichever type of analysis is used the purpose in analysing past data is to **identify trends** which can be projected forward into the future.

It is important to identify different types of trend which occur. These are shown in Figure 3.4.

- The **underlying trend** (sometimes described as the **secular trend**) defines the general drift of the data, for example, whether demand has been growing, static or declining, and the *rate* at which these changes have been occurring (for example, a market growing at 5 per cent per annum).
- **Cyclical trends** can often be identified. These are caused by the longer-term recessions and booms which are found in many industries. The cycle is usually described in terms of its **frequency** (for example, four years from recession to recession) and its **amplitude** (for example ± 10 per cent around the underlying trend).
- Many organisations experience **seasonal trends** which are cyclical changes within one year. Seasonal trends are described in the same way as cyclical trends.

Having identified the historical trends, projection methods simply project these trends forward into the future.

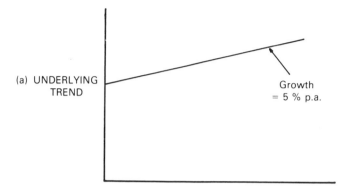

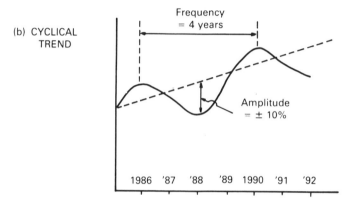

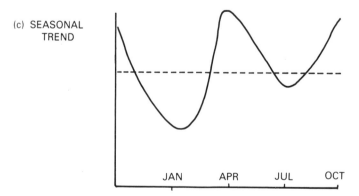

FIGURE 3.4   Trends used in forecasting

EXERCISE 3.8

Read Illustration 3.5, Super Bolts Company and using the information provided:

1. Assuming that the past rate of growth in the **market demand** continued into the future make your estimate of the underlying trend in market demand by 1994 (do this graphically).
2. Why is a time series analysis inadequate in this case?

CAUSE-AND-EFFECT METHODS

Cause-and-effect methods differ from time-series methods in the way that past data is used. Data is analysed to establish which factors caused demand in the past. The most commonly-used statistical method is that of **multiple regression** which seeks to produce a mathematical equation explaining the relationship between a dependent variable (such as demand) and those factors which caused the dependent variable to have the value which it did. These **causal factors** are called independent variables. As an alternative, the mathematics of the forecast can be relatively straightforward and understandable if a graphical representation is used. The steps in the analysis are as follows:

● Use multiple regression methods to establish an equation which satisfactorily describes the relationship between the dependent variable (demand) and appropriate independent variables (such as motor-car production). It should be noted that in practice this can be an extremely lengthy process and in many case may prove very difficult. A graph will often prove useful as an alternative.

● Using forecasts of these independent variables for the period ahead, the equation can be used to forecast the likely demand. This may also be done graphically.

EXERCISE 3.9

Using the information provided in Illustration 3.5 undertake a **cause-and-effect** forecast of the **market demand** for Super Bolts by 1994 by following these steps:

1. Explain why the independent variables should be:
   (a) UK production of motor cars (A)
   (b) number of bolts per axle (B)

ILLUSTRATION 3.5   Super Bolts Company: forecasting

The Super Bolt Company was a small precision engineering company who specialised in the manufacture of precision bolts for the axles of motor cars. In 1984 there was only one other company who manufactured these bolts – the Axle Bolt Company. The Managing Director of Super Bolt Company was keen to assess the likely future demand for Super Bolts in order to decide whether any new investment in machinery was needed. The company had detailed records of its sales over the previous ten years together with the total UK demand. The company also received information about the UK production of motor cars, together with the motor industry's own forecast for the following ten years. All these data are shown in the following graphs:

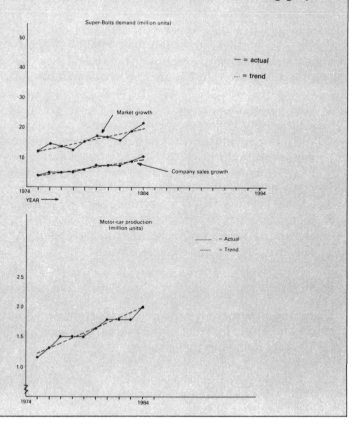

Several facts emerged from an analysis of these data. First, although the demand was clearly cyclical in nature there had been an underlying growth in *company sales* of about 10 per cent per annum which compared favourably with the overall market growth of 5 per cent per annum (as a result company market share had risen from 33 per cent to almost 50 per cent in ten years). Second, the pattern of demand was clearly dictated by the production of motor cars which showed similar cyclical movements but on average, had also grown by 5 per cent over the previous period. Third, the motor trade were clearly expecting the growth in production to slacken. Their forecast suggested an average growth rate of about 2 per cent per annum in the period ahead.

During the period 1974–84 there had been no significant change in axle design. However, one major axle producer had recently launched a new '1995' axle. This new design required twice as many bolts as the traditional axle and it was being claimed that all motor cars would be using this axle by 1995.

2. Use the forecast of (A) to forecast the underlying trend in market demand for Super Bolts if (B) remained constant (do this graphically).
3. Why is this forecast different from that which you obtained by time series (projection)?

OTHER FORECASTING METHODS

It can be seen from the illustration that a forecast which relies exclusively on either time-series and/or cause-and-effect methods may well fail to take proper note of any **new** developments in the environment (in this case, the new axle). It is usually necessary to supplement the forecast with other analyses which take care of these new factors. In the illustration the advent of the new axle will influence demand for bolts. Previous experience of the rate of adoption of new products could be useful in forecasting demand for bolts. Very often it is impossible to be too precise about the impact of new factors and the forecast may need to be refined as new information becomes available in the future.

EXERCISE 3.10

Continuing the forecasting exercise for Super Bolts:

1. Amend your forecast of the underlying trend in market demand from the previous exercise to take account of the impact of the '1995-axle' (do this graphically).
2. How certain are you of the accuracy of your forecast?
3. Forecast the underlying trend in company sales by 1994 making your assumptions clear.
4. How might the company's business plans need to change as a result of your forecast?

3.3.4 Identifying opportunities and threats

One of the pitfalls of strategic planning is that the detailed work of forecasting, etc., can obscure the overall purpose of these analyses, namely, to sort out the major opportunities and threats surrounding an organisation. In particular, it is essential to establish the extent to which the organisation's plans are properly matched to the environment and whether forecast environmental changes will create significant **threats** to the organisation's survival.

A changing environment also creates many **opportunities** and these need to be identified and assessed as possible future ventures. The most important opportunities and threats can be usefully summarised as part of a SWOT (Strengths, Weaknesses, Opportunities and Threats) analysis and shown in Illustration 3.7, British Telecom, at the end of the next section.

3.4 Assessing an organisation's capabilities

Understanding an organisation's capabilities is a key part of business planning in two main ways:

1. It helps to identify areas of particular **strength** which could form the basis for the company's future operations. Perhaps some strengths are under-exploited.
2. Areas of **weakness** are also important to identify. These could represent significant constraints on pursuing certain business ventures **or** areas where the company may choose to follow policies of improvement (for example, through training, capital investment, etc.).

There are a number of different analyses which can be used to establish an understanding of an organisation's capabilities. Since capability is largely concerned with **resources** it is sensible to begin the discussion with a brief review of the types of resources which an organisation has at its disposal.

3.4.1 Resources available to companies

Table 3.5 lists the types of resources which are available to organisations and which influence the ability of the organisation to pursue different types of business ventures:

PHYSICAL RESOURCES

These include buildings, machines, etc. In assessing the capability of the organisation it is necessary to identify the age, condition and location of these physical assets rather than simply listing them.

HUMAN RESOURCES

People are a key resource of organisations. The number of personnel, their skills and the extent to which working agreements allow/preclude flexible use of people all contribute to the overall picture of the organisation's capabilities.

SYSTEMS

The systems within an organisation are often the key to its success and are needed to organise the resources of the company. Business planning plays an important part in assessing the company's systems and the extent to which changes might be needed.

INTANGIBLES

Many organisations have significant strengths in intangible assets such as 'image' or 'brand-name'. The value of intangible resources should not be underrated. Indeed in many service companies these intangibles can be the key asset of the company. Potential purchasers are often willing to pay substantial sums of money for this 'goodwill', underlining their real value.

TABLE 3.5 Resources available to organisations

	Operations	Marketing	Finance	Personnel	R & D	Others
Physical resources	Machines Buildings Materials Location Stock	Products/ services Patents, licences Warehouses	Cash Debtors Stock (Equity)† (Loans)†	Location	Size of R & D Design	Location of buildings
Human resources	Operatives Support staff Suppliers	Salesmen Marketing staff Customers	Shareholders Bankers	Adaptability Location Number of employees Age profile	Scientists Technologists Designers	Management skills Planners
Systems	Quality control Production control Production planning Purchasing	Service system Distribution channels	Costing Cash management Accounting	Working agreements Rewards	Project assessment	Planning and control Information
Intangibles	Team spirit	Brand name Goodwill Market information Contacts Image	Image in City	Organisational culture Image	Know-how	Image Location

† Equity and Loans are owed by the company but an understanding of how the company is financed is an important part of a resource audit.
Source: G. Johnson and K. Scholes, *Exploring Corporate Strategy* (Prentice-Hall, 1984) (with permission).

3.4.2 Reasons for good or poor performance

It can prove very difficult to assess why a company's performance has been good, bad or indifferent. Some reasons will undoubtedly be concerned with the organisation's environment or the objectives that they have been pursuing as discussed in the previous sections. There are also several reasons why the company's capabilities and performance might have been affected by its resources:

- The **type of resources**, for example, old machines, unskilled work-force or out-of-date products may be reasons for poor performance and important areas for improvement in the business plan.
- **Poor utilisation** of resources; for example, perhaps materials are wasted, capacity fill is low, skilled people are used to do unskilled jobs, etc. Often these problem areas can be improved by redesigning some of the company's business systems. For example, wastage in the cutting-room of a clothing factory may be improved by better planning of the flow of orders to allow for less wastage in off-cuts.
- **Poor control** of resources; for example control systems concerned with quality, stock, costing, or production planning may be ineffective causing the organisation to perform badly. Again, the remedy – improving control systems – may be easy to identify, but more difficult to change.

Table 3.6 gives some examples of how an organisation's resource capability might be assessed by looking at a combination of these three factors.

EXERCISE 3.11

Choose any organisation with which you are familiar. You work for a firm of consultants and have been asked by the organisation to prepare a report on their resource capabilities. From your general knowledge of the organisation prepare a list of **specific** questions you would wish to ask on your visits to the company. Use Table 3.6 as a checklist but ensure that your questions are specifically related to your chosen company.

The purpose of investigating the issues identified in Table 3.6 is to assess whether the company's past performance could be regarded as satisfactory. It is not possible to answer this question without some *bases*

TABLE 3.6 Assessing an organisation's resource capability

Resource area	Type of resources	Utilisation of resources	Control of resources
Buildings	Age of buildings, location and quality of accommodation	Capacity fill	Security, maintenance
Plant and machinery	Age and type of machines	Lay-out of production system, job design	Production control systems
Financial	Financial structure of company	Profitability, use of working capital	Costing systems, budgets, investment appraisal systems.
Materials	Access to sources of supply	Suitability of materials used. Yield during processing (waste)	Purchasing systems. Stock control
Products/services	Stage in product life-cycle	Demand situation for product/service. Effectiveness of marketing effort	Stock control. Quality control. Losses (e.g. damage or theft)
People	Age and skill profile of employees	Labour productivity. Allocation of jobs to people (e.g. duplication of effort)	Quality of leadership. Control of outlets. Industrial relations climate
Intangibles	Extent to which intangibles are a real strength	Exploitation of image, brand name, market information, research knowledge, etc.	Control of image (public relations) Information systems.

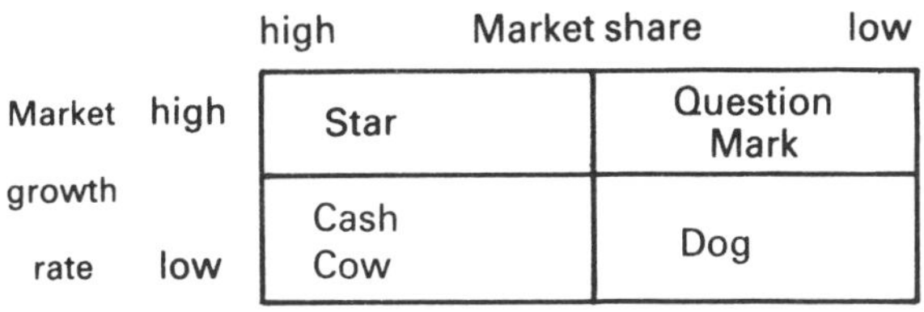

	high	Market share	low
Market high	Star		Question Mark
growth			
rate low	Cash Cow		Dog

FIGURE 3.5 Product portfolio analysis

against which the performance can be measured. Typically this would be done in the following ways:

● By comparing company performance and capability over a number of previous years. This *historical* approach can be quite useful. For example, if labour productivity is regarded as a key measure of company performance, the current level of output per employee could be compared with that for previous years. Such a comparison should be extended to all those resources which are regarded as critically important in determining the company's capabilities.

● The danger of relying on such an historical comparison is that it is very introspective since it pays no attention to changes in capability and performance which may be taking place in competitive companies, industries or countries. Since most organisations operate in a competitive situation these relative measures are particularly helpful in understanding the company's capabilities.

3.4.3 Product portfolio analysis

The discussion so far has assumed that a company's capabilities can be fully understood by analysing **separately** all its various resources. Such an analysis is unlikely to be adequate since the company's capability is also determined by the **mix** or **balance** of resources which it possesses. For example, a company may have significant marketing strengths in terms of selling high-volume, cheap, repeat-purchase products. In the same company the production departments may be regarded as being particularly good at producing high-quality, durable products. Whereas, these two resources could each (separately) be regarded as a strength the **combination** of these resources would be regarded as a **weakness**. High quality, durable products are not required for high-volume, low-price markets.

Product portfolio analysis is a useful means of assessing the balance of an organisation's activities and stems from the work of the Boston Consulting Group (BCG) in the 1960s. The analysis classifies a company's products or businesses in terms of two important factors related to the market situation, as shown in Figure 3.5.

- The **growth rate** of the market. Rapidly-growing markets may be regarded as desirable but they also require significant levels of investment in terms of money, production capabilities (including people) and the development of appropriate products or services.
- The **market share** which the company possesses in the market segments in which it operates. It is argued that market share is a key ingredient of success in the market place. Companies with greater market-share are, on the whole, at a significant competitive advantage because of their better cost-structure, and their influence in the market.

These two factors (growth rate and market share) are the basis on which the company's products or activities can be classified as one of the BCG categories as seen in Figure 3.5, namely:

Question Marks are those activities on which the company's future may depend. They are something of an unknown quantity and require investment (and therefore risk) if they are to be developed into the *stars* of the future.

Stars are those products/businesses which are in the full flood of success. Although stars may be highly profitable, the continuing growth needed to follow the market may still require a net outflow of funds from the company.

Cash Cows are products/businesses in maturity, reaping the benefits of a strong market position. As the name suggests they should be significant contributors of funds to the organisation.

Dogs are also in maturity, (or decline) but do not enjoy the strong market position of the cash cows. They may still be net contributors of funds but are areas of potential worry to the company. They may need to be revitalised (for example, by investment) or disposed of.

Such an analysis should prompt two important questions to be answered in preparing business plans:

1. Is the balance of activities adequate? For example, are there sufficient cash cows providing the security and funds in support of areas with greater future potential (such as question marks).
2. Does this spread of activities represent the company's resource capabilities properly? For example, a preponderance of question marks would require particular strength in research and development whereas the management of cash cows requires properly-

ILLUSTRATION 3.6 Dixons plc: product portfolio analysis

The following information is abridged from the Directors' report for Dixons plc in 1984.

1. *Retail Division*

Sales £217m (1982/83 £151m)   Profit £14.8m (1982/83 £7.5m)

The division has had an outstandingly successful year, with a sales increase of 44 per cent to £217m, and profit almost doubled. These increases have resulted from new concepts of shop design and merchandising, a greatly enlarged product base and more retail shops.

During the year new stores were opened, fourteen were re-sited or extended and ten modernised. The division also acquired the Orbit group of stores. The division had 274 branches at year end.

Dixons successfully entered the market for microwaves and substantially increased its market share in photography, where it currently holds a commanding position. The division has also achieved market-share increases in televisions (sales up 76 per cent), video cassette recorders (up 28 per cent) and portable audio products (up 65 per cent). In the two merchandise categories that Dixons entered the previous year, home computers (up 348 per cent) and keyboards, the division has maintained its market lead. Dixons will, during the current year, become the first multiple to market personal computers nationally.

2. *Distribution Division*

Sales £78m (1982/83 £69m)   Profit £642,000 (1982/83 £880,000)

In pharmaceutical wholesaling the year began favourably with sales well ahead of the previous year, and margins becoming more stable. However, in August 1983 the Government imposed a 2.5 per cent price reduction and suspended further price increases. This, together with an increase in importing to pharmacies, caused an erosion of margins.

Margin pressures combined with a downturn in some key markets, led to a reduction in the profitability of our butane gas refill, snuff blending and associated distribution activities.

ILLUSTRATION 3.6 *continued*

3. *Property division*

Sales £11m (1982/83 £9m)   Profit £2.3m (1982/83 £2.2m)

Our thrust in recent years has been in the retail sector, the area of our greatest expertise. This sector has demonstrated remarkable stability and resilience, and there is now a considerable increase in demand. We are at various stages of progress on a substantial number of developments throughout the country with a high level of either pre-letting or serious interest. The division has a clear competitive edge in its field. As a result our cash flow is growing and the prospects for increased profits are favourable at this time.

4. *Overseas division*

Sales £29m (1982/83 £31m)   Profit £2.3m (1982/83 £3.7m)

In the USA the construction of the division's major office development in Broad Street, New York, was successfully completed. The building should be fully let in 1985 as planned. Because of high interest rates, housing sales in the USA have been lower than forecast. As a result sales so far in our residential development in Arizona have been below budget. However, the project as a whole will take another two years to complete. We are considering joint property ventures in the USA with local partners.

5. *Processing division*

Sales £19.3m (1982/83 £11m) Profit £401,000 (1982/83 £314,000 loss)

The processing division returned to profit in 1984. The division launched its new film-processing service to independent retailers under the 'Horizon' banner. This venture is proving highly successful and almost 800 Horizon franchises are now in operation. The division also opened its first high-volume film-collection shop in London, trading as 'Photoquick' and additional outlets are being sought. These two developments exploit market movements towards the retail sector and have increased the division's overall market penetration.

> The division also acquired Colortrend whose prime market is mail order. They trade under the 'Truprint' brand which has developed considerable consumer awareness and loyalty.
>
> Source: Abridged from Directors' report 1984.

developed financial-control systems to ensure that significant amounts of cash **are** being generated from these activities and channelled into more cash-hungry ventures.

EXERCISE 3.12

Read Illustration 3.6, Dixons plc.

1. Carry out a product portfolio analysis of Dixons attempting to locate the business activities and the divisions at the appropriate point on the matrix. Explain your reasons.
2. Do you think that Dixons have a balanced portfolio?
3. How might future plans be affected by this analysis?

3.4.4. Identifying strengths and weaknesses

There are dangers that the analysis of a company's capabilities may become too detailed at the expense of a proper identification of the **key strengths and weaknesses** (which must be seen as the end-point of this capability assessment). A strengths-and-weaknesses analysis summarises the most important conclusions being drawn from the resource analysis of a company.

The analysis is particularly useful if it takes into account the strengths and weaknesses of the organisation relative to its major competitors. This is often described as assessing the **distinctive competence** of the company, that is, those strengths which give the company an edge over its competitors and particular areas of weakness to be avoided.

EXERCISE 3.13

Read Illustration 3.7, British Telecom.

1. What were the major strengths and weaknesses of British Telecom in 1984?

2. How effective was BT's response to the opportunities and threats in the telecommunications market?

ILLUSTRATION 3.7   British/Telecom: SWOT analysis

In 1981 the Government announced its intention to privatise British Telecom (BT). Until this time BT had a complete monopoly of all telecommunications with the exception of large PABX systems with over 120 extensions. Privatisation, which came in 1984 provided both threats and opportunities for the company:

- BT had to compete with companies like Plessey and ITT in the market for all telecommunications equipment and service from private telephones to complex switching equipment. On the positive side, the market for large exchange systems was opened to them.
- BT began a sales drive. They appointed representatives on a bonus scheme to attack the business market with a new range of microprocessor-controlled switching equipment and generous leasing terms under the Merlin trade-name.
- BT mounted the 'phonepower' campaign to promote higher call usage. This was aimed at making business customers aware of the use of the telephone in their marketing strategies. BT provided training courses for telephone-selling tailored to customers' needs.
- BT provided a wider range of telephones under the 'Infone' label available in shops. For the business customer it promoted car-phones and radio-paging.
- To counter its poor image for service and reliability BT introduced Telcare to monitor customer opinion. The company also mounted a programme of staff training to counteract the complacency resulting from many years of monopoly.
- BT began replacing the old cable network with optical-fibre cables and new switching equipment to provide faster and more efficient calling for the business customer. BT was likely to retain the monopoly of the domestic market for some time, for it was too expensive for a competitor to install new cables for each house. However other companies were likely to install new cables for the lucrative business market. Mercury, one of BT's competitors was considering a plan to lay cables along the railway lines between major business centres.

• When BT became a private company in 1984 certain restrictions were imposed by the government. First BT had to maintain loss-making services such as telephone boxes, services in rural areas and operator services. Second, they had to provide an equipment-testing service for all equipment, including that of their competitors. Thirdly, they had to be seen to be trading fairly; customers and competitors complained to the government watchdog OFTEL if BT tried to undercut on contracts.

Source: BTEC student assignment, Sheffield City Polytechnic, 1986.

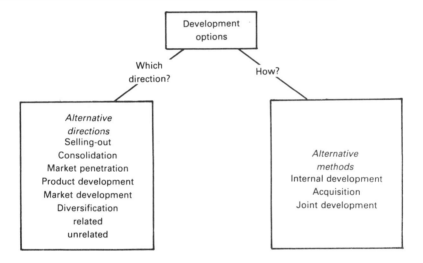

FIGURE 3.6   Identifying future options

3.5 Identifying future options

The discussions so far in this chapter have been concerned with understanding a company's position in relation to the three major forces which will dictate its future; the organisation's objectives, the business environment and the resource capability. Within these constraints there are likely to be a number of different options which a company could follow (with varying degrees of success) in the future.

In deciding which activities to pursue there are two related issues to be considered as shown in Figure 3.6:

PRODUCT

		Present	New
M	*Present*	Selling-out Consolidation Market penetration	Product development
A			
R			
K			
E	New	Market development	Diversification related unrelated
T			

FIGURE 3.7   Directions for development

1. the **direction** in which the company might choose to develop, for example, perhaps new products should be developed or parts of the business sold off.
2. The **means** by which this could be achieved (for example, internal development or acquisition).

3.5.1 Development directions

Figure 3.7 summarises the development directions which organisations might choose to consider, described in terms of the product/market plans of the company. So, for example, there may be a number of opportunities within the current products/markets which might help to **consolidate** the organisation's position. Other development opportunities might require the development of **new products**, the extension into **new markets** or even **diversification** away from the current products/markets. The purpose of this section is to indicate briefly what the various options might entail and why companies might choose to follow them. Readers interested in a fuller discussion of these options should follow up the reading recommended at the end of this chapter. Table 3.7 summarises the key points from the following discussions.

Before considering new developments it is advisable to think about the consequences of a 'Do-nothing' plan, in other words, if the organisation continued its current plans what would the organisation's performance be? This is a very useful basis with which to compare other plans. Clearly organisations who face a rather bleak 'Do-nothing' situation have a greater incentive to change than might other organisations.

TABLE 3.7   **Some common reasons for choosing development
options**

Option	Common reasons for choice	Examples
Do nothing	(a) Is easy, requires little change	
	(b) May well be good enough	
Consolidation or market penetration	(a) Maintaining or improving share in a growing market	Quality improvement or cost-efficiency as competitive weapons
	(b) Switching emphasis in static or declining market	
Selling-out	(a) Company circumstances irretrievable	
	(b) More resources needed	
	(c) Speculation-selling at the top of a market.	Property companies
	(d) Personal reasons	Retirement of the owner
	(e) To balance the company's activities	Company buying and selling its subsidiaries
Product development	(a) Company's particular strengths lie in its market knowledge and contacts	Retailers
	(b) A statutory requirement to serve certain markets	Public services
Market development	The company's particular strengths lie in its product or technology	Electronics, Process industries (Steel, Chemicals, etc.)
Related diversification	(a) Control of suppliers (quantity, quality or price)	Component manufacture in motor industry
	(b) Control of markets	
	(c) Improved information (technological or market information)	
	(d) Cost-savings	Integrated steel plants
	(e) Profit or growth	
	(f) Indirect competition	
	(g) Resource utilisation	
Unrelated diversification	(a) Resource utilisation	
	(b) Escape from current product/markets	
	(c) Spreading risk	
	(d) Personal values of leaders	

It is also quite sensible for organisations to look at development plans which most closely relate to the company's current activities (That is, the present products/present markets box in Figure 3.7). It may well be that these opportunities are sufficient to satisfy the company's objectives and are within the company's capabilities.

Often organisations which have had a period of significant growth may feel that a **consolidation** is necessary in order to improve certain aspects of its business such as quality or cost control. This might be very sensible if market growth is declining and competitive activity increasing. British motor manufacturers were in this situation during the late 1970s and early 1980s.

In some instances an organisation may feel that **selling-out** is the only sensible way forward. Perhaps the situation has deteriorated so much that survival is threatened or maybe necessary developments will not be possible without the resource backing of a much bigger organisation. The example of Acorn in Chapter 1 illustrated this point. Where **speculation** is a key aspect of an organisation's activities (for example, commodities or property) selling-out at the top of the market may be a good strategy. Sometimes the owner of the company has reached retirement and sells the family business. Many of the large conglomerate companies will buy and sell subsidiaries as a means of keeping a properly-balanced range of interests.

Often organisations find themselves in relatively static market situations yet still have a desire to grow. This may only be possible by **market penetration** (at the expense of competitors).

Although organisations might have a natural tendency to follow plans which are closely related to current activities this may prove impractical or undesirable. In these circumstances the alternatives of **product development** and/or **market development** may prove attractive:

● *Product development* includes many strategies ranging from minor modifications or upgrading of current products or services to launching genuinely new products. However, in all cases the rationale is the same – trying to exploit the company's knowledge of certain markets by additional or replacement products. Retail companies would normally use this as a central part of their future development plans. The development of traditional estate agencies into 'property shops' – offering allied services of insurance, mortgages, etc., is also a good example.

● *Market development* also includes a number of different types of development. For example, it could involve moving into new market sectors as the most successful clothing retailers have done, or geographical spread, or often finding new uses for existing products, an example being the use of stainless steel for car-exhaust pipes. In all cases the rationale is one of further exploitation of a company's current products or technologies by opening up new market opportunities.

In reality many developments require a combination of both product and market development. For example, a public house might extend its market coverage by serving lunches or even opening as a coffee bar outside licensing hours.

EXERCISE 3.14

Read the Illustration 3.8, Marks & Spencer: Product and market development.

1. What trends caused Marks & Spencer to move away from consolidation in the clothing market (refer to Table 3.7)?
2. Which aspects of this plan would you classify as product development and which as market development?
3. Would you advise them to choose other development options?

If organisations are prepared to forgo the security of **both** their current products **and** their current markets there are two types of options worthy of consideration which would fall under the general heading of **diversification**:

● There are options which are **related diversifications** in the sense that they are within the 'industry' in which the company operates. So, for example, a manufacturer of children's sweets might consider **backward integration** into sugar supply or **forward integration** into wholesaling or retailing or perhaps **horizontal integration** into chocolate manufacture. The possibilities for related diversification can be quite numerous as shown in Figure 3.8.
● Other organisations may choose developments which lie beyond the industry in which they are currently involved. Indeed some companies such as Imperial Tobacco and Lonrho have developed over a number of years by a process of unrelated diversification. There are a variety of reasons why unrelated diversification might be regarded as desirable and these are also outlined in Table 3.7.

EXERCISE 3.15

Read Illustration 3.9, Lonrho (p. 103).

1. How would you describe the type of diversification undertaken by Lonrho since 1909?
2. Why have they developed this way? (See Table 3.7)

ILLUSTRATION 3.8   Marks & Spencer: product and market development

In the spring of 1985 Marks & Spencer became the first retail stores group to earn more than £300m in pre-tax profits.* Maintaining the position of Britain's leading retailer had meant continued change in both the product and market field. Marks & Spencer were responding to social trends, such as women working, leisure, increased credit and couples shopping together for household items. They were also changing the profile of goods sold – away from the traditional clothing towards household goods with a higher retail mark-up. The changes can be summarised as follows:

- **'Satellite' stores:** smaller and 'down-the-road' from the main store, these are likely to specialise in specific products. In 1986 six Home Furnishing shops were opened together with nine St Michael 'Nurseries' catering for all baby needs.† They are seen as the answer to 'land-locked' big stores which cannot be extended.
- **Out-of-town stores:** bigger and with more parking facilities and a wider range of goods. The first was opened in the Metro Shopping Centre at Gateshead in 1986.
- **Shops-within-shops:** small self-contained mini-stores – for household plants, for example – within big stores.
- **Financial services:** continued extension of the charge-card scheme, and wider use of the data-base on customers which it provides for promotion activities.
- **Mail order:** An experiment in the West Country, whereby a mail order form was provided with a standard Marks & Spencer household catalogue, may be extended to other branches that do not carry the full product range.
- **Refurbishment** on a large scale to improve the décor of existing stores. The emphasis will be on maintaining a friendly atmosphere.
- **More export business** and development in special food and clothing lines, for example, speciality wines and ski gear'.

*The *Sunday Times*, 12 May 1985.

† Marks & Spencer publicity for account holders.

FIGURE 3.8 Development by related diversification: alternatives

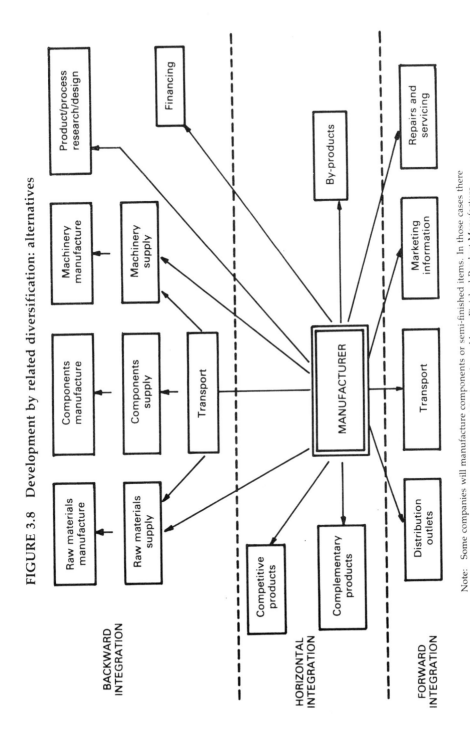

Note: Some companies will manufacture components or semi-finished items. In those cases there will be additional integration opportunities into Assembly or Finished Product Manufacture.

Source: G. Johnson and K. Scholes, *Exploring Corporate Strategy* (Prentice-Hall, 1984) (with permission).

3.5.2 Methods of development

A company needs to give consideration to the alternative methods by which it could develop along any of the alternative directions already discussed. For example, a company owning several newspaper shops within a city might decide that it would wish to develop by market penetration. This would mean growth at the expense of other news-agents. Three methods could be used:

1. *Acquisition* of other newsagents' businesses either with the purpose of running them as a going concern or shutting them down and servicing the customers through one of the company's existing shops.
2. *Internal development* of the company's business (in other words, the company develops through building up business itself). In these circumstances market-share could be gained by opening up new shops in competition with existing traders. If some areas of the city are developing while others are declining such developments may be possible even within an overall no-growth situation. Alterna-tively, it may require more aggressive policies being followed in the current shops in order to woo customers away from competitors.
3. *Joint developments* with another company may make sense. For example, perhaps the company will offer existing sole-trader news-agents the possibility of trading under *their* company name and benefiting from company advertising in return for a part-stake in their business.

Table 3.8 outlines some of the major advantages and disadvantages for organisations of these various methods of development.

EXERCISE 3.16

Read Illustration 3.10, Distillers.

1. Write a briefing paper (about 700 words) explaining the relative merits of acquisition and internal development as methods of pursuing the diversification into new product areas.
2. Which of the various diversifications mentioned do you prefer? Why?
3. How were Distillers' diversification problems resolved in 1986?

ILLUSTRATION 3.9 Lonrho: range of activities

LONRHO

1909 ——— 75 YEARS ——— 1984

From its original base in 1909 as the London & Rhodesia Mining Company Lonrho had diversified in a major way in its first 75 years. These were its main activities in 1984:-

Property

World-wide property investments

Printing and publishing

22 provincial Newspapers and 1 national (Observer) Printers of Company bonds and prospectuses, postage stamps, school textbooks

Mining and refining

Precious metals mining and refining in Africa; coal mining, off-shore oil and gas exploration in the Bahamas

Motor distribution

Sole distributor of Audi and VW cars, buses and trucks in the UK, and for Spanish Seat cars. Large Austin Rover dealer Agents and distributors for European cars and farm machinery in Africa

Transport

Freight handling and warehousing at Rotterdam. Marine insurance. Air freight company operating from the UK

Agriculture

Tea, sugar and coffee production in Africa. Growth in vegetable production and cattle ranching for export from East Africa. Leather and other products

Engineering

Steel production, making sinks and fridges in the UK. Water treatment plant in Belgium for export to Arabia; car and motorbike assembly in Nigeria. buses in Zimbabwe. Paint production in Zambia. Manufacturers of water components

Textiles

Manufacture and retailing of bed linen in the UK and sacking material in Malawi

Wines and spirits

Whisky in the UK, vineyards in France, breweries in Kenya, coca-cola bottling plants in Nigeria

Hotels and leisure

Hotels and conference centres in Mexico and Bermuda. The Metropole Hotel Group in the UK. Casinos in London

Source: Company statement 1984

TABLE 3.8   **Relative merits of different methods of development**

Method	Advantages	Disadvantages
Acquisition	1. Speed 2. Buying 'know-how' 3. Overall cost may be low 4. Competitive position may be left undisturbed	1. Difficult to control new company 2. Difficult to integrate old and new 3. No candidates to acquire
Internal Development	1. Slower development helps to acquire knowledge and skills 2. Spreads cost 3. Less disruption	1. Slow 2. May never match performance of established companies because of late entry. 3. Upsets competitive position – possible backlash
Joint development	*Shares:* 1. Risk 2. Cost 3. Expertise (allows specialist roles)	1. Difficulties of working together 2. The weaker partner dictates pace of development

3.6 Summary

This chapter has outlined the type of analyses involved in strategic planning which help organisations to *think ahead*. The analysis of the company's current situation can usefully be divided into three parts although these are very closely related to each other. Analyses should look at the variety of **objectives** which individuals or groups would like the organisation to pursue; the organisation's **environment** – in particular the opportunities and threats which exist and the company's **capabilities** – its major strengths and weaknesses. Although these analyses, are concerned with an organisation's past performance and current position they are nevertheless forward-looking in purpose since they seek to identify those **key issues** about the company's situation which will dictate the type of activities which need to be planned for the future.

The various development options available to the organisation in the future can be usefully developed from this historical analysis as has been shown in the latter parts of the chapter. This is the reason for entitling this chapter 'Thinking Ahead' – since it is the part of business planning which lays the foundations on which **decisions** about the future of the

ILLUSTRATION 3.10 Distillers: diversification

In 1985 the Distillers Whisky Company were concerned because of their poor profits growth of the previous five years. The company had failed to generate any new products. It had been adapting different whisky brands, slowly contracting capacity in its Scottish distilleries which had been reduced from forty-five to twenty-four*

The Company had considered various areas for diversification. In 1984 they had attempted to gain a large holding in the Bank of Scotland, but the move was not favourably received by the banking authorities.* Another obvious area for diversification was food. Like every large supplier Distillers had been squeezed by the large supermarkets' purchasing power. Moving into food would expose them to the same risks, particularly as stores such as Tesco preferred own-branding. Despite these disadvantages, the addition of some food items would give Distillers a more balanced portfolio of products. A third possibility was for Distillers to consider a major new-product launch in the drinks market, possibly for young drinkers. Distillers had bought an American distribution company in 1984, which, together with its European subsidiaries, would provide an ideal vehicle for new ventures in the drinks market.

During early 1986 the company received a great deal of attention from rival take-over bids from the Guinness company and Argylls who saw Distillers as a useful diversification to their own interests in the food and drink markets. The battle was finally won by Guinness in a controversial take-over of the Distillers company.

* The *Sunday Times*, 10 March 1985.

company can be based. Chapter 4 is concerned with decision-making in business planning.

Recommended key readings

Gerry Johnson and Kevan Scholes, *Exploring Corporate Strategy* (Prentice-Hall, 1984), provides a comprehensive coverage of strategy-making in organisations.

M. E. Porter, *Competitive Strategy* (Free Press, 1980), provides an extensive discussion of how organisations might analyse their competitive position.

Ray Thomas, *Business Policy* (Philip Allan, 1983) 2nd edn. Chapter 3 is a useful discussion of the role of objectives in strategy-making.

Liz Rick and Frank Neal, *The Business Environment* (Nelson, 1983), is specifically written for BTEC students.

Gordon Bolt, *Market and Sales Forecasting* (Kogan Page, 1981) 2nd edn, is a useful book for those readers wishing to learn more about the use of forecasting in business planning.

Ray Wild, *Production and Operations Management: Principles and Techniques* (Holt, Rinehart & Winston, 1984) 3rd edn. Chapter 21 provides a useful discussion of performance measures which is relevant to the issues concerning resource analysis.

CHAPTER 4

Making decisions

4.1 Introduction

This chapter is concerned with how decisions about an organisation's future are made. It has been a common misconception that planning and decision-making are the same thing. This is not the case as should be apparent from earlier chapters of this book. Making decisions about the future is simply one of the tasks within business planning. A great deal has been written about decision-making techniques for business and it is the purpose of this chapter to show how a variety of decision-making approaches can be useful within business planning. It is not intended to give an exhaustive and detailed description of decision-making techniques. If readers are interested in following up particular aspects of decision-making the references at the end of the chapter should prove useful.

Figure 4.1 shows that there are two related aspects of decision-making which are an essential part of business planning. The chapter is divided into these two themes:

1. Choosing the **preferred plan** is an important part of business planning. Some readers may regard this as fairly self-evident. However, one of the shortcomings of business planning is that this particular aspect of decision-making has tended to be over-emphasised at the expense of the other factor in Figure 4.1. Often **optimisation techniques** can be useful in identifying the most sensible course of action for an organisation. Business planning at all levels will depend heavily on analyses which help choose the preferred plan. For example, the foreman in a machine shop will need to choose the best way of allocating jobs to machines and

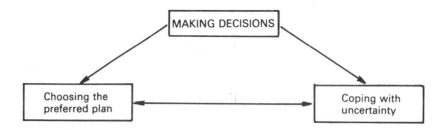

FIGURE 4.1   Decision-making as part of business planning

operators (**operational planning**). Equally, at a **strategic level** decisions have to be made between the various options which an organisation could follow – for example, would it be better to open up new shops in the south-western region or start a new operation in France?

2. Business planning is of little value to organisations if it is confined to identifying the preferred course of action. Most business planning situations are subject to considerable levels of **uncertainty** and, therefore, it is essential that business plans take proper account of this uncertainty. An analogy would be someone making a journey who was only in possession of a description of the **best route**. If there were no hitches then they should arrive safely. However, without a **map** they may be unable to cope with any unexpected events (such as roadworks causing a diversion).

   Business planning must provide this map as well as the most preferred route. There must be fall-back plans in case things go 'wrong'. This will involve assessing the uncertainty which the organisation faces, the **risks** which it is prepared to take and the degree of **flexibility** which is required in future plans.

These two aspects will now be discussed separately.

4.2   Choosing the preferred plans

Decision-making is an important aspect of planning because it assists in the process of choosing the most preferred courses of action for an organisation. This is necessary at all levels of business planning. However, it is impossible for these decisions to be made without some *criteria* against which the various options can be assessed. Analytical techniques of decision-making can then help in assessing possible courses of action against these criteria.

4.2.1 Decision criteria

There are three different types of criteria which can be useful in assessing the relative merits of various alternative courses of action:

1. The **suitability** of an option is concerned with the extent to which the option addresses the problem. For example, in strategic planning this would involve an assessment of whether a particular strategic option builds on the strengths of the organisation and exploits genuine opportunities in the environment (as discussed in Chapter 3).

   At an operational level the assessment of suitability is often described as a 'technical' appraisal of the situation. For example, whether a new machine would be capable of meeting the required quality and output targets; whether a librarian is capable of being retrained to handle on-line computer data-bases, etc.
2. The **acceptability** of an option is related to the likely consequences of following a particular plan. For example, whether the plan would achieve the levels of profitability or employment which people expected. At an operational level, acceptability is often a key issue when working practices are likely to be changed by new technology.
3. The **feasibility** of a plan is to do with whether the plan will be possible in practice. For example, whether the organisation has sufficient money for the investment which the plan requires; or the necessary management skills to cope with different ways of operating.

When using these various criteria to assess different business plans against each other it is necessary to ask a number of specific questions for each criterion. Examples of typical questions are outlined in Table 4.1.

EXERCISE 4.1

Read Illustration 4.1, Supergrip Tools.

1. How far do you agree with the suitability, acceptability, and feasibility of each option as perceived by the new management?
2. Apply the analysis to a further option, namely, a merger with a larger tool company with international interests.
3. What specific analyses would you wish to undertake to assess these three alternatives more rigorously?

TABLE 4.1   Some important questions when assessing the future

---

1. *Suitability of options*
   - Will the plan tackle existing problems. Will it avoid or remedy resource **weaknesses** and/or **threats** in the environment?
   - Will the plan exploit the **strengths** of the company and/or the **opportunities** in the environment?
   - Will the plan fit the dominant **objectives** of the organisation? If not can these objectives be adjusted to fit the plan?

2. *Acceptability of options*
   - How will financial performance be affected (for example, profitability)?
   - How will financial **risk** change (for example, liquidity)?
   - Will the financial **ownership** of the company change (for example, new shareholders, more loans)?
   - Will the **functions/responsibilities** of any group of people change significantly?
   - Will other **stakeholders** be affected (for example, suppliers, customers)?

3. *Feasibility of options*
   - Can the necessary **funds** be found?
   - Is the organisation **capable** of the required performance levels?
   - Can the necessary **market position** be achieved in the face of **competition**?
   - Will the necessary **skills** be available?
   - Will the **technology** be available?
   - Will all the necessary **materials and services** be obtainable at satisfactory levels of price and quality?

It is important to remember that although these decision criteria are applied as part of the process of making decisions they are also concerned with the practicality of the business plans. As such they are closely related to the discussions which will follow in Chapter 6. The remainder of this section is devoted to a discussion of how various analytical techniques can contribute to deciding the most preferred course of action for a business.

4.2.2 Option ranking

Ranking is a very simple way of assessing systematically the **relative** merits of various alternative plans. As such it is useful at all levels of planning. In strategic planning it can be used to compare a variety of development options against the assessment criteria just discussed. At the operational level it can be helpful in deciding how people or items should be selected from a queue. Ranking has the particular virtue of

ILLUSTRATION 4.1　Supergrip Tools: assessment of options

Supergrip Tools was formed in 1979 when four junior managers in an old-established (Sheffield) tool company decided to buy the firm with the aid of a £350,000 bank loan, following liquidation. The new management team were energetic and enthusiastic, and succeeded in keeping the firm going, but over the first five years they were faced with major difficulties:

1. The old company had been family-owned and controlled. Working practices were orientated towards providing a living and an easy existence for the family. Several managers were coasting in anticipation of their pension. On the positive side, many of the seventy-five staff were loyal and highly skilled toolmakers, on whom the firm's reputation for quality workmanship depended.
2. The history of the company had led to a large and fragmented product range. The company manufactured a total of 1750 different products, ranging from heavy hand-tools such as vices, to lighter items such as chisels.
3. The company had 1500 customers but only 250 of these had sizeable accounts. They ranged from those who bought Supergrip tools but sold under their own brand name, to wholesalers, retailers, and even the Ministry of Defence. The salesmen were expected to sell all products to all potential buyers in their particular area of the UK (no exports).
4. When the old company went into liquidation many of the creditors remained unpaid. This made it difficult to get supplies. Similarly, many customers were reluctant to begin trading again, fearing that the new company would not survive for long.
5. Although the factory buildings were acceptable, much of the machinery used to manufacture the tools was old and inefficient.

The 'rescue' operation for Supergrip had been successful, and a satisfactory level of sales maintained. However, the management were aware of the desperate need for new investments and developments for long-term survival, especially in the light of the static UK market demand for tools, and increasing import penetration. Two major categories of option are considered below in terms of their suitability, acceptability and feasibility.

ILLUSTRATION 4.1 *continued*

	A. Rationalise existing product range and customers	B. Expand into export market.
Suitability	Supergrip could economise on: 1. Sales and administration by concentrating on those customers with larger orders 2. Eliminating short production runs 3. Only selling under own brand name Does **not** address problem of static UK market.	Would give access to developing markets for quality tools, particularly the Middle East and thus solve problems of static demand.
Acceptability	Would salesmen be prepared to acquire right skills to specialise? Work-force would need to adapt to narrow product range. Some skills would be redundant.	Would require major changes in skills and approach for a traditional company. Management team needs to be prepared to take risks, travel and develop contacts. Workers would have to adapt to make types of tools needed for export market.
Feasibility	Does company have skills to assess market – which tools and customers to concentrate on and which to eliminate? New investment needed as existing machinery cannot cope with long production runs, but this is the 'cheaper' alternative.	Major difficulty in acquiring necessary exporting skills. Possible retraining or buying an already-established export manager. Would need considerable financial backing, high set-up costs for export drive; also payment delays. Could they gain foothold in this very competitive market?
Conclusion	Not particularly suitable, but more acceptable and feasible given the existing resources than (B).	The most suitable solution, but greater element of risk. Acceptability and feasibility in doubt.

Source: Abridged from a case study by P. Jennings, Sheffield City Polytechnic.

being a simple and easy technique to use, but some of its dangers need to be avoided. For example, it is almost always necessary to **weight** the various factors which are being used in the analysis. In some instances one or more factors may be of overriding importance (in the waiting-list example which follows, urgency of complaint could become such a factor if the imminent death of any patient was likely). Another obvious danger is that the relative importance of the various criteria may need to change over time and the plan must be adjusted to take account of this.

EXERCISE 4.2

Read Illustration 4.2, Hospitals Waiting List Management.

1. Assuming that only one person per week is treated, and one new person joins the list, produce a *ranked* waiting list of the five patients for *each* of the next ten weeks (commencing 3 January 1986).
2. How long did each patient have to wait for treatment?
3. What criticisms would you have of this system and how would you improve it within current resource constraints?

4.2.3 Decision-trees

Decision-trees could be regarded as another type of ranking technique. The major difference lies in the fact that alternative courses of action are ranked by progressively **eliminating** other options (by applying further criteria which need to be met). Decision-trees can be used at various levels within business planning. In strategic planning they are useful in assessing the **suitability** of the various development options discussed in Chapter 3. For example, a company may decide that the most suitable development options are those which produce growth, with minimal investment and in related products or markets. By applying each of these three criteria many development options are eliminated on the grounds that they do not satisfy one or more of the criteria. Figure 4.2 shows an example of how a decision-tree can be used in this way. Choosing growth as an important criterion automatically ranks options 1–4 more highly than 5–8. At the second stage the desire for low investment would rank 3 and 4 above options 1 and 2 and so on. In operational planning they can be used to clarify many different planning problems in all business functions. They can help with assessing choice of suppliers (purchasing), or distributors (marketing), or in planning new product development. Many business microcomputers now have useful decision-tree packages to help with business planning. Decision-

ILLUSTRATION 4.2   Hospitals: waiting list management

One of the most difficult planning problems in the National Health Service is the management of waiting lists. The following describes one approach to ranking patients in a waiting list in an Orthopaedic Department of a hospital. Each patient in the waiting list is allocated a 'score' depending on an agreed set of factors relevant to the patient's condition and situation. For simplicity these can be divided into three categories:

1. *Disability* (*D*) Which takes into account the effect of the patient's condition on his earning capacity, family, community and general 'psyche'.
2. *Urgency* (*U*) of the condition. This is a clinical judgement based on the severity of the condition, its liability to progress, or the extent to which the patient would be at hazard.
3. *Time* (*T*) spent on the waiting list in weeks – on the grounds that less urgent cases still have the right to treatment albeit after a longer wait.

After extensive testing of various combinations and weightings of these factors the following formula was derived as a way of scoring individual patients:

$$S = D \times (2.2)^U \times T$$

S = Patients score

D = Disability factor (1–5) and is assessed by the surgeon at the out-patients clinic and can be adjusted if circumstances change.

U = Urgency factor (0–5) and is allocated from a table of common orthopaedic conditions.

T = Time already on waiting list (weeks).

Source: A. Fordyce and R. Phillips, 'Waiting List Management by Computer', *The Hospital*, September 1970.

A. *Waiting-list – 3 January 1986*

Patient	Condition	Disability (D)	Urgency (U)	Entered list	Score (S)
1. Peter Abell	Hammer-toe	1	0	29 Nov.	5
2. Mary Booth	Arthritic finger	2	2	6 Dec.	39
3. Andrew Carpenter	Spina bifida	2	4	13 Dec.	140
4. Bill Dodd	Stress fracture	5	5	20 Dec.	515
5. Liz Evans	Dislocation of knee	3	1	27 Dec.	7

B. *New patients (Jan/Feb).*

Patient	Condition	Disability (D)	Urgency (U)	Entered list	Score (S)
6. Ann Firth	Arthritic hip	3	3	3 Jan.	
7. Sue Green	Bunions	1	0	10 Jan.	
8. Ian Hubbard	Tendon repair	1	5	17 Jan.	
9. John Inkpen	Snapping tendon	5	2	24 Jan.	
10. Jenny Jones	Metabolic bone disease	2	4	31 Jan.	
11. Alan Katz	Arthritic knee	4	3	7 Feb.	
12. Sandra Lound	Un-united fracture	5	5	14 Feb.	
13. Gill Mayor	Neuralgia of foot	1	2	21 Feb.	
14. Fred Norman	Deformed big toe	4	1	28 Feb.	

NB 3 January 1986 was a Friday.

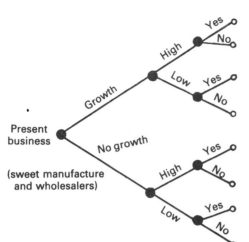

Growth   Investment   Diversification

1. Manufacture cakes, etc.

2. Strengthen distribution, buy more outlets

3. Purchase cakes, etc. and distribute

4. Purchase complementary sweet products

5. Convert some factories to cake manufacture

6. Convert to new product range

7. Substitute some manufacture for buying-in cakes

8. Same as (7) but with sweets

A simplified
decision-tree for a sweet manufacturer

FIGURE 4.2   The use of a decision-tree in strategic planning

Source: G. Johnson and K. Scholes, *Exploring Corporate Strategy* (Prentice-Hall, 1984) (with permission).

trees are also useful in assessing the probable benefits of various courses of action where some uncertainty exists as to future events. This particular use will be discussed in Section 4.3.6.

4.2.4 Linear programming (LP)

Linear programming is a very useful technique in business planning where the following situation exists:

● There is a clear objective, such as the minimisation of cost, or the maximisation of revenue.
● There are numerous courses of action to choose from.
● There are many restrictions on the resources available.

Many operational planning problems are of this type as the following examples illustrate:

● Choosing the **cheapest** mix of materials needed to make a metal alloy (such as steel) when ingredients are available in many different forms (for example, pure alloying elements, metal scrap, etc.)

● **Timetabling** in a school or college where there are a restricted number of rooms, and teachers can only teach a limited number of subjects.

● Deciding on the best **advertising media** when readerships and advertising rates vary and several different products are to be advertised.

● **Allocating jobs to machines** when different jobs take different times and machine capacities are limited.

● Deciding on the best **product mix** to maximise the profitable use of a given capacity when both product costs and market prices vary.

● Designing the best combination of new **funding** for a business expansion when the cost of capital varies and there are limitations on the amounts available from each source.

The technique identifies the optimum solution to a problem taking due regard of the various resource constraints. Simple linear programming is often best expressed graphically as shown in Illustration 4.3. Many planning problems would have more variables involved and a computer would help with the analysis. Nevertheless the principles are the same.

EXERCISE 4.3

Read Illustration 4.3, Rotherson's Newspapers.

1. Assume that the price of the *News* falls by 1*p*. What will the optimum production now be?

2. If the price of the *Post* remains constant what is the price of the *News* at which a range of different product mixes between points *C* and *D* on the graph would be **equally** profitable?

3. What other factors would influence the product-mix decision in practice?

4.2.5 Break-even analysis

Break-even analysis is a simple, and widely used, linear-programming technique which is helpful in exploring how a company's cost structure would be affected by different decisions – for example, whether machinery is purchased or leased (see Figure 4.3). The relationship between

ILLUSTRATION 4.3   Rotherson's Newspapers: production planning

Lord Rotherson's newspaper company produced two newspapers, the *Post* and the *News*. The *Post* was an up-market paper, comparable with the *Daily Telegraph*, and sold for 25p. The *News* competed in the tabloid market, and sold for 14p. The same presses produced both papers, and had a capacity of 80,000 copies of the *Post*, or 160,000 copies of the *News*, per hour. The presses could run for a maximum of 10 hours per day. The variable costs of producing the papers, mainly for newsprint, were 8p and 5p for the *Post* and *News* respectively. Fixed costs were £120,000 per day, mainly for labour. So far as these were attributable, each paper accounted for half.

The problem was to decide how many of each newspaper to produce. Maximum possible sales were estimated at 500,000 and 1.2m per day for the *Post* and *News* respectively. Lord Rotherson had categorically ruled out the closure of either paper. The following graph shows how the optimum product mix could be decided assuming an objective of maximum profit.

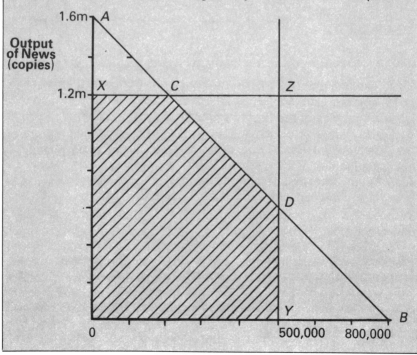

1. The line *AB* shows the *maximum output* at different product mixes ranging from 1.6m copies of the *News* only to 800,000 copies of the *Post* only.
2. Lines *XZ* and *YZ* show the constraints of demand for each newspaper.
3. The hatched are (*OXCDY*) represents the feasible region within which the product mix can be decided.
4. Overall profits will vary along the line *ACDB*, therefore maximum achievable profit will occur *either* at *C* or *D* and can be calculated. Remembering that the financial contribution for each copy of the *News* and the *Post* is 9*p* and 17*p* respectively we have:

   At Point C: *News* = 1.2m @ 9p = £108,000
   Post =   .2m @ 17p = £ 34,000
   Total   £142,000

   At Point D: *News* =   .6m @ 9p = £ 54,000
   Post =   .5m @ 17p = £ 85,000
   £139,000

5. The optimum production is therefore at Point C – 1.2m copies of the *News* and 200,000 copies of the *Post*.

Source: Adapted from a case study by Glyn Owen, Huddersfield Polytechnic (with permission).

output and profit (or loss) is different in the two cases shown in the figure because of the very different levels of fixed costs. This is very valuable information for business planning. For example, situation *A* in Figure 4.3 might represent the cost structure if new machinery such as a photo-copying machine is leased with an output-related leasing charge while situation *B* represents the purchase of the same machine. The decision whether to lease or buy the machine is clearly dependent on the likely output which will be maintained on the machine. The leasing option has a lower break-even point (*X*) but involves higher running costs. If output is likely to be significantly greater than (*Y*) the purchase decision looks favourable.

Break-even analysis can be used as a quick and easy way of looking at many other business planning problems such as the use of maintenance contracts (as against in-house servicing), whether to hire new full-time staff or use over-time, etc.

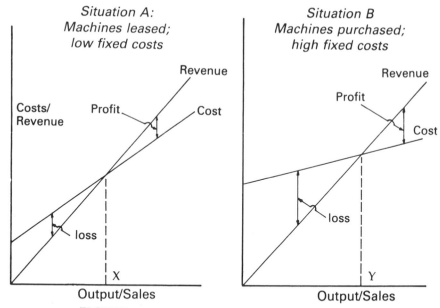

FIGURE 4.3   Break-even analyses: an example

4.2.6 Investment appraisal

During the 1960s and early 1970s many UK companies and public service organisations were growing fairly rapidly and as a result a key part of their business planning was the planning of their *capital spending*. Most large organisations developed elaborate procedures for capital investment appraisal. These techniques have one thing in common – they all attempt to assess which course of action is likely to produce the maximum benefit for the costs incurred over the lifetime of the investment. In commercial organisations this would tend to be calculated in terms of expenditure and income and be a measure of the **long-term profitability** of an investment. In public service organisations the assessment of benefit may prove to be rather more qualitative.

Since most organisations tend to have more bids for spending than funds available, investment appraisal has had to centre on **comparing** the relative merits of different plans. Figure 4.4 shows two commonly-used techniques applied to the case of a small manufacturer planning to spend £200,000 on improvements to the production process. These improvements are expected both to reduce cost and to extend market opportunities and, therefore, to increase the net cash flow of the company. **Pay-back period** analysis assesses how long it will take to pay

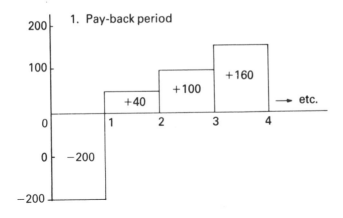

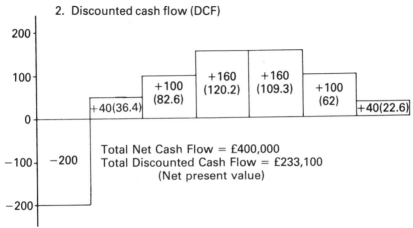

Figure 4.4   Investment Appraisal Techniques

Note: Figures in brackets are discounted at 10% per annum

back the initial investment of £200,000 through these **additional** earnings – in the example, a little less than 3.5 years.

Perhaps the most widely-used investment appraisal technique has been **discounted cash flow** (DCF) analysis which seeks to measure the net cash generated by investment over its useful life adjusted to give more value to cash generated early rather than later. In the example the total net cash flow of the investment is £400,000 which when discounted at 10 per cent per annum is valued at about £230,000 (net present value). This would be compared with the value of investing the £200,000 in other ways – perhaps opening up new branches or adding new product lines. Readers wishing to learn more about these techniques should follow up the references at the end of the chapter.

ILLUSTRATION 4.4   Council Car Park: investment appraisal

In January 1987 a local council was considering building a new car park. Plans had been drawn up by the surveyor's department and if construction was to start immediately the car park would be operational by early 1989. The following information was available:

(a) The site could be bought for £3m: £1m payable in each of the years 1987–9. The construction costs were estimated at £1m in 1987 and £2m the next year.

(b) The council intended to use the car park for all-day parking at a cost of £1 per day (except Sundays). The maximum capacity would be 5,000 cars and they expected an average 80 per cent utilisation rate over its entire life. The running costs would be £800,000 per annum.

(c) At the end of a five-year operational life the car park would be renovated at an estimated cost of £500,000. The car park and site, the real value of which was expected to rise at 5 per cent per annum, would be sold at market value to an independent operator.

(d) The government had recently issued a directive to local councils requiring a 6 per cent return on capital for such projects.

(e) The car park was in response to a demand from local traders and was expected to relieve congestion in the city centre.

The Council Treasury tackled this problem by first setting out the costs and revenues for each of the seven years of the project on the enclosed table. The object of this first stage was to estimate the cash flow for *each year* of the project, commencing in 1987. In order to estimate the present value of the project in 1987 the annual cash flows were discounted by 6 per cent per annum in line with the required minimum rate of return by central government. (The council itself was more concerned about covering costs, providing local jobs and improving city centre environment.) By multiplying the cash-flow figure for each year by the discount factor they obtained a discounted cash flow for each year and the total net present value (NPV) for the whole project.

	Year						
	1987	1988	1989	1990	1991	1992	1993
Cash in							
Cash out							
Net cash flow (A)							
Discount factor (B)	1.000	0.943	0.890	0.840	0.792	0.747	0.705
Discounted cash flow (A × B)							
Net present value (NPV)	=	Sum of previous line					

EXERCISE 4.4

Read Illustration 4.4, 'Council Car Park. Investment appraisal'.

1. Draw up a table of the net annual cash-flows for the scheme for each of the years 1987–93. If you have a spread-sheet package available, set up this data on the spread-sheet as shown in the illustration.
2. Using a discount factor of 6 per cent per annum calculate the **annual discounted cash flow** for each of the years 1987–93. [Use discounting tables for this purpose – the discount factors are shown in Illustration 4.4].
3. Calculate the **net present value** of the scheme by adding these annual discounted cash flows. If your spread-sheet has an NPV function check out your NPV calculation using that function.
4. Assume that the government required a rate of return of 10 per cent per annum – does the project still look favourable (i.e. is the NPV still positive)?
5. At what rate of return (approximately) is the NPV equal to zero? (Use the internal-rate-of-return function on your spread-sheet package.)

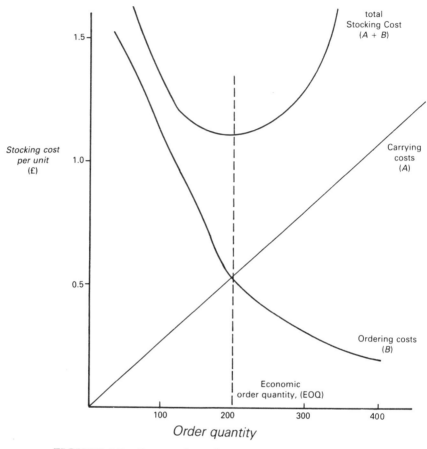

FIGURE 4.5   Economic order quantities: an example

4.2.7 Least-cost analyses

Many business planning problems are concerned with deciding how the least-cost can be achieved when more than one activity is needed to execute a particular aspect of the plan. Some of the techniques already mentioned – such as linear programming – can be helpful in this respect. However, it is useful to look at one situation where such an analysis would be used quite regularly – **economic order quantities** (EOQ).

Controlling the cost of holding stock requires a balance to be struck between the different costs involved:

● If low levels of stock are held, the **carrying** cost of stocks will be low but the **ordering** costs will be high since orders need to be

ILLUSTRATION 4.5   Greenup Fertilisers: economic order quantities

Jack Benjamin was stock control manager for Greenup Fertilisers based in Okehampton, Devon. This small company sold 50kg bags of peat-and-bone-meal mix which it obtained from its supplier in Bristol. The company had a regular delivery round and all customer requirements were known well in advance. Consequently, no buffer stocks were maintained and it was not normally necessary to vary the quantity ordered from the supplier. Partly because of the regular nature of their business, Benjamin had been able to negotiate a fixed price, fixed supply contract. He had based his order size on the following information:

1. Purchase price (per bag) = £15
2. Ordering cost (per order) = £20
3. Holding cost (per kg per annum) = £0.05
4. Quantity demanded per annum = 10,000kg.

Jack Benjamin was congratulating himself on the smooth operation of his stock-control and purchasing system when a letter arrived announcing that the landlord was raising the rent on the warehouse. This would mean that the holding cost would rise to £0.45 per kg. of fertiliser. He now had to decide how this would affect his supply schedule. Jack had determined the most economical order quantity (EOQ) (number of bags) of his last order by using the formula:

$$EOQ = \sqrt{\frac{2\,CR}{H}}$$

where EOQ = order quantity
  C = cost of order
  H = holding cost
  R = rate of usage

$$EOQ = \sqrt{\frac{2 \times 20 \times 10,000}{0.05}}$$

ILLUSTRATION 4.5 *continued*

> *EOQ* = 2828 kg = 56.56 bags.
> No. of orders per annum = $\frac{10,000}{2828}$ = 3.5 times per annum.
>
> He now made a further calculation using this formula and the changed information.

placed more frequently and quantity discounts may also be sacrificed as a result.
- However, if high levels of stock are held, the ordering costs may be reduced, but the carrying costs of stock will rise because of the need to provide more space, the cost of money tied up and the greater risk of ending up with obsolescent stock.

Clearly there is an **optimum** re-order quantity which lies between these two extremes. Figure 4.5 shows the example of a store buying dresses from manufacturers. The cost of holding stock rises to almost £1.50 per item if very large orders of 400 are being placed. However, the ordering costs, in terms of both administration and loss of quantity discounts, can be equally high with orders of less than 100. In the example the optimum policy is to place orders of around 200 items which has the minimum overall cost of about £1.20 per item.

EXERCISE 4.5

Read Illustration 4.5, Greenup Fertilisers.

1. Now that the rent has been increased should Jack order a different quantity?
2. What are the implications of this change for the relationship between Greenup and the supplier?
3. What was the effect of the cost changes on the cost lines in Figure 4.5?

The same logic and analysis would apply to other similar business planning problems where cost minimisation is important. For example, decisions in the area of **quality control** concerning the optimum level of inspection where cost-savings resulting from reduced inspection would result in increased costs through rejects and customer returns. **Mainten-**

ance planning is also helped by an assessment of the relative costs of breakdown as against regular maintenance. There are many other similar uses in business planning.

4.2.8 Analysing competitive performance

The discussions in this section have so far concentrated on analyses which attempt to find the 'best' course of action. For example, whether machines should be leased or purchased, whether overtime is preferable to setting on new full-time staff, etc. However, many business planning situations are rather too complex to place too much dependence on these theoretically 'best' decisions. The example of the reorder level for purchasing dresses (Figure 4.5) might provide useful guidance on the size of orders to be placed, but may need to be tempered by other factors which could influence the situation. Maybe competitors are using more-frequent purchasing to 'play the market' and pick up bargains. Or perhaps buying small quantities of particular lines is not problematic since they command premium prices and additional costs can be absorbed.

For this reason a great deal of business decision-making will rely on an assessment of the company's plans **relative** to what other organisations are doing (particularly competitors). This issue was mentioned in Chapter 3 in the analysis of an organisation's capabilities. Decisions on whether or not changes need to be made in the way which an organisation uses its resources can be assisted by such comparisons. Many of the analyses referred to in Table 3.6 would prove useful. For example, a company may well decide that restructuring or reallocation of jobs is needed because the company's labour productivity compares unfavourably with competitors or maybe the sales per square metre of shop space in Debenhams should be improved if compared with John Lewis shops, etc.

In these examples the performance of competitors is used as a yardstick against which business planning decisions are made and performance targets set – in other words it is an attempt to match the best performance of others rather than being the 'best' plan in any absolute sense. Such analyses are extremely valuable in business planning.

4.3 Uncertainty, risk and flexibility

One criticism which could be levelled at a good deal of business planning in companies is that it is over-concerned with planning the 'most preferred' course of action and does not pay enough attention to how the organisation can assess and cope with the uncertainties which it faces in the future. The danger of ignoring this latter aspect of business planning is that the company's plans become little more than an 'ideal' which soon prove to be worthless and discredited. This section will look at how business planning **can** take account of the uncertainties in business life and provide help in coping with those uncertainties.

Readers may find it useful to distinguish between the use of the terms 'risk' and 'uncertainty':

- **Risk** refers to situations where there are a known set of possible outcomes or events that might occur in the future. However, it is not known which of these outcomes will actually occur. For example, when bidding for a major contract there may be only *two* outcomes (gaining the contract or not).
- **Uncertainty** refers to situations where the set of outcomes is only partially known. In other words unexpected things might happen.

It is not important to be dogmatic about the distinction between these two definitions, since in some senses most future business situations are of the latter type (uncertain). However, the distinction is helpful since the extent to which a business plan is dealing with risk or uncertainty will dictate the way in which the planning should be undertaken.

If a situation is essentially one of **risk** it is much easier to use statistical analyses to assess and quantify the risk as a basis against which decisions can be made. It will be seen later that such analyses are helpful in areas such as stock control and quality control.

In contrast if the situation is largely one of **uncertainty** the business planning will need to cope with this in different ways. In general plans need to be more **flexible**. Some useful approaches will now be reviewed.

4.3.1 Scenarios

In Chapter 3 business forecasting was discussed as an important way in which a company could assess developments in its business environment and the likely impact on the organisation (for example, in terms of sales, profits, etc.). It should be appreciated that these quantitative approaches are most likely to be successful when the future bears some identifiable relationship to the past. Forecasting techniques rely on an identification of this relationship as a basis for speculating about the future. However, there are many situations in business planning (particularly at a strategic level) where such a relationship would be difficult to establish. This is obviously the case when the future is likely to be very different from the past. New product development would often present this problem.

In such circumstances planning methods which are essentially **qualitative** can play an important part. **Scenario planning** is one such technique which is gaining favour in business planning. The technique considers a number of different ways (scenarios) in which a company's business environment **might** develop in the period ahead. For **each** of these scenarios the following issues are then described in detail:

- The impact on the industry concerned, for example, what the behaviour of suppliers, unions, competitors, customers, etc., might be for that scenario.
- The extent to which these changes would be generally favourable (or otherwise) to the company.
- The type of response (business plan) which the company might need to make if that scenario occurred.

EXERCISE 4.6

Using the information in Illustration 4.1, Supergrip Tools, consider the following scenarios and write a report for management on their implications for the firm:

1. The £ falls against other major currencies.
2. The government introduces a new scheme of generous cash grants for the replacement of old machinery (60 per cent of cost).
3. There is a political scandal resulting in the Arab nations cancelling contracts with British firms.
4. The government plan an increase in public expenditure for the forthcoming year.

It should be noted that this whole approach is fundamentally different from the traditional business planning based on forecasting described in Chapter 3. Forecasting is concerned with identifying a single course of events and the likelihood of those events occurring (for example, the chances of demand exceeding a certain level). In contrast, scenario planning is built on the belief that it is very difficult to predict with any precision what the most likely course of events will be (amongst the various scenarios). The emphasis in planning is therefore placed on:

- Understanding the impact of a **variety** of possible futures and being prepared to meet **any** of them.

● Continually **monitoring** events as time proceeds in order to identify which of the various scenarios appears to be unfolding in practice and choosing appropriate responses from the variety of business plans previously considered.

4.3.2 Contingency planning

In many organisations the underlying approach behind scenario planning has been adopted for many years in a more limited way in the process of **contingency planning**. In public service organisations, contingency planning is a most important part of decision-making. In simple terms, contingency planning requires that detailed plans are worked out to cope with a series of situations which are not necessarily regarded as desirable but nevertheless may happen. In extreme cases, such as the emergency services of fire, ambulances, etc., the vast majority of their planning is of a contingency nature. Fire brigades even have detailed plans on how to cope if their own fire station burns down!

This kind of planning is entirely in line with the discussion in the previous section on scenario planning. Whereas an organisation has a 'most preferred' plan for the future it faces such a high degree of uncertainty that it needs to have other plans worked through in detail and ready to implement if necessary (contingency plans).

The key to good contingency planning is to identify clearly the circumstances in which each plan should be used. For example, the level of security which might be needed at a football ground is uncertain and varies from match to match. In planning the provision of police officers, clubs would tend to opt for a **base level** of provision which would apply to all matches. This would then be supplemented by additional requirements for selected matches. Some of these additional needs would be predictable (local 'Derby' matches), whereas there would always be an unpredictable need should particular games become unruly. This unpredictable demand would need to be called up at short notice and the planning at both the football clubs and the local police forces would need to be able to respond to these circumstances – however infrequently they might arise.

EXERCISE 4.7

Read Illustration 4.6 Uncertainty in the Travel Business. Imagine yourself as the personal assistant to the Marketing Director of a major holiday company:

1. Rank the contingency plans (a) to (d) in order of priority (that is, which would you use first, etc.). Give your reasons.

P 1 — 22

P 149 – 150 ✓

P 173 – 194

P 211 – 213 ✓

Global strategy
P 192. (SWOT)

Tech/g P 194
→ critical success factors

ILLUSTRATION 4.6   Uncertainty in the travel business

Package-tour companies need to commit considerable funds by booking flights and accommodation in one year, in the hope that the public will buy holidays in the following year. If 90 per cent of holidays are not sold by May or June companies have contingency plans to minimise the loss. Examples of some of the policies adopted are:

(a) Discounting slow-selling holidays. In 1985 Thomson offered an estimated 8 per cent reduction on late bookings ('late deals').

(b) Cancellation of certain holidays. In June 1984 Ventura cancelled the whole of their Spanish mainland programme because bookings had not reached the required level.

(c) Rearrangement of flight and hotels. In 1983 Horizon chose to cancel rather than discount slow-selling holidays in the belief that discounting would damage its relatively up-market image and discourage people from early booking. Clients were offered alternative holidays or compensation.

(d) In 1984 Budget Holidays offered large discounts to clients who were prepared to select an area to visit, but to leave the exact location and accommodation to be determined when they reached the airport.

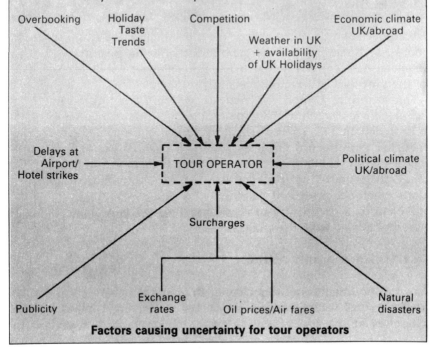

Factors causing uncertainty for tour operators

ILLUSTRATION 4.6 *continued*

Breakdown of cost of a typical £200 14 day holiday to Majorca (1985)

	£
Air transport	79
Hotel + transfer	80
Commission to travel agents	20
Overheads	17
Profit (average)*	4
	200

* On 'up-market' holidays the profit is higher

Data Source: BTEC student assignment, Sheffield City Polytechnic, 1986.

---

2. What advice would you give to your boss on the likely *longer-term* effect of implementing these contingency plans.
3. Are there any *other* contingency plans s/he should be considering?

4.3.3 Sensitivity analysis

Sensitivity analysis (often called 'What if?' analysis) is an increasingly popular technique. It has the great virtue of being easy to use and to understand. It is also very easy to use 'spread-sheet' computer packages for the purposes of sensitivity analysis.

The principles behind the analysis are very straightforward. The technique allows each of the important assumptions underlying a plan to be **questioned**. In particular it seeks to test out how **sensitive** is the predicted performance (such as profit) to each of the assumptions. Figure 4.6 (pp. 133–4) shows how a sensitivity analysis can be undertaken. Perhaps one of the greatest advantages of sensitivity analysis is that it can usually be presented graphically (as in Figure 4.6) and therefore proves to be a useful way of communicating the important planning messages arising from the analysis.

4.3.4 Statistical quality control

It is not the intention of this chapter to give a detailed description of quality control techniques (for which the reader must follow up the references at the end of the chapter). However, it is important to

● Sensitivity analysis is a useful technique for assessing the extent to which the success of a company's preferred strategy is dependent on the key assumptions which underlay that strategy.

In 1982 the Dunsmore Chemical Company was a single product company trading in a mature and relatively stable market. It was intended to use this established situation as a Cash Cow to generate funds for a new venture with a related product. Estimates had shown that the company would need to generate some £4m cash (at 1982 values) between 1983 and 1988 for this new venture to be possible.

Although the expected performance of the company was for a cash flow of £9.5m over that period (the **base case**), management were concerned to assess the likely impact of three key factors:

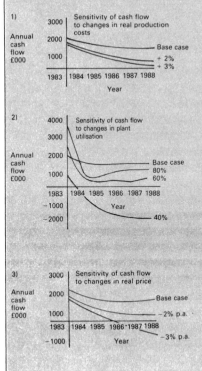

1. Possible increases in **production costs** (manpower, overheads, and materials) which might be as much as 3% p.a. in real terms.
2. **Capacity-fill** which might be reduced by as much as 25% due to ageing plant and uncertain labour relations.
3. **Price levels** which might be affected by the threatened entry of a new major competitor. This could squeeze prices by as much as 3 per cent per annum in real terms.

It was decided to use sensitivity analysis to assess the possible impact of each of these factors on the company's ability to generate £4m. The results are shown in the graphs.

From this analysis the management concluded that its target of £4m would be achieved with **capacity utilisation** as low as 60 per cent which was cer-

Fig. cont. overleaf

FIG. 4.6 *continued*

tainly going to be achieved. Increased production costs of 3 per cent p.a. would still allow the company to achieve the £4m target over the period. In contrast, **price** squeezes of the order of 3 per cent p.a. would result in a shortfall of £2m.

The management concluded from this analysis that the key factor which should affect their thinking on this matter was the likely impact of new competition and the extent to which they could protect price levels if such competition emerged. They therefore developed an aggressive marketing strategy to deter potential entrants.

Source: The Dunsmore example is from the authors. The calculations for the sensitivity test utilise computer programs employed in the Doman Case Study by P. H. Jones (Sheffield City Polytechnic).

Figure 4.6   Sensitivity analysis: an example

Source: G. Johnson and K. Scholes, *Exploring Corporate Strategy* (Prentice-Hall 1984) (with permission).

recognise that business planning should be concerned with ensuring that critical elements of a plan (such as quality) can be properly controlled during implementation. Statistical methods of quality control are used very extensively within business organisations (particularly in the manufacturing sector). They rely for their success on two conditions being true:

● Although the quality of a product (for example, the diameter of a steel bar or the number of crisps in a bag) is **variable** it varies in a predictable way (in other words, a **probability distribution** can be constructed).

● The company is willing to state an **acceptable** range of variability in the product (for example, each bag of crisps must contain between 25g and 30g).

Quality can be controlled by the use of **sampling** in product inspection. The size of sample will be dependent on the risk the company is prepared to take that individual products do not conform to required standards, since this risk can only be completely removed by 100 per cent inspection.

ILLUSTRATION 4.7   Crackle Crisps: statistical stock control

Fred Bolton, Quality Control Manager of Crackle Crisps was concerned that their chief rival, Strollers had the production process under much tighter control. Taking a sample of bags, Crackles ranged between 24.4. and 43.8 grams (see below) as against Strollers which ranged between 24.8 and 32.1 with an average weight of 28.5. The nominal weight for both (printed on the packet) was 25 grams. This caused Fred to comment rue-fully:

Strollers must be saving hundreds of potatoes! Their equipment is more accurate so they are able to set a much lower average weight. I dare not set a lower average weight or the Weights and Measures inspectors will be down on us like a ton of bricks! The firm can't afford new equipment with better tolerances, but has agreed to invest in two automatic check weighers to check bag weights before sealing.

Weight of a sample of 48 packets of Crackle Crisps (in grams)

32.9	35.8	31.8	33.4
32.5	29.7	30.7	39.4
33.1	25.7	43.8	26.8
38.1	41.4	30.7	28.1
24.2	30.4	31.9	26.9

ILLUSTRATION 4.7 *continued*

32.4	24.9	38.3	28.8
31.1	32.3	30.5	28.9
31.8	34.9	40.9	32.3
31.5	28.8	35.7	34.1
27.9	31.0	24.4	34.6
37.9	31.9	33.2	42.5
32.4	32.9	29.7	33.7

Tally chart

Weight in gms	Frequency
24 up to 25	
25 up to 26	
26 up to 27	
27 up to 28	
28 up to 29	
29 up to 30	
30 up to 31	
31 up to 32	
32 up to 33	
33 up to 34	
34 up to 35	
35 up to 36	
36 up to 37	
37 up to 38	
38 up to 39	
39 up to 40	
40 up to 41	
41 up to 42	
42 up to 43	
43 up to 44	

EXERCISE 4.8

Read Illustration 4.7 Crackle Crisps. You work in the Quality Control department and Fred Bolton has asked you to advise him on how they should tackle the problem of controlling bag weights:

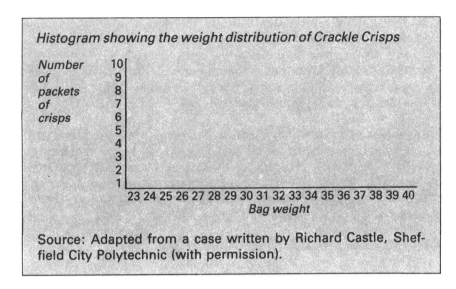

Histogram showing the weight distribution of Crackle Crisps

Source: Adapted from a case written by Richard Castle, Sheffield City Polytechnic (with permission).

1. Using the sample data provided complete the tally chart and histogram provided in the Illustration. Calculate the mean weight and the standard deviation from the mean.
2. Assuming the values calculated in (1.) and assuming a normal distribution advise Fred about the percentage of bags which fall below the nominal weight of 25g. (You will need normal distribution tables or a computer package.)
3. With the existing equipment can Fred afford to reduce the average weight setting by 2g? Is this likely to lead to complaints and reduced sales? (NB In 1985 the Weights and Measures legislation allowed for **individual** packets to weigh less than the stated weight provided that the average weight of any production run did not fall below the nominal weight.)
4. Given the fierce competition in the crisp market was it a good idea to invest in automatic check-weighers (at £5,000)?

4.3.5 Statistical stock control

Another key aspect of a business plan could be ensuring that the stock of certain products is properly controlled. It is often necessary to devise a system to reduce the risk of a **stock-out** (zero stock) without carrying excessive stocks. The problem is very similar to the quality control issue. In this case it relies on the following situation prevailing:

● That both the **sales demand** and the delays in obtaining **new stocks** (from suppliers or the production system) vary in a predictable manner (that is, probability distributions can be constructed.)
● The company understands the importance of not having a stock-out in any item, for example, is it catastrophic to customer relationships or is it simply an irritation?

The statistical analyses can then help determine the reorder level (that is, the minimum level to which stock should fall before reordering). With the increased use of computerised control systems such techniques are an invaluable aid to ensuring that business plans work smoothly, particularly in organisations with a large number of stock items (retail shops, spare-parts suppliers, etc.).

4.3.6 Decision-trees

Decision-trees have already been mentioned in Section 4.2.3 as a means of ranking various plans, and assisting with the choice of plans. They are also extensively used to assess the overall risk which would be involved in following a particular plan where each element of that plan is subject to some degree of uncertainty. Again it should be recognised that this particular use of decision-trees depends on being able to assign probabilities to each course of action with some degree of confidence. For this reason operational planning applications have tended to be the most common use of decision-trees.

ILLUSTRATION 4.8   Ace Construction: decision trees

Ace Construction had bid for the contract to build a specialised bridge over a canal in the Midlands. They were undecided as to what they should do regarding the provision of the specialist skills needed to construct the bridge. They wanted to use a decision tree to get a clearer picture of the issues. The following information was available:

● If they won the contract and fulfilled it successfully they estimated the profit to the company as £200,000 (excluding any special costs such as training or recruitment).
● The cost of training their own work-force would be £20,000 if

commenced immediately but some £40,000 if done at a later date.

● It was unclear as to whether there were competitive bids for the contract. If there were, the contract could be lost to competition unless guarantees about an early starting date could be given. This would require a ready-trained work force **or** last minute recruitment (costing an additional £100,000).

The company estimated the probabilities of these various outcomes as follows:

● They thought it 80 per cent likely that the Country Council would proceed with the bridge construction.
● There was a 70 per cent chance that the company would win the contract against competition providing they could guarantee work-force skills could be made available.

The Decision-tree below shows the range of outcomes.

At the outset the company had three choices available regarding work-force provision:

1. Train work-force at outset.
2. Train work-force later.
3. Recruit new (trained) work-force if and when necessary.

The table on p. 140 can be used to show the profit or loss for each course of action on the decision tree.

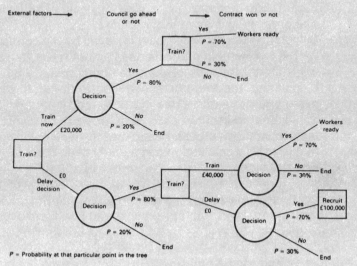

A Decision-tree for Ace Construction

ILLUSTRATION 4.8 *continued*		(£'000) Profit/(loss) by decision		
Outcome	*Probability*	*Train now*	*Train later*	*Recruit*
1. Bridge not built	0.2	(20)		
2. Bridge built by competitor	0.24	(20)		
3. Contract won	0.56	180		
Weighted average profit and/or loss	N/A	92		

EXERCISE 4.9

Read Illustration 4.8, Ace Construction.

1. From the data provided in the decision-tree complete the table provided by:
   (a) Confirming that the probability of each of the three outcomes is as shown in the table
   (b) Calculating the profit (or loss) incurred by the company for the two remaining decisions it could make (regarding training) for each of the three outcomes.
   (c) Calculating the weighted average profit (or loss) of these two decisions. (This is calculated by multiplying the estimated profit in each of the rows in the table by the probability factor shown in the left-hand column for that row. This calculation has already been done for the first decision.)
2. What is the best decision to make at the outset of the project (that is, based on the data in your table)?
3. Are there any other factors which might influence your decision?

4.3.7 Simulation and model-building

Much of the contribution of operation research to business planning, particularly in the production/operations functions of organisations has been through the ability to **simulate** likely future events, particularly with the aid of computer models. These techniques are used extensively to help in the planning of **traffic-flows** which occur in many business situations. The most obvious use is by traffic engineers when redesigning traffic systems in towns and cities, including the phasing of traffic lights, use of one-way streets, etc. But traffic-flow problems also occur in many operational systems and are important aspects of planning in service organisations who deal directly with the public such as banks, supermarkets, or hospitals. **Queueing theory** is used extensively when constructing simulation models.

In principle simulation models could also be useful in strategic planning to forecast the likely outcome of various strategies by building a model of all the interactions between the company and its environment. Such models have, hitherto, proved extremely difficult to produce because of the great complexity and uncertainty involved in strategic planning. Nevertheless there are certain aspects of business planning at the strategic level where models can make a useful contribution – financial modelling being a good example.

4.3.8 Financial modelling

Financial modelling is one area where models have been useful in business planning. Typically financial models attempt to highlight the most important financial consequences if particular business plans were put into operation. This would usually be expressed in terms of a **forecast** of the key financial performance indicators such as profit, cash-flow or other items like stock-levels. With the advent of cheap microcomputers and the ready availability of software packages such as spread-sheets, financial modelling is now within the scope of all businesses however small, although few have yet grasped this new opportunity.

EXERCISE 4.10

Imagine that you are a sole-trader operating a market stall selling clothing. You operate a standard mark-up of 33 per cent on your purchase prices. Your only overhead is the rental charge for your stall which is £5,000 per annum (paid in four quarterly instalments – in advance). Your current turnover is £70,000 per annum and you hold two months' stock on average. At the beginning of 1986 you have a bank balance of £2,000.

1. Construct financial models which would help you to assess your quarterly profit, cash-flow, stock-value and bank balance. [Use a spread-sheet package if possible].

2. Estimate each of these four variables at the end of each of the four quarters of 1986 assuming that sales turnover will grow at 10 per cent each quarter.

4.3.9 Planning for flexibility

It is important that readers do not gain the impression that the risk and uncertainty surrounding businesses can be removed by the use of a few magic techniques. In most business situations, and particularly in **strategic planning**, there will always remain some uncertainty surrounding business plans. If this uncertainty is likely to be high – perhaps if an organisation is entering a new market – it is important that the business plans provide enough **flexibility** to cope with this uncertainty. It may well be that this flexibility will be more important than necessarily following what might be regarded as the 'best' plan. Readers may like to refer back to the ICI illustration where the company became too committed to a plan which subsequently turned out to be unwise. Very often a company might deliberately choose to sub-contract work, or hire short-term contract employees until they are clearer whether a new product or service is likely to be successful, despite the fact that these arrangements are more costly than employment of new full-time staff.

Planning for flexibility **must** be seen as a key part of business planning at all levels. A major factor which adds to the uncertainty in business planning is the extent to which plans are likely to run into difficulties during implementation, in particular, the extent to which people are able and willing to perform at the level anticipated in the plan. This is a very important consideration in business planning and is given extensive discussion in Chapter 6.

4.4 Summary

This chapter has been concerned with the decision-making aspects of business planning at strategic, management and operational levels. It has shown that decisions need to be made both on the most preferred courses of action and also on the way unwanted or unexpected events might be coped with. Without proper attention to this latter aspect, business planning runs the risk of being regarded as an intellectual exercise rather than a positive help in securing a company's future.

It is equally important that business planning is not regarded as having finished once decisions have been made. The following chapters of the book look at the way that business plans can address the realities of making plans work out in practice at all levels.

Recommended key readings

Steve Cooke and Nigel Slack, *Making Management Decisions* (Prentice-Hall, 1984), is a comprehensive book about decision-making.

C. Gilligan, B. Neale and D. Murray, *Business Decision-making* (Philip Allan, 1983), is a shorter book than Cooke and Slack and is particularly useful in extending the discussion of many of the techniques covered in this chapter.

P. G. Moore, *Basic Operational Research* (Pitman, 1976) 2nd edn, provides greater detail on certain techniques, in particular **stock control** (chapter 7), **linear programming** (chapter 3) and **decision trees** (chapter 8).

Ray Wild, *Production and Operations Management: Principles and Techniques* (Holt, Rinehart & Winston 1984) 3rd edn, is useful for his coverage of techniques. **Stock control** (chapter 17), **quality control** (chapter 19) and **maintenance planning** (chapter 20) all receive a full treatment.

Terry Hill, *Production/Operations Management* (Prentice-Hall, 1983), is a shorter book than Wild but his treatment of techniques is good. Readers should find his discussion of **stock control** (chapter 8), **quality control** (chapter 10) and **maintenance planning** (chapter 11) of value.

Brian Ogley, *Business Finance* (Longman, 1981), discusses **breakeven analysis** (p. 229) and **investment appraisal** (chapter 14). In addition readers should find chapter 5 a useful résumé of the **sources of finance** for business development.

B. K. R. Watts, *Business and Financial Management* (M. & E. handbooks, 1984, 5th edn), also deals with **break-even analysis** (Chapter 14) and **investment appraisal** (Chapter 12).

D. R. Myddleton, *Financial Decisions* (Longman 1983) 2nd edn, also looks at **investment appraisal** (Chapter 4).

Completing jobs on time

One of the criticisms of many organisations is that they are extremely poor at completing jobs **on time**. Customers complain of consistently late deliveries and the apparent lack of responsiveness of many companies to their needs. The ability to complete jobs on time is clearly influenced by the way in which work is planned within an organisation, and this is the issue for discussion in this chapter.

There are three different aspects of the problem, any of which could affect the ability of a company to complete its jobs in time (see Figure 5.1.):

1. Most business decisions involved **leads and lags**. For example, having decided to open up a new retail outlet there will be a period of time before the shop can be operational, during which premises are rented, and fitted out; stock is purchased and laid out; new staff are recruited, etc.
2. Most tasks within business consist of a number of smaller tasks. Therefore, the **sequence** in which these tasks is carried out is often a critically important part of planning. For example, the assembly of a motor-car requires a complex planning procedure for the assembly of components.
3. It is necessary to ensure that tasks are undertaken at the right time. This aspect of planning is known as **scheduling**. For example, when launching a new product on to the market, the television and press advertising, and the efforts of the sales force must coincide properly with the availability of the product from the factories. Each of these tasks must be done at the right time.

A. *Leads and lags*

| Thinking | Deciding | Action |

B. *Sequencing*

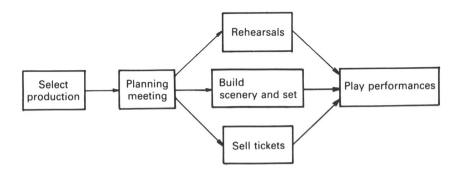

(Example: a theatre)

C. *Scheduling*

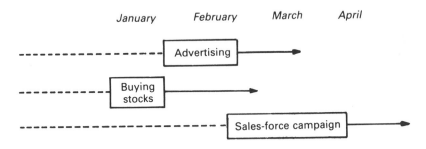

FIGURE 5.1   **Completing jobs on time: the three key planning tasks**

5.1 Leads and lags

5.1.1 Reasons for leads and lags

Business activities require the gathering together of the different **resources** (such as people, materials, money etc.) needed to undertake that task. This process requires **time** before the task can be started and the planning of leads and lags is important in ensuring that a business continues to run smoothly. It is necessary in all parts of a business although there is a considerable variation in the length of time needed to gather together resources depending on the circumstances (see Table 5.1):

TABLE 5.1   Some common reasons why leads and lags occur

Reason	*Examples*
The size of the task	Major projects
Unexpected events	Breakdowns, surges in demand (for example, because of weather)
Infrequent events	Special orders
Bad planning in other companies	Delays in deliveries
Inability to stock the 'product'	Service industries
Bad planning	

- The *size* of the task can be important. At one extreme **routine operational tasks** within a business, such as serving the next customer, or the regular weekly maintenance of a machine, should involve a very minimal lag between the task being requested and actually being undertaken. The task should have been properly anticipated and the resources planned to be available at the right time and place. In contrast there are many situations where lead-times are likely to be very long – often many months or even years. For example, major civil engineering projects, such as building a new motorway, have a long delay between making the decision and commencing the work. Finance needs to be arranged, work-force recruited, negotiations for materials begun, etc.
- There are many occasions within business when events could not have been so easily anticipated. An **unexpected** machine breakdown, a big surge in demand because of unusual weather conditions, or perhaps the sudden death of one of the key people in a company would all be examples. Because these types of events

are unexpected it is almost impossible to forecast precisely **when** they might occur. Therefore it is unlikely that the business will be able to respond immediately.

● A company may be aware that certain events **may** happen (the example of unusual weather above) but it cannot justify the additional costs of having resources permanently available to meet all such infrequent events. So a manufacturer of soft drinks will plan to produce more in summer and hold additional stock to meet the occasional heat wave. However, they could not justify having the productive capacity or stock levels to cater for an unbroken three-month period of hot weather in the UK. When this does occasionally happen there is often a shortage of stock before manufacturers increase output by overtime working, etc.

● Lead-times are also likely to be longer for tasks which are performed infrequently, for other reasons. A good example is a manufacturer who may offer a standard range of goods ex-stock whereas 'specials' will be made to order and therefore require longer lead-times when ordering.

● Problems in gathering together resources can also occur because of **bad planning** in **other companies**. Unfortunately, it is too often the case that the purchasing of material or components may involve unexpected delays because suppliers are unable to meet their promised delivery times, or because items are out of stock. These delays are likely to set off a chain reaction by delaying the production process, lengthening the delivery time to the customer, etc.

● Sometimes it can be difficult to avoid unexpectedly long lead-times. In service industries particularly where the **'product' cannot be stocked**, delays may occur if demand is unexpectedly high. For example, a large part of the business of a skilled electrician or plumber may consist of dealing with emergency breakdowns and repairs. Since these emergencies are not anticipated, the previously-mentioned planning problems are present but compounded by the fact that their services cannot be 'stocked' for future use – they are only available in one place at any one time.

● Finally, it needs to be recognised that on some occasions the reasons for leads and lags is **bad planning within the company itself**.

The discussion so far has highlighted circumstances in which lags might be expected. However, there are many situations in which good planning can anticipate and avoid unnecessarily long lead-times. Figure 5.2 summarises the different ways in which business planning contributes to the planning of leads and lags.

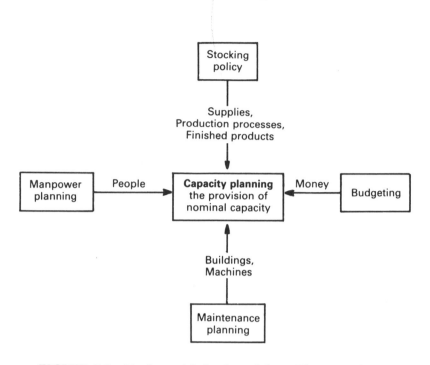

FIGURE 5.2 Coping with leads and lags: The contribution of different planning methods

Notes

Planning method	Purpose	Examples
Capacity planning	To decide output capacity by balancing the need to minimise lead-times with the need to produce goods economically	Buildings machinery; supplies; products; people; money
Stocking Policy	To avoid delays between ordering and delivery	Raw materials; Buffer stocks (between production processed); finished goods
Maintenance planning	To avoid disruption due to breakdowns	Planned maintenance of machines
Manpower planning	To avoid delays due to lack of key personnel	Recruitment and training
Budgeting	To ensure the money is available on time	Funds flow forecasting; credit control; payments policy; inflation

The central problem concerns the **output capacity** of the organisation since the greater the available capacity the shorter will be the leads and lags in completing jobs. However, the effective capacity of a company, in turn, is dictated by the way in which the various production resources are planned:

● Provision of **nominal capacity** through what is usually described as capacity planning. The nominal capacity of an organisation can be considered as its output capacity in normal circumstances. However, the actual output capacity may be lower or higher than this nominal level depending on how the other factors are planned.

● **Manpower planning** determines the availability of people in both the long term (for example, through recruitment policy and succession planning) and the short term (for example, overtime planning).

● **Stocking policy** for materials, work in progress, and finished goods determines the processing and sales capacity of the company in the short term. A company holding high stocks of finished goods has these available for almost immediate sale.

● **Maintenance planning** for machines and buildings determines the usable short-term capacity in two ways. First, failure to maintain equipment properly increases the risk of breakdowns. Second, maintenance-time reduces the time available for output (that is, capacity).

● **Budgeting** is concerned with planning the availability of money at the right times. This provides a key constraint on capacity. For example, it may not be possible to build up stock-levels as quickly as desired because of lack of cash in the short term.

EXERCISE 5.1

You are the assistant to the owner of a major independent seaside hotel. The owner has asked you to brief her on ways in which she can ensure an available capacity of 220 visitors throughout the season (current nominal capacity is 200 visitors).

1. List the factors which will determine the effective capacity of the hotel (see Figure 5.2).
2. Outline ways in which each of these factors could affect the chances of establishing and maintaining the 220-person capacity.

5.1.2 Capacity planning – the provision of nominal capacity

Capacity planning lies at the centre of all planning methods used to cope with leads and lags. Many problems could be eliminated if companies were able to plan sufficient capacity to cope with all the tasks they are likely to be asked to undertake. However, it is both unrealistic and uneconomic for organisations to do this. The costs of providing capacity in terms of machines, buildings, or manpower which would not be fully utilised are prohibitive, particularly when competitors are running a 'lean' and efficient organisation. As a result there is pressure on companies to trim down their capacity to the minimum with which they can manage.

One of the skills of capacity planning is to understand how the various factors which affect the company's capacity need to be planned and the different lead-times which are likely to occur in each area. As a general guide the lead-times are likely to follow a pattern as shown in Table 5.2. The speed at which nominal capacity can be varied is dependent on the **factor** which is limiting capacity (buildings, labour, etc.) and also the **method** by which capacity can be changed:

● The size, location and type of **buildings** can limit the effective capacity of an organisation. If the provision of buildings needs to be changed the organisation has several choices. As a general rule the longest lead-time will be needed if **new buildings** are to be custom-designed and built, whereas **leasing** of vacant premises may prove a relatively quick solution to this problem (particularly in service companies where it may be easy to move equipment). Between these extremes there may be other options such as purchasing vacant premises or adapting current buildings for different use. Clearly the decision on which option to choose will be determined by many factors including the **relative costs** of each option. However, the lead-time inherent in each particular method could well be a crucial factor in the decision.
● **Product availability** may be the reason for limited capacity or output. For example, a manufacturer of magnetic recording tapes may not have mastered the technology to produce good-quality metal tapes which are growing in popularity. Developing a new system from scratch through *research and development* (R & D) could entail an unacceptably long lead-time. In contrast, selling tapes under licence from another manufacturer is a much quicker way of unlocking this particular 'capacity' limitation.

TABLE 5.2 Changing nominal capacity: methods and lead-times

Lead-time	Reason for capacity limited	Methods of changing capacity
Long	Buildings	Build, purchase, lease or adapt
	Product availability	Research and development; licensing agreements
	Finance available	New sources of finance
	Machinery/equipment	Purchase; lease; build/adapt; subcontract
	Labour (major change or new skills)	Recruit, redeploy, retrain
Short	Suppliers	New suppliers, change specification
	Labour	Casual, overtime, part-timers

● It has been mentioned previously that the ability to raise **finance** quickly can be a major factor causing delays in starting new ventures. Some sources of finance can be switching on more quickly than others. So, for example, cash may be obtained more quickly by bank-loans than by issuing new shares.

● *Machinery* and *equipment* may cause a limitation of an organisation's capacity. Purchasing or leasing new equipment could entail lengthy periods of commissioning which together with other possible delays may produce very long lead-times. It may be possible to adapt a current machine for a different job or even build a new machine/system 'in house'. An example of the latter might be the decision to write a custom-built software package to run on the company's current mainframe computer rather than wait for a dedicated microcomputer designed to fulfil that particular task (for example, an order-scheduling system). In some cases companies will quite sensibly choose to *subcontract* certain parts of a job – that is, use the capacity already available in other companies – rather than delay the job while new capacity is provided internally.

● Supplies of **materials** may limit capacity. The search for new suppliers may be difficult and cause delays. An alternative might be to change the specification (if appropriate) in order to reduce lead-times. A wholesaler of fruit and vegetables might decide that the business being lost through delays in supply of tomatoes from Guernsey is becoming unacceptable. S/he may purchase Spanish tomatoes (which had, hitherto, been regarded as below the normal quality requirements).

● **People** are a significant resource of all organisations and may be a reason for a limitation of capacity. In some cases this may require a long lead-time to change – if major changes in the number of people or types of skills needed are required. In other situations this may not prove very problematic if additional capacity can be made available at short notice. For example, many service organisations such as hotels, restaurants and theatres will use part-time or casual staff as a high proportion of their work-force. In this way they are able to 'flex' their capacity quickly as the demand shifts through the seasons.

There are certain aspects of manpower planning which contribute significantly to the consideration of leads and lags in capacity planning. For example, **succession planning** is concerned with the planned replacement of key individuals when they gain promotion, retire, leave, or die. Equal difficulties can be experienced with the **reduction** of capacity in certain areas of a company's activities because of problems of **redeploying** employees (this, of course, was one of the underlying issues behind the miners strike of 1984–5).

EXERCISE 5.2

Read Illustration 5.1, The Midland Bank. Form two groups.

The Bank is faced with a serious shortage of data-processing staff. One group should work out arguments why existing employees should be sent on an intensive training course. The other should think of reasons why the bank should recruit new employees from outside. Each group should have some time to prepare their arguments and present them to the Chief Personnel Director.

These various aspects of capacity planning are an essential 'core' of the planning of lead-times since they are concerned with the **provision** of nominal capacity. However leads and lags are also strongly influenced by the way in which the **use** of that capacity is planned since this affects the actual available capacity. These are the aspects referred to in Figure 5.2:

ILLUSTRATION 5.1   The Midland Bank: succession planning

Long-term planning for key human resources is a major task for companies in the financial services sector. In 1985 the Sheffield Region of Midland Bank employed 1145 people and extended from Derbyshire to the Lincolnshire coast, incorporating the cities of Sheffield, Rotherham and Doncaster, together with a large agricultural area. The bank, along with many other financial institutions, operated a system of internal promotion for filling jobs for two major reasons:

1. Those in senior posts would have a thorough experience of all aspects of the business.
2. There would be a constant and secure supply of suitable candidates for 'key' positions – potential branch managers.

The career structure was in the shape of a pyramid, theoretically open to all, but in practice many (mainly women) remained in the lower clerical grades. In all there were 18 job grades, in three classes:

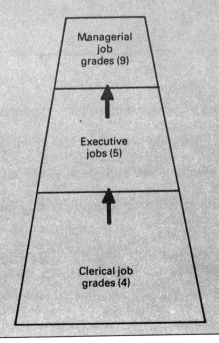

ILLUSTRATION 5.1   *continued*

Initial recruitment was within the age range 16–22, and all subsequent appointments were by internal promotion. The only occasional outside appointments were specialists such as surveyors and data-processing staff. In this way the bank could be sure that, as branch managers' posts became available, there would be enough suitable candidates who had been trained and tested out over a 15-year period. The advantages of succession planning were thought to outweigh the possibility of getting fresh ideas by making external appointments.

However there were some problems with such a system when it came to responding to unexpected changes in the product and labour markets. In the 1950s the bank had solved the problem of shortage of suitable managers (caused by low recruitment during the war) by raising the retirement age. In the 1980s with the continuing rise in unemployment and changing expectations of women who wanted to progress to management they were faced with a surplus of middle management. In 1982, they introduced a discretionary early-retirement scheme to improve morale and promotion prospects.

Source: The Midland Bank.

- The **stocking policy** of an organisation will influence the leads and lags being experienced in supplies, production processes and supply of finished products.
- **Maintenance planning** will affect the extent to which the expected capacity of machines and buildings are **actually** available.
- **Manpower planning** will contribute to the maintenance of the levels of skill needed by the organisation.
- **Budgeting** will be necessary in order to plan the details of **when** money will be needed.

These more detailed aspects of lead and lag planning will now be considered separately.

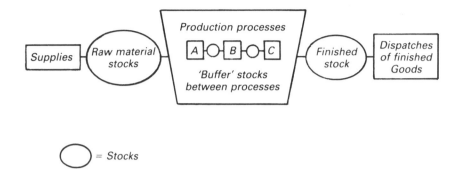

FIGURE 5.3   Different types of stock within a manufacturing
company

5.1.3 Stocking policy

Stocking policy is concerned with leads and lags which might occur in supplies, within the production system and with the supply of finished products. In a manufacturing company there are three different types of stock which could be held, as Figure 5.3 illustrates.

1. **Raw materials** stocks can be held in order to reduce delays caused by lateness in deliveries from suppliers.
2. **'Buffer' stocks of semi-finished items** can be held between the various production processes involved in manufacture in order to avoid any delays in the production process.
3. Stocks of **finished goods** may be held to improve the delivery time to customers.

The planning of these various stocks is not an easy task since, like most planning decisions, it requires a proper balance to be struck among a number of competing factors. For example, the advantages and disadvantages of high levels of stock could be described as shown in Table 5.3.

TABLE 5.3   High stock levels: advantages and disadvantages

Advantages	Disadvantages
Improves delivery-time	Stocking is very expensive
Production easier to plan efficiently	Danger of deterioration or obsolescence
	Lack of space (bulky goods)

The relative importance of the various items shown in Table 5.3 will vary from one situation to another. In reality the situation is complicated since companies may be attempting to plan a very large product range (perhaps 10,000 lines) often in many different markets or locations. Most organisations cope with this complexity by concentrating their stocking policy on those items which are used or produced in significant quantities. Lower-volume items such as 'specials' are not normally available from stock.

EXERCISE 5.3

Read Illustration 5.2, Sheffield Parks.

1. For 'other plants' the Recreation Department decided to produce and stock to a level lower than the maximum forecast demand of 65,000. Calculate **why** they came to this conclusion.
2. What else could the recreation officers do to cope with this unpredictable demand and their long lead-times?

5.1.4 Maintenance planning

One of the issues which needs to be planned within companies is the balance between regular planned maintenance and emergency breakdown maintenance. Again this requires a balance to be struck between the cost of maintenance and the disruption caused by breakdowns. Planned maintenance will tend to be concentrated on equipment which is *critical* to the organisation's activities. This may be a machine which is heavily worked and central to the production process. It may also be necessary for items which are used infrequently but where it is **critically important** that they function when needed (fire-fighting equipment is a good example).

In contrast, other equipment may not warrant the expense of planned maintenance. Whereas occasional breakdowns may be an irritation, it

ILLUSTRATION 5.2 Sheffield Parks: planning for uncertain demand

In 1975 Sheffield City Council Recreation Department produced a wide range of trees and shrubs for its own parks and woodland. It also supplied the Housing and Environmental Planning Departments, whose unpredictable demand made it difficult to formulate a stocking policy. In the words of one of the recreation officers:

'We try to provide both of these departments with a good service, but it's far from easy. Our biggest headache is trying to decide when they'll need trees for each of their schemes – we all know how unreliable building schedules are. However, we still have to decide whether or not to grow new trees and once we've started growing them it's virtually impossible to hold them back or speed them up. So if we're not careful we can have a pretty big write-off on our hands despite our attempts to plan in advance.'

These problems were particularly important because it took five years to propagate a tree. In 1975 it cost £1.25 to grow a tree but £4 to 'buy-in' ready for planting out. For other plants the home grown price was 35p and the buying in price 45p. Despite these difficulties it was important to formulate a stocking policy for 1978–80. The demand estimates were:

	Minimum	Most likely	Maximum
Trees	6,000	10,000	20,000
Other plants	30,000	50,000	65,000

In deciding how many trees to plant they were guided by two criteria:

1. To ensure that the maximum possible cost to the council was minimised.
2. To avoid excessive 'write-off' costs which might be politically embarrassing.

They produced the following two tables to help with their decision regarding trees (remember home-grown trees cost £1.25 and bought-in trees £4):

ILLUSTRATION 5.2   *continued*

A.   *Total cost matrix*

		Demand (trees)			Maximum possible cost (£s)
		6,000	10,000	20,000	
	6,000	7,500	23,500	63,500	63,500
Production	10,000	12,500	12,500	52,500	52,500
	20,000	25,000	25,000	25,000	25,000

B.   *Write-off costs*

		Demand (trees)			Maximum possible cost (£s)
		6,000	10,000	20,000	
	6,000	0	11,000	38,500	38,500
Production	10,000	5,000	0	27,500	27,500
	20,000	17,500	12,500	0	17,500

It could easily be seen that they ought to produce 20,000 trees since this gave the minimum possibility of having **either** an excessively high total expenditure **or** a high write-off.

Source: Kevan Scholes, *Growing Trees and Shrubs* (Case Clearing House, Cranfield).

causes little or no disruption to the company, either because tasks can await repair of the equipment, because repair is quick and easy, or perhaps **replacements** are cheap and easily available. Clocks are a good example, as attitudes to maintenance have changed considerably over recent years for a number of these reasons.

5.1.5 Manpower planning

Manpower planning is clearly an important part of the planning of nominal capacity as discussed in section 5.1.2. However, manpower planning is also concerned with ensuring that this capacity is actually achieved in practice. This can be regarded as the parallel of maintenance planning in terms of the people within a company.

For example, a major retail store might be attempting to up-date its image and move with the times by dropping its furniture department and introducing sports goods. In addition it might be keen to increase self-service in as many parts of the store as possible. The speed with which these changes could be introduced would be strongly influenced by the manpower·planning in certain key areas:

- *Redeployment* would need to be planned in order to ensure that new departments have their proper share of sales assistants.
- *Training,* both in terms of product knowledge and customer service would need to be undertaken extensively.
- *Recruitment and/or redundancy* may prove necessary if the skills cannot be made available by redeployment and retraining.
- *Overtime* working may be needed as a short-term measure.
- *Part-time staff* may prove valuable in the new sports department.
- *Morale* may be a reason for delay in introducing new product lines. Employees may feel uncertain about their future prospects. In these circumstances the organisation's approach to *counselling* individuals and *negotiating* with unions could have a big effect on the acceptability of change and the lead-times involved. The introduction of new technology into offices has very often been delayed by insufficient attention to this particular aspect of manpower planning.

These issues will be discussed more fully in Chapter 6 along with the practical problems of implementing business plans.

EXERCISE 5.4

Read Illustration 5.3, The flexible firm.

1. The manager of a major departmental store which is planning to extend opening hours up to 8 p.m. has asked you to submit a report on how this might be achieved. Use the ideas in Illustration 5.3 to explain how staffing levels could be varied to match peak shopping-times.
2. Would the store be affected by current employment legislation if these ideas were adopted?

ILLUSTRATION 5.3   The flexible firm: flexible work-force

In 1984 it was reported that companies were creating more flexible work-forces by relying on a core of full-time staff, but expanding the work-force when necessary by the addition of temporary, part-time and subcontract workers. Research by the Institute of Manpower Studies at Sussex University suggested that companies were looking for a mix of three kinds of flexibility:

Functional – so that they could redeploy people between different functions of the business.

Quantitative – so they could vary the number of people employed to cope with short-term changes in demand.

Financial – to take on and lay off employees as cheaply as possible.

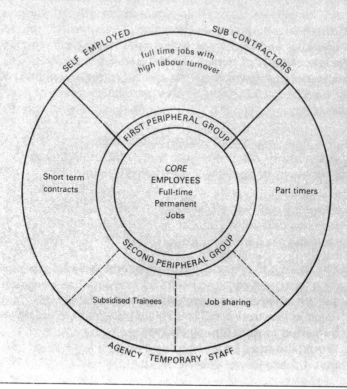

In the flexible company employees were categorised. Job-security was highest for the core full-timers (in the centre of the diagram), reduced in the first periphery, reduced further in the second periphery, and non-existent outside. The periphery expanded and contracted with demand:

- *Core* These jobs had career prospects and job security. In return employees were expected to be flexible, to switch jobs and location. Core-skills were not easily purchased from outside.
- *First periphery* These were full-time jobs, but not careers, including secretaries, supervisors, assemblers and other jobs where labour turnover is relatively high. This helped to reduce or boost numbers where necessary.
- *Second periphery* These three categories provided the major flexible element.
- *External groups* such as agency cleaners, nurses or office staff, and self-employed subcontractors.

The share of part-time employees in total employment increased between 1973 and 1981 in nearly all the twenty-four countries belonging to the Organisation for European Co-operation and Development (OECD). In some industries, sub-contracting was preferable to part-time employment. Rank Xerox was pleased when executives left to form their own companies, and then sold their services back to Rank Xerox. In 1984 the company had forty-eight ex-employees working from home, including two former directors, and wanted to increase the numbers to 150. It reckoned that for each £10,000 of full time labour costs in central London it must add another £17,000 for non-wage overheads. Savings had come in other ways; it had sold an office building that housed fifty people and cost £330,000 a year to run.

John Atkinson, of the Institute of Manpower Studies warned that there are dangers in this policy. He advised firms to guard against some employees' pay, security and other opportunities being secured at the expense of others. This can damage morale, and then company performance.

Source: *The Economist*, September 1984.

5.1.6 Budgeting

The nominal capacity of an organisation in the long run is dependent on the proper planning of the financial resources needed to sustain that level of capacity as already mentioned. However, in the short term the actual capacity attainable is dependent on money being spent and received at the right time. This short-term financial plan usually exists as a series of **budgets** within an organisation which spell-out the detailed financial aspects for each part of the organisation. Although budgets fulfil several purposes in the context of this chapter their most important use is as a forecast of when money will be spent and received. So, for example, **credit control** is a very important aspect of the cash management of the business – ensuring that the credit being extended to customers is properly controlled and that customers pay on time. The opposite side of the equation is the **payments policy** which the company is operating to its suppliers. The lead-time for payment extended to the company by its suppliers needs to be monitored in relation to the lag in payments which occurs from customers (credit). Some businesses (supermarkets, for example) get cash over the counter whilst receiving as much as three-months credit from their suppliers. In contrast, small manufacturers supplying major companies like Ford or Marks & Spencers are very often in the opposite position receiving very little credit and yet having to extend credit to **their** customers.

At a detailed level the **cash management** within a company needs to be carefully planned to ensure that the sequencing of payment, and receipts day-by-day does not overstrain the company's liquidity position. Of course, this is a problem which most people encounter in planning their personal finances and attempting to avoid rude letters from the bank manager. The wide availability of **spread-sheet packages** for computers now means that cash management is somewhat easier to conduct. However, this does not remove the very real difficulties which exist in this area because of the uncertainty which surrounds the precise timing of certain receipts of cash (and often payments too).

One of the special problems which occurs in planning future financial requirements is that the value of money changes over time. This is called **inflation**. An important part of budgeting is to forecast the likely levels of inflation in the various costs which the company incurs and the prices it is likely to command in the market. When inflation is low the process of adjusting to new price-levels can be relatively painless. However, in periods of high inflation (as experienced in the UK in the mid-1970s) there can be significant lags between a company experiencing cost increases and being able to recoup these extra costs through price changes. During this period in the 1970s the situation was made more difficult for many companies by a prices-and-incomes policy which legally required large companies to seek permission for any price changes. Although these price changes were usually approved, this process caused delay and made financial planning more difficult.

EXERCISE 5.5

Read Illustration 5.4, Mosquito Sports.

For this exercise you will need to be in pairs; one to play the role of Jim Bond and the other to be the financial adviser. Your tutor or the rest of the group will be the bank officials who are considering your request for finance to cover the period 1985–8. You should present your case for finance verbally, but supported by facts and figures in the form of a cash budget for each of the years 1985–8, similar to the cash-flow statement in Jim's accounts. This should be presented professionally in a file.. You should also be prepared to explain the reasons why this expansion of your business 'makes sense.

5.1.7 Seasonality

Seasonality of demand is such an important issue to many businesses that it warrants separate discussion and is a suitable topic on which to conclude this section. Seasonality can create major planning problems in any of the company's resources:

- The utilisation of buildings and machinery during slack seasons. Should they be closed down entirely (as some seaside hotels do) or should alternative uses be found (for example, attracting conference trade to those same hotels)?
- Planning the manpower requirements. Most companies in very seasonal businesses will plan their work-force with a minimal core of full-time staff and hire part-time staff and use overtime to meet the periods of peak demand. In many companies (particularly in the tourist industry) their need for part-time staff coincides with a large number of students seeking vacation employment.
- Budgeting can provide special difficulties for seasonal businesses. Toy manufacturers for example, have extensive cash requirements during the early part of the year as their production is geared up for the following Christmas boom.

ILLUSTRATION 5.4   Mosquito Sports: cash-flow planning

Jim Bond opened his Sheffield sports shop, Mosquito Sports, in leased premises in 1982, which proved to be very good timing as it coincided with a boom in sports and fitness in the UK, and the build-up to the 1984 Los Angeles Olympic Games. The shop was a phenomenal success in its first three years of operation. It had followed policies of offering substantial discount on branded goods, and sales had reached £338,000 in 1984 and he anticipated sales to grow at a further 20 per cent per annum for each of the next three years.

As a result of this rapid growth the shop itself had become too cramped to display the stock effectively and Jim wanted to take over the adjoining shop. However, he was uncertain precisely how much money would be required to expand his operation in this way. He did have some useful information though (see also enclosed accounts for 1984):

- He estimated that if he took the new shop, the overheads of the business would increase by about £15,000 per annum because of increased rates, rent, heating, etc.
- He would need to spend about £10,000 on repairs, alterations and fitments.
- His prices were determined by applying a straight mark-up of 25 per cent on the purchase price of his supplies.
- Jim traded strictly on a cash-for-goods basis to ensure that he had no money tied up in customer credit. However, he was extended 30 days credit by all his suppliers.
- Jim was worried about the high level of stocks which he was holding which were valued at £80,000 in his 1984 accounts. However he felt that he would need to hold four months' stock if he were to continue with his current product range and obtain the best prices from his suppliers.

- Seasonality caused by buying peaks in the financial year – in the NHS and education services this is often in March.
- Marketing and selling effort also tends to be very unbalanced through the year. Sales managers will normally plan the activities of the sales-team to reflect this. So sales-training or new-product

---

Company Financial Accounts (1984)

A. Profit and Loss Account (1984)

Sales revenue	£338,000
Cost of goods sold	£270,000
Overheads and wages	£25,000
Depreciation	£3,000
Interest payments	£2,000
Profit before tax	£38,000
Tax	£15,000
Net profit after tax	£23,000

B. Balance Sheet (31 December 1984)

Fixed assets		Long-term liabilities	
Equipment and		Share Capital	£25,000
Fittings	£22,000	Loans*	£30,000
		Retained earnings	£25,000
Current assets			£80,000
Stock	£80,000		
Current liabilities			
Creditors	£22,000		
Total net assets	£80,000		

* £20,000 loan repayable December 1985
£10,000 loan repayable December 1986

C. Cash-flow Statement (1984)

Sources		Uses	
New Share Issue	£5,000	Purchase of Goods	£305,000
New LT loan	£10,000	Running costs	£25,000
Sales Revenue	£338,000	New Fittings	£5,000
Increased creditors	£5,000	Re-pay overdraft	£6,000
	£358,000	Interest payments	£2,000
		Tax	£15,000
			£358,000

training will normally be undertaken out of season as will much of the preparation work on advertising campaigns, consumer and trade promotions, etc.

- The work-force may be switched from production to maintenance work out of season.

In all these areas work-scheduling is an important way of ensuring that
peak demand can be met whilst avoiding the problems of wasting
resources during periods of slack demand – and this general issue will
now be discussed more fully.

5.2 Planning the sequencing and scheduling of tasks

The previous section has shown how the provision of productive capacity and the effective utilisation of that capacity are both subject to
leads and lags. However, this is not the only issue which will determine
whether an organisation manages to complete its jobs on time. Most
jobs within a business are broken down into a series of smaller tasks in
order to ensure that they can be done efficiently. As a result it becomes
necessary to plan the **sequence** in which these tasks should be undertaken. At the same time it is important to plan precisely **when** each task
should be executed. This is known as **scheduling**.

There are important links (and conflicts) between these two planning
tasks of sequencing and scheduling. Indeed many planning techniques
address **both** issues simultaneously. For this reason it is intended to
discuss these two aspects together in the following way:

- Consideration will be given to the **factors** which influence the
  way in which tasks should be planned (sequencing and scheduling). These factors are outlined in Figure 5.4 and are discussed in
  Sections 5.2.1 and 5.2.2.
- A number of **planning techniques** will be reviewed in terms of
  the contribution they make to planning the sequencing and scheduling of tasks. Particular attention will be paid to the way these
  methods attempt to reconcile the often conflicting factors of Figure
  5.4.

5.2.1 Sequencing

There are several factors which can influence the order in which tasks
should be undertaken (see Figure 5.4):

- Some tasks *must* precede others because they are **prerequisites** for
  later tasks to be undertaken. For example, a bar of steel cannot be
  put through a rolling mill until it has first been heated in a furnace.

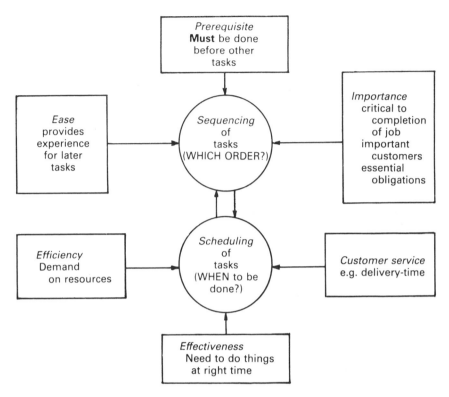

FIGURE 5.4   Factors influencing the sequencing and scheduling of tasks

An insurance policy cannot be issued until a person or property has been 'valued' to assess the risk involved.

● Sometimes the sequence of tasks is dictated by the **ease** with which tasks can be done. When writing a textbook it is common practice to start with the chapters which are regarded as more straightforward rather than working systematically from beginning to end. Many aspects of business are similar to this – particularly where the tasks require a **creative** element such as design or product development. The learning process which is involved in such activities means that later tasks can be built on the experience gained from the earlier tasks.

● Because some tasks are **more important** than others, the planning of the other tasks is regarded as subsidiary to these major tasks. For example, in the building trade there is a mixture of both indoor and outdoor jobs which at many stages of construction could be undertaken in parallel with each other (that is, the sequence is not important). However, during periods of good weather (particularly in winter) priority will be given to outdoor jobs as it is important to take advantage of the weather in order to minimise the risk of later delays.

● In a similar way some customers are **more important** than others and their orders may be *given priority*. This can often be in conflict with an efficient scheduling of work within the company as discussed below.

● With many service industries there is a **threshold** of performance which must be maintained but a genuine desire on the part of the providers to exceed this threshold. In these circumstances the planning tasks which are essential to achieve the threshold must be given priority over other tasks. An example would be a Social Services department within a local authority where its statutory obligations must take priority over those aspects of service which, although desirable, are not mandatory. Training programmes are often structured in a way which recognises this idea of a threshold. There will be a core programme of tasks which should achieve this threshold, but additional (sometimes optional) activities which will take trainees beyond this minimum.

EXERCISE 5.6

Read Illustration 5.5, Western Jean Company.

1. Suggest a method of scoring an employee's qualities on section 2 of the checklist.
2. How would you establish a **threshold** – a minimum level of performance – which employees should achieve before proceeding from sales assistant to assistant manager?
3. Should any sections be added to, or deleted from, this form?
4. Compile a list of additional skills and/or qualities you would add as a minimum threshold for **store managers**.

5.2.2 Scheduling

There are different reasons why the scheduling of tasks (i.e. when tasks are done) is important. Again readers are referred to Figure 5.4:

● The scheduling of work will dictate the time at which resources (people, money, machines, etc.) need to be made available. The

ILLUSTRATION 5.5   Western Jean Company: training thresholds

Many companies require a *threshold* level of knowledge before staff are considered adequately trained.

In 1985 Western Jean Company was a medium sized company which distributed and retailed jeans and related clothing. It had 18 retail outlets and 270 employees, predominantly young people. The company provided training in retail management for all employees, together with regular performance appraisal. In the words of the Sales Director:

> 'This is a business for young people, we want our staff to fit our customer profile, and project a youthful, up to date image. Thus we aim to train and promote promising sales assistants to be retail managers as quickly as possible.'

The performance appraisal form used by Western Jean is shown below. This was used by the company to assess the level and knowledge of employees at certain stages in their training.

WESTERN JEAN COMPANY

Performance Appraisal for Staff Training

Name: *BRANCH:*

Training period ___ days.   From _____ to _____ inc.

Section 1.
(a) *Enthusiasm for the job*   (b) *Reaction to training*

Section 2: Qualities shown by the individual sales assistant.

Product Knowledge	Sales Technique	Merchandise Knowledge	Procedures
Style	Greeting	Merchandising policy	Security
Sizing	Establishing needs	Shop layout	Tidying
Manufacturer	Satisfying needs	Presentation	Till

Cont. overleaf

ILLUSTRATION 5.5   *continued*

| Material | Closing sale | Credit cards |
| Pricing | Goodwill building | Health and safety systems |

Personal Organisation
Personal sales graph

Personal training record

Sales Qualities
Use of customer benefits

Enthusiasm
Positiveness
Phraseology

Section 3: Overall Qualities of the Individual Sales Assistant.
Strengths   *Weaknesses*

I agree/disagree with this assessment. Signed _____
                                                          (Trainee)
Source: Company information.

reverse is also true – that is, the schedule must reflect the reality of the company's resource availability. The **efficient** running of any organisation requires proper scheduling of resource utilisation to avoid periods of over-use followed by low utilisation. It is very rare that the work-load of an organisation remains at a constant and predictable level over long periods of time. One of the purposes of scheduling is to predict these changes and to minimise the disruption to the company. For companies operating in highly seasonal markets (for example, at seaside towns) this is an important part of their planning.

● Some business activities are relatively infrequent events but **must** occur at precisely the right time. The timing of a major television advertising campaign **must** match the market conditions, and the company's readiness to supply the product. Correct timing might also mean a specific day or even the right time-slot within a day. All these scheduling considerations are seen in the heavy advertising given to children's toys during late November and early December, particularly using advertising slots within children's viewing times – late afternoon (weekdays) and Saturday mornings.

● **Customer service** is very strongly affected by the scheduling of tasks (such as orders) within companies. This is most clearly illustrated in terms of the delivery-time quoted for individual orders and is an issue where conflict can exist within the production-planning system between the **efficient scheduling** of work and the **sequencing** of particular customer orders. This issue will be discussed more fully later.

EXERCISE 5.7

You have been elected by your Students' Union to organise a graduation disco in December for students who finished their courses in the summer.

1. Assuming it is now 1 October, write a schedule in the form of a flow-chart putting the tasks below in the correct order over a two-month period. Give your reasons.
2. The group want to be paid half their £750 fee in advance. *Normally* tickets are not sold till the week before. How would you tackle this problem?
3. Referring to Figure 5.4, explain why you have chosen to plan the tasks this way.

Tasks:
Form committee of helpers
Book pop group
Book venue
Decide on price
Arrange for tickets to be printed
Allocate responsibilities in the committee
Organise advertising
Catering arrangements
Volunteers to help on the door
Arrange for payment of overtime for Union porters

There are a number of planning methods which are very useful in the sequencing and scheduling of tasks. These will now be discussed in the following sections.

5.2.3 Network analysis

Network-analysis methods are extensively used in businesses where a complex variety of tasks needs to be undertaken to produce the company's product or service. The best examples are organisations where

project planning is central to their activities. Civil engineering, building, or the planning of major events (sporting events, concerts, etc.) all have a major need for planning of this type.

Network analysis (also known as **critical path analysis**) has been used widely since the Second World War. It is a technique which breaks down a project into its component tasks and shows these in the form of a network. By considering resources and times needed to complete each of these tasks it is possible to locate the **critical path** of tasks which determines the minimum project-time. It has been used extensively in planning new product launches, construction of new plants, research and development projects and in many other ways. Figure 5.5 is an example of a network used for a new product launch. Network analysis can contribute to planning in a number of ways:

- It forces planners to think carefully about those tasks which **must** precede others (**prerequisites**).
- The critical path is a useful way of identifying the **most important tasks** to be undertaken at any time if delays are to be avoided. Clearly, if work is proceeding on several arms of the network at the same time the critical path will change with time, particularly if some tasks are completed more quickly than expected and others are delayed. The network needs to be constantly up-dated.
- The network will also be used to forecast **when** future tasks are likely to be required. Thus the network is helpful in **scheduling** tasks. Figure 5.4 includes time-estimates which would be used for this purpose.

EXERCISE 5.8

Referring to the network analysis in Figure 5.5:

1. Beginning at point 1. what is the **shortest** time in which the launch could be achieved using current time estimates?
2. Draw the **critical path** onto the network (that is, the sequence of tasks which dictates this shortest time).
3. You have been asked to reduce overall launch-time by three months. To what extent would one-month savings in each of the following help you to achieve the overall saving:
   Engineering design
   Prototype development
   Procurement programme
   Customer market research

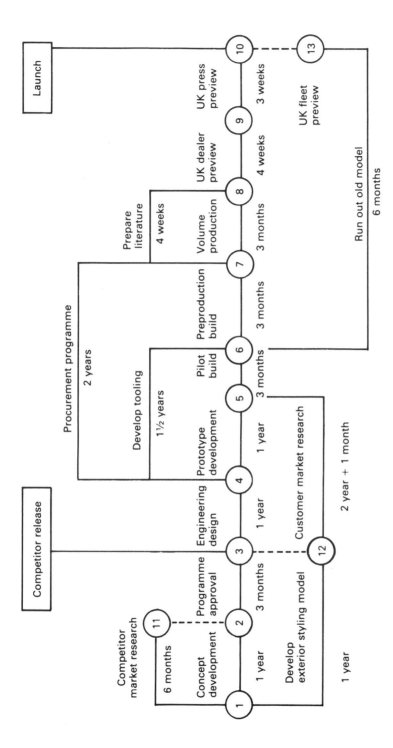

A network analysis for the launch of a new car.

FIGURE 5.5 Network analysis: an example

Source: G. Johnson and K. Scholes, *Exploring Corporate Strategy* (Prentice-Hall, 1984) (with permission).

5.2.4 Production planning

In project-based companies, techniques such as network analysis will be central to production planning. However, in many organisations the production cycle is completed in a much shorter period of time. Nevertheless the production process is usually divided into several subsidiary tasks and, therefore, the **sequence** of these tasks needs to be planned. At the same time the situation is complicated by the fact that the proper **scheduling** of work within the production system will influence important factors such as delivery time (customer service) and whether products are available at the right time to tie in with other business activities, such as the advertising campaign. Production planning within companies attempts to reconcile these various aspects of sequencing and scheduling in a number of ways (see Table 5.4):

● Often companies will have a written **production route** for each product or service. This will have been determined as a result of a number of different considerations. For example, some tasks must precede others, the physical layout of the production system (see below) or where quality might be affected by the sequence of activities (for example, in preparing meals in restaurants certain tasks cannot be undertaken earlier in the production process without affecting the quality of the meal).

● In many service industries it can be difficult to predict in advance the detailed requirements of a job. For example, in a solicitors office the sequencing of tasks needed to handle the conveyancing of a house sale is very predictable and will normally be undertaken by relatively junior staff following clearly laid-down procedures. However, other legal work is far less predictable and may not lend itself to such a streamlined 'production' system. In these circumstances the production planning is done on a 'one-off' or *ad hoc* basis and is likely to be changed as the job proceeds. This can bring difficulties for the company and the clients since the ability to assess the time involved and the associated legal costs is much reduced. As a result the costing of such jobs is often done on a 'swings-and-roundabouts' basis where some jobs are subsidising others.

● Many production-planning systems are half-way houses between fully-planned task-sequencing and an entirely *ad hoc* approach. Whereas the sequencing of tasks will be different in detail for each product or service which the company offers these tasks can usually be grouped into **blocks**. The sequencing of these blocks remains largely unchanged from one product to another.

TABLE 5.4   Sequencing and scheduling in production planning

Type of system	Advantages	Difficulties
1. Fully planned production routes	(a) Most efficient system (b) Takes care of prerequisite tasks	(a) Inflexible – may not be responsive to real priorities (for example, rush order) (b) May not allow for key targets in other parts of business (e.g. advertising) (c) 'one-offs' difficult to cope with
2. *Ad hoc* system	(a) Very flexible allows a 'tailor-made' solution each time (b) Easy to change and accommodate priorities	(a) Inefficient use of resources (b) Difficult to understand (for example, for new employees)
3. Mixed system (Planned but allowing for 'fine-tuning' and variations)	Attempts to combine the best aspects of (1) and (2)	

The detailed differences are accommodated within these separate blocks. In a brewery the three major blocks would be **preparation of ingredients** (hops and malt), **fermentation**, and **clarification and containerisation** (barrels, bottling, etc.). These blocks **must** be undertaken in this sequence. However, the **detailed** planning of each block will be changed with each different brew (beer, lager, etc.).

● Although the **level of priority** of some orders will diminish the level of service given to other customers (for instance, in delivery-time) it should be possible to schedule the work of the various production departments to maintain quoted delivery times to all customers (albeit different ones for each customer). However, in practice problems often arise because orders are completed on an *ad hoc* rather than a planned basis, usually as a result of pressure from an important customer. The results of this are that other orders are delayed and delivery-times not met. In some extreme cases it is not unknown for the situation to be so out-of-hand that customer-pressure – rather than the efficient use of resources or even processing the oldest orders first – becomes the key criterion

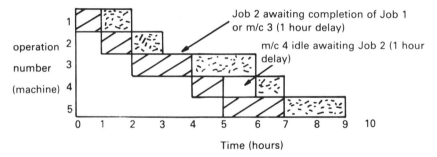

Job 1 = ///

Job 2 =

Notes:
1. The chart shows two jobs each consisting of the same five operations in the same sequence and taking the same time.
2. Operations 1, 2 and 4 take 1 hour.
3. Operations 3 and 5 take 2 hours.

FIGURE 5.6   Gantt charts in production planning

in deciding the day's production schedule. There is a lesson for potential purchasing managers here!

Production schedules are often depicted on Gantt or bar charts (either manual or computerised) as shown in Figure 5.6. The loading of any one machine or department can be seen at a glance as the various jobs are added to the chart. In the example there are problems with the utilisation of machines 2 and 4 because of the longer operational times of the operations which follow (3 and 5). The production scheduling could be arranged to use this slack by infilling with jobs which require these two operations without placing any further load on machines 3 and 5.

EXERCISE 5.9

Read Illustration 5.6, Esprit Hammers. You are in charge of planning the manufacture of hammer heads and you have two different hammers to make which have the following estimated operational batch-times:

	Esprit 1	*Esprit 2*
Heating	30 minutes	30 minutes
Hardening	30 minutes	1 hour
Tempering	15 minutes	30 minutes
Grinding	30 minutes	1 hour

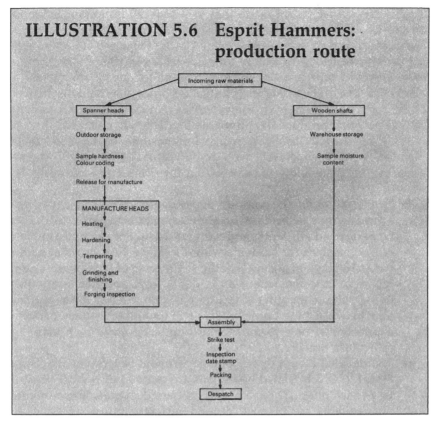

ILLUSTRATION 5.6 Esprit Hammers: production route

You are required to manufacture six batches of Esprit 1 and three batches of Esprit 2. By drawing a Gantt chart as in Figure 5.6 determine:

1. The shortest overall time to manufacture these nine batches.
2. The percentage utilisation of equipment for each of the four operations.
3. If you were able to reduce batch-time by additional capacity *which* operation would you increase capacity on first?

5.2.5 Location, layout and work-flow

The planning of location and layout of a company's facilities is very closely interlinked with the flow of work needed within the company and also the production planning processes discussed above. This is not to suggest that the layout should dictate the other two (or vice versa). Ideally these three issues should be planned to be properly consistent with each other.

Whatever decisions are made they will have an important influence on the way in which tasks can be sequenced and scheduled within a company. This discussion can be related back to Figure 5.4. For example the decision to relocate a factory, or a department within a company, or even a person within a department may affect any of the factors in Figure 5.4. The efficiency of the production processes could be changed as transport costs change, customer service may be affected if communications between production and marketing, etc., are changed.

There are various levels at which location and layout need to be planned, each of which will have important consequences to the sequencing and scheduling of tasks within the company:

- The **location** of the various departments (or divisions) of the company may determine the sequencing of activities if work is to be performed efficiently and without delay. For example, in planning timetables for students within a Polytechnic or college, care has to be taken to ensure that the sequencing of work within a day minimises the movement of students from one site to another. Equally the **scheduling** of lecture times must allow for movement time between sites. Some readers will undoubtedly have personal experience of how resource constraints can make such planning difficult in practice.

- The detailed **layout** of any one department or location affects the extent to which related operations are carried out in close proximity to each other. There are many different choices. Some production systems are planned around **different processes** as in the brewery example and also in many process industries such as steel or chemicals. Other systems have layouts which are designed around the **fixed location of the product**. Large products such as aircraft, products which have a fixed location (for example, coal) or services which are offered in a fixed venue (for example, theatre or football) all tend to be planned in this way. Another commonly-occurring layout, found in many craft industries, is where the layout is designed around the skilled operator (craftsman) and all the materials and tools are brought to the operator's location and replenished as they are used.

  The reason for describing these different choices of layout is to show that the sequence in which tasks can be undertaken will be strongly influenced by the layout chosen by the company. The layout used by craftsmen is the most flexible and allows the operator the maximum discretion on how the total job is undertaken. The other extreme is a production-line operation where the sequencing of tasks is entirely predetermined as the product is progressively assembled on the production line. The **scheduling** of work is also affected in a similar way. A highly inflexible layout makes it more difficult to alter production schedules and priorities.

● The layout of the individual work-place is the most detailed level at which the sequencing and scheduling of jobs might be affected. In an office, inappropriate siting of typewriters, support machinery, and filing systems may result in an extremely inefficient use of secretaries' time as they are constantly moving from one part of the work-area to another.

One of the key questions which needs to be answered during planning is the extent to which the work-flow should dictate the layout or vice versa. As a general guide where the nature of the work is predictable and repeated frequently it will probably be worthwhile planning the layout to fit this 'normal' work-flow. In contrast if jobs are infrequent and/or unpredictable it is unlikely that one 'best' layout can be determined as each job will have to be fitted in to whatever layout is chosen.

EXERCISE 5.10

Read Illustration 5.7, Morrells Meat, and refer to Figure 5.4.

1. Compare the layout and production planning at Morrell's meat with:
   (a) A traditional butcher's shop
   (b) A supermarket supplying pre-packed frozen meat.
   (Hint: compare the four operational tasks identified in Illustration 5.7)
2. Which factors dominate the layout and the sequencing and scheduling of tasks in each of the three situations?

5.2.6 Organisation and Methods (O & M)

One of the major contributions of organisation and methods (O & M) in business planning is in scrutinising work methods and the extent to which they could be performed more efficiently. It is interesting to note that public-sector service organisations have been the major users of O & M (often through their management services departments). Typical O & M studies might look at such issues as layout, the flow of work through offices, and (particularly relevant to this discussion) the information and communications which exist between sections or departments. In many services the efficient flow of information from one section to another can be the key factor in ensuring that the service is operating successfully

ILLUSTRATION 5.7 Morrells Meat: location layout and work-flow

Before 1974 Morrells Meat Ltd was a conventional father-and-son butchers' business in Leeds. In that year they moved to larger premises in a residential area to cater for customers who wanted to buy in bulk for their freezers (3lb minimum sale) but still wanted personal service. With this in mind the Morrells designed the layout of their shop as shown in the diagram.

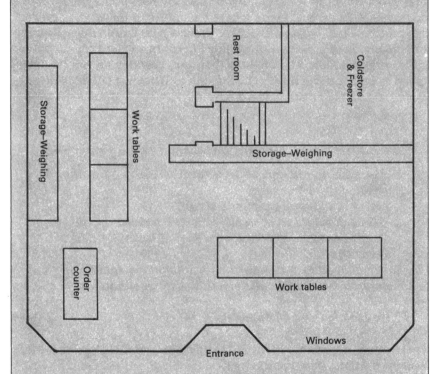

Order of work
1. Customer enters shop and gives order to assistant at order counter.
2. Assistant costs it and takes the money.
3. When one of the three butchers is ready he comes to the counter, takes the customer with his order sheet to the

work table. Here he discusses the customer's requirements and cuts, weighs, trims and bags the meat.
4. An assistant is available to carry the meat to the customer's car.

Source: Adapted from *Morrell's Meat* Nigel Slack, (Templeton College, Oxford) (with permission).

(diagnosis and treatment of patients in hospitals is a good example). O & M studies very often suggest changing the lines of communication, often resulting in a new sequencing of the various tasks needed to provide the service. Although this is usually described as 'removing unnecessary bureaucracy' or 'cutting through red tape' there are many occasions where this fresh look is really a result of circumstances having changed since the initial system was designed. For example, it may be decided that the separate departments within a local authority have become big enough to allow them to handle their own recruitment and training of staff without the need to channel applicants through a centralised personnel department. In contrast, the purchase of new equipment (such as microcomputers) which had been left to the discretion of individual departments may be centralised for a period of time because compatibility of equipment is felt to be a key objective. This obviously changes the sequence of events needed in purchasing such equipment.

5.2.7 Work measurement

Although work measurement is an important aspect of business in its own right (for example, in job-costing) it is clearly essential in providing information on the time which jobs will take and, therefore, the scheduling of those jobs. So, for example, both network analysis (Figure 5.5) and Production Planning (Figure 5.6) are dependent on time estimates for the tasks/jobs involved.

Work measurement and method study (see previous section) are often described collectively as **work study** and they have made valuable contributions to the development of production planning systems, particularly in manufacturing companies.

EXERCISE 5.11

Re-read Illustration 5.6, Esprit Hammers. You are a work-study officer with the company and have been asked to advise on ways in which the volume of work can be increased. As part of this task you intend to undertake both method study and work measurement in the company:

1. In which departments would you undertake these studies?
2. List a series of questions which you would wish to have answered in each department?

5.2.8 Route planning

Although route planning is not a technique as such it is worthy of separate discussion since it is an important area of planning in most companies, for example, in sales-call planning. Similar considerations apply to the routing of certain mobile public services such as mobile libraries, family doctors' visits or meals-on-wheels. Route-planning needs to be influenced by consideration of both the **sequencing** (who comes first) and **scheduling** (when to arrive) aspects of planning.

In deciding what is the 'best' plan for a route there are a number of different criteria which could apply (refer back to Figure 5.4):

- The **minimisation of cost** as measured by distance travelled (or travelling time) – this is the efficiency criterion.
- Allocating priority according to the **importance** of each visit; attempting to ensure that any delay or shortfall occurs with the less important visits. 'Importance' may be measured by customer size, or perhaps the likelihood of losing business or sometimes new calls may be given higher priority above the repeat-calls on existing customers or patients.
- In relation to the route-planning of **competitors**. For example, it would be unwise for an ice-cream salesman to follow his major competitor's route 15 minutes behind them (this is the **effectiveness criterion**).
- Some routes are **easier** to plan than others. This could well be an important criterion in opening up a new overseas market. This would provide the experience on which a more comprehensive sales-calling pattern would be developed at a later date.
- Some calls may be **prerequisites**, that is, they **must** precede other calls. For example, when visiting a dealer network in a particular town it may be necessary for the representative to visit the main

dealer first in order to check out the level of activity of subsidiary dealers before visiting them.

The decision as to which of these criteria should be dominant in planning routes will vary considerably from one situation to another. Where sales-calling is a relatively routine affair – perhaps where the salesman's major job is merchandising activities with retail outlets rather than securing orders – the cost-efficient use of sales-force time will tend to dominate the planning. However, if there is an important element of hard-selling – where a new product is being introduced or a new geographical area opened up – it is likely that the planning will be influenced by some of the other factors already outlined.

Identical considerations apply to the planning of physical distribution of a company's goods either between its own warehouses and stores (as in retailing companies) or to customers.

EXERCISE 5.12

Read Illustration 5.8, Bridgers Plant Hire.

1. Work out a calling schedule for the eight outstanding orders, indicating the sequence of the calls and the expected arrival time at each customer.
2. Why have you chosen to plan the calls in this particular way?
3. If you had to complete the calls in the minimum possible time (irrespective of any other consideration) – what changes would you make to the schedule and what time would you finish the day's calling?

5.3 Summary

This Chapter has been concerned with the way in which business planning can help organisations to complete their jobs on time. Three aspects of timing, **leads and lags, task sequencing** and **work scheduling** have been discussed and it has been shown that they are closely related to each other. Many planning techniques are concerned with more than one of these issues as has been illustrated.

The most important message which readers should try to remember is that there is little point in organisations deciding to follow any of the business opportunities discussed in the previous chapters unless they are prepared to plan out in detail **when** the various tasks need to be

ILLUSTRATION 5.8 Bridgers Plant Hire: sales routes

Bridgers Plant Hire operated from a depot in Bolton and serviced an area of approximately 30 miles radius (most of the industrial areas of South Lancashire). The company specialised in the hire of machinery for the building trade such as powertools, mixers, scaffolding, etc. The firm prided itself on its guaranteed 24-hour delivery service. As the depot closed on Wednesday the following enquiries were left outstanding:

Location	Time of Enquiry	Type of Order	Regular Customer
1. Blackburn	9.30a.m.	Mixer	No
2. Bury	10.30a.m.	Scaffolding	Yes
3. Burnley	11.00a.m.	Power saws	Yes
4. Preston	1.30p.m.	Power tools	Yes
5. Oldham	2.30p.m.	Mixers	No
6. St Helens	3.00p.m.	Scaffolding	No
7. Leigh	4.00p.m.	Scaffolding	Yes
8. Chorley	5.00p.m.	Mixers	Yes

The following chart gives times to travel between these various centres (minutes):

	Blackburn	Bolton	Burnley	Bury	Chorley	Leigh	Oldham	Preston	St Helens
1. Blackburn	0	30	30	30	30	60	60	30	30
2. Bolton	30	0	60	30	30	30	45	60	45
3. Burnley	30	60	0	30	60	90	60	45	105
4. Bury	30	30	30	0	60	60	30	90	75
5. Chorley	30	30	60	60	0	15	75	30	45
6. Leigh	60	30	90	60	15	0	75	45	15
7. Oldham	60	45	60	30	75	75	0	105	75
8. Preston	30	60	45	90	30	45	105	0	30
9. St Helens	30	45	105	75	45	15	75	30	0

The depot opened at 8a.m. and loading usually took 1 hour. Unloading time at a customer's was normally about 15 minutes.

undertaken. This theme of looking at the practical details of making plans work is continued in the next chapter which looks at **how** plans can be made to work in practice.

Recommended key readings.

Ray Wild, *Production and Operations Management: Principles and Techniques* (Holt, Rinehart & Winston, 1984) 3rd edn, covers scheduling comprehensively in Chapter 12 and network analysis in Chapter 13.

Terry Hill, *Production/Operations Management* (Prentice Hall, 1983). Scheduling is covered in Chapter 7 and network analysis in Chapter 7.

P. G. Moore, *Basic operational research* (Pitman, 1976) 2nd edn, is also useful for a fuller treatment of network analysis (Chapter 2).

Brian Ogley, *Business Finance* (Longman, 1981), provides a very useful discussion of budgeting (Chapter 8) and management of cash (Chapter 9).

D. R. Myddleton, *Financial Decisions* (Longman, 1983) 2nd edn, is a good reference to follow up the management of working capital (Chapter 3) and cash management (Chapter 2).

CHAPTER 6

Implementing plans

Planning is of little value to organisations if it is regarded as complete once decisions have been made about the organisation's future. Indeed if this were the case it is almost certain that the majority of plans would fail. It was mentioned in Chapters 1 and 2 that business plans (whether they be at a strategic level or an operational level) can be difficult to put into effect. Many people within an organisation need to feel committed to making the plans work. It is very likely that the implementation of business plans will be hindered by groups or individuals if it is felt that they cut across the vested interests of that group. It is for these reasons that planning must also be concerned with thinking through **how** the organisation's plans can be made to work in practice.

Figure 6.1 illustrates that the success of business plans ultimately hinges on the ability to gain co-operation from people – both employees and others such as suppliers or distributors. However, this co-operation is determined by the way in which the other issues are planned. The ability to motivate people to perform and the realistic assessment and development of their skills are of central importance. For example, British Telecom's business plan might include extending sales of non-standard telephone equipment (such as cordless phones, message-recording machines, etc.) to householders. Whether or not they are successful in this respect depends on the extent to which people are able and willing to put that plan into action. There may be many factors which could make it difficult to achieve this plan:

● The sales team may be unused to selling such equipment – they need training in product-knowledge and sales techniques to improve their **skills**. Many employees may not be **motivated** to implement the plan – perhaps they feel very half-hearted about the new equipment and do not appreciate the need to change sales

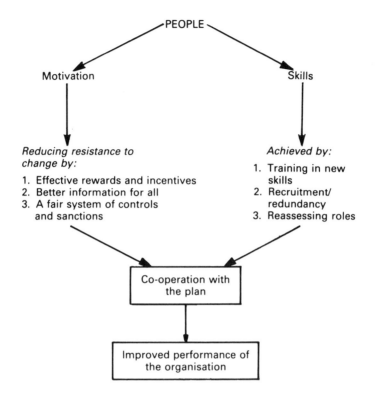

FIGURE 6.1   Major factors influencing implementation

policy, or perhaps they fear that the new equipment may threaten jobs and, therefore, they are resisting the change.

● Perhaps there are no **incentives** to follow the plan. The change may require more effort from employees or distributors and they need to be persuaded that it is worthwhile. Suppliers may regard as unattractive, the prices they are being offered to add additional features to equipment. Sales staff might be losing commission on their 'normal' sales by switching their attention to new products.

● It may be that the sales department's targets cannot be met if they are selling fewer more expensive systems.

EXERCISE 6.1

Refer to Figure 6.1. Think of an organisation with which you are familiar and any change which they have recently introduced (perhaps a new product line, or a new system of planning work, etc.):

1. Which of the factors in Figure 6.1 contributed most to the success or failure of the change?
2. How could the change have been planned better?

Each of the issues in Figure 6.1 will now be considered separately but it must be remembered that there is a strong link between these various factors.

6.1 Gaining co-operation with business plans

Plans will not work out successfully if people do not have any commitment to make them work. Indeed plans can be undermined by individuals or groups who feel strongly opposed to those plans. Gaining people's co-operation with business plans can be usefully considered under the following headings:

- People's **involvement** in planning processes
- Overcoming **fears** about the consequences of new plans
- Reassessing people's **roles** and **skills**.

6.1.1 Involvement in planning processes

Chapter 2 discussed the way in which the various 'stakeholders' of an organisation (employees, shareholders, etc.) might be involved in business planning to a greater or lesser extent. The ease with which business plans can be implemented can be strongly influenced by the degree of involvement which people have had during the planning process. In many cases people who have not been involved in the planning process are expected to implement a new plan. Many managers in companies feel the need to keep their future plans secret especially where they involve major changes, and present them to the work-force, suppliers and distributors as a *fait accompli*.

EXERCISE 6.2

Read Illustration 6.1 'Lucas Aerospace'.

1. Do you agree with the Combined Committee that the company rejected their plan because it challenged basic managerial prerogatives.
2. Assess the pros and cons of involving workforce representatives in company planning in an industry of this kind.

ILLUSTRATION 6.1 Lucas Aerospace: participation in planning

In the 1970s Lucas Aerospace produced mechanical, electrical and electronic systems for the aerospace industry. About half of its business was related to military aircraft and defence systems. In 1976 25 per cent of work came from Ministry of Defence contracts but this was threatened by proposed cuts in the defence budget.

The company dealt mainly in small-batch precision engineering, producing specialist accessories for the aerospace industry. In 1977 the workforce of 13,000 contained a high percentage of skilled engineering workers and technicians. The company had a reputation for being a relatively progressive employer, with a profit-sharing scheme and procedures for consultation at plant level. However, these discussions were limited to bargaining with individual unions over pay and conditions. In 1969 the unions had formed a Combined Shop Stewards committee which provided a forum for discussion of the company plans, but this was not recognised by the company as a negotiating body as they preferred to deal with each union separately.

In the early 1970s the combined committee became concerned about the company's rationalisation policies; 5,000 redundancies had already taken place by 1974 and further restructuring was expected. Since they had not been involved in the company's plans the combined committee decided to produce an 'alternative' corporate plan which was made public in 1976. The plan was wide-ranging and long-term, and included feasibility studies of possible new products – such as kidney machines, remote-handling gear for undersea oil-rig maintainance and a hybrid diesel electric engine – using the skills of the work-force. One objective was to reduce the company's reliance on the volatile aerospace industry. Another was to use the skills of the work-force rather than use machinery to replace or deskill them. The plan also included radical ideas for new ways of organising and controlling production involving project teams which would eventually break down traditional skill and job definitions.

ILLUSTRATION 6.1   *continued*

The company response to the 'Alternative Corporate Plan' was widely interpreted as a rejection. In its reply the company stated its intention to 'concentrate on its traditional business'. It did not wish to discuss the report at managerial level but referred the suggestions in it to 'local consultative machinery'.

Source: *Lucas Aerospace Alternative Corporate Plan.*

If plans are to be implemented successfully careful thought needs to be given to the political situation within the company. It is often useful to assess who will feel most affected by the plan and how they will try to help or prevent the plan being implemented. In this way business planning can try to take much greater notice of the **vested interests** within and around the organisation and the way in which they will have to be managed. In other words there must be a positive strategy for gaining the acceptance of the plan by all those most directly affected.

The management of UK and USA companies are often accused of being too keen to make decisions without thinking through the way in which they will manage the resistance to the changes which their plans involve. In contrast Japanese companies, although sometimes painfully slow to produce their plans, tend to implement them more easily. The major reason for this difference often lies in the extent to which resistance to change has been managed **during** the planning process. In particular Japanese companies tend to have a much **wider** involvement of people in planning than has typically been the case in many UK/USA companies. Not only is this likely to smooth the final implementation of plans but often vital knowledge about the workability of plans rests with those who will have to carry them out (for example, production teams, sales force, etc.). In public-sector organisations this wider involvement is often formalised in the decision-making procedures (for example, the governing body of a school will represent a wide variety of interests.)

It is important for readers to remember that there is a price to pay for such wider involvement, namely, the time-delays involved in implementing plans as planning becomes a much more overtly **political** process within the organisation.

Involving people more fully in planning has the advantage of improving their understanding of the realities of the company's situation and the reasons why plans and practices need to be changed. For example, changing a traditional waiter-service restaurant to a fast-food operation will require considerable changes in the working practices for employees. They are more likely to accept the need for these changes if they are aware of the market-pressure from competitors which brings about the need for the changes. Many organisations now have regular newsletters which seek to keep all their employees, suppliers and customers up-to-date on the most important developments in the organisation's plans.

The UK motor industry in the 1970s was an interesting example of the difficulties which can be faced when unions have a high level of involvement in **operational** planning but are kept in the dark on the **strategic** position of the company.

EXERCISE 6.3

Read Illustration 6.2, British Leyland.

1. Why did British Leyland have difficulties in implementing the 1975 plan?
2. In what ways could the implementation of their plans have been improved?

6.1.2 Overcoming fears

Many people feel threatened by plans which increase the uncertainty surrounding their jobs. The initial reaction of many office-workers to new office technology has tended to be coloured by the uncertainty and worries about not being able to cope with new systems. Some of these worries may be overcome by training but there may also be the real fear that conditions of work may deteriorate. For example, a secretary whose job contains a variety of typing, administration and reception duties may fear being tied to a video display unit (VDU). Such fears should be recognised and people reassured that the consequences of new plans will not all be bad. Many people tend to see only the negative side of change without recognising that change may bring new opportunities too. Plans to introduce office automation into an organisation although threatening, could potentially allow for a much more interesting working life for many employees and a chance to learn new skills as more routine tasks are automated. During the planning of such change the company might decide to hold a series of meetings with employees where these functions of **education and reassurance** can be undertaken **positively** rather than just hoping for the best after changes have been made. For major changes it is often helpful if the consultations take place at an early stage of planning. Strategic planning often uses brief

ILLUSTRATION 6.2   British Leyland: styles of work-force control

In the 1960s the car industry was expanding. British car producers had no problems in selling their output; their major difficulty was in the recruitment of the skilled labour necessary to achieve this output. The best means of obtaining the workers needed was via the unions, who were given almost complete autonomy over day-to-day work organisation. Considerable slack was built up in companies like British Leyland (then BMC) with reports of workers sleeping through night shifts, and empire-building and excessive perks by management.

In the 1970s the market situation changed dramatically, with British companies struggling for survival in a far more competitive market. In 1975 British Leyland was only saved from liquidation by a £1,000m loan from the government. Michael Edwardes was appointed as the new Chief Executive. His policy was one of asserting direct control through a major 'shake-up' of systems and working practices. Management were pruned and pressurised to become more market-orientated, and workers' autonomy on the production line was replaced by strict – some said harsh – managerial control. Troublesome shop stewards were sacked.

Workers strongly resisted these changes; in fact, the 'washing-up time' dispute of 1981 was less about the five minutes in question, than about the new management policy of controlling work so closely that even the workers' time in the washroom was being measured. The strength of the resistance was shown by the spontaneous acts of vandalism in the paint-shop at Linwood. However, despite the harshness of the new regime, workers and unions were on the whole forced to accept that the loss of their autonomy was secondary to the survival of British Leyland in the market place.

'discussion documents' as a means of 'testing the water' and allowing people to get an early idea of what is afoot and to influence the plans.

There are some circumstances where resistance to change is likely to be so great that there is a significant chance that the plans will not be able to be fully implemented at that time. It may be necessary to implement the plans in one or other of the following ways:

- **Step-by-step** – although it may be regarded as desirable to implement a plan in its entirety it may prove impossible because of resistance from groups (such as unions) who feel threatened by the plans. However, partial implementation may be acceptable and form a useful base from which to proceed to the full implementation of the plan at a later date. This situation is very common and can be a most successful way of overcoming resistance to change. For example, the union representing the employees in a chain of supermarkets may be unconvinced that the introduction of automatic check-out machines (reading bar-codes on goods) is practical. Equally they may be worried about the implications for jobs. It may prove necessary to operate the system on a limited-time trial (say, two months) at one supermarket before agreement can be gained to the complete change-over to the new system. If the trial is successful it will have served a useful purpose, namely, breaking down fears and prejudices and improving the climate for implementing the plan more fully.
- **Postponement** – sometimes the implementation of plans may have to be postponed simply because certain groups such as unions, or customers are not convinced of the necessity of the new plans and are sufficiently powerful to oppose any changes. It may be that it is only when circumstances change that the plans can be implemented. This often means that the market pressure on the company has to be so obvious that opposition to change is lowered. The British Leyland illustration shows this. Sadly, the recognition of the reality of this market pressure often comes too late – making changes much more difficult.

Those responsible for ensuring the success of business plans need to give careful thought to how they are to gain the acceptance of other people to the plans. The above section has given some examples of how this might be achieved.

6.1.3 Reassessing roles and skills

The previous section has looked at how people's resistance to change might make the implementation of business plans difficult. However, there is very often another equally important reason why people may have difficulties making plans work. This concerns the extent to which people are **capable** of carrying out the tasks which the plan requires.

New plans may change the **balance of skills** needed within the organisation. The value of certain people's skills is therefore diminished whilst new skills may need to be acquired. For example, if a city's library service starts to pursue a positive policy of seeking out disadvantaged sections of the community it clearly requires a different approach from simply running libraries. More emphasis will need to be given to social skills and less to the 'traditional' librarianship skills.

Therefore another important aspect of gaining people's acceptance of business plans is a realistic assessment of how the plans are likely to affect people as individuals, the roles they play within the company and the extent to which their skills will be used. It is not good enough to assume that people will simply adjust to new circumstances by themselves. Planning must pay attention to the way in which the impact of the plan on individuals can be managed to ensure their continued value to the company. This means that good business plans should address the following:

- An assessment of the capabilities of individuals and the extent to which they will be able to cope with the company's plans. For example, if the Housing Department of a local authority decided to change from a highly centralised organisation to a series of smaller, more autonomous, district offices, the success of this plan would hinge on having good District Managers who could shoulder the responsibilities of running their district. This would be a new **role** within the organisation for which some people would be rather better suited than others. Certainly the bureaucrat who relied only on formal procedures and detailed instructions from superiors would find the District Manager's role difficult to cope with because of the need to exercise more flair and judgement. So the business plan must identify which individuals have the capability to fit the roles which are essential to the success of the plan.
- In many circumstances the business plan would have to identify the extent to which people would need to be **retrained** to carry out the new tasks which the plan required. This may be a relatively straightforward matter – for example, if a new machine were to be introduced into a production department – or may require something very much more extensive as might be necessary if a company decided to extend its operations to a new country – requiring language training, etc.
- Some jobs may become redundant when new plans are implemented. The plan must include consideration of the best way to cope with this. For example, the Recreation Department of a local authority may decide to reduce its commitment to traditional sports, such as football, whilst building up amenities for newer sports such as aerobics, squash or snooker. What should be done

with the employees who specialise in football – the ground-staff, coaches, etc.? Clearly, there are several choices, and the plan must indicate what is to be done. Some could be **retrained** and **redeployed** to the newer sports, others may have to be offered **redundancy**.

● Some plans require skills which are unlikely to be available without **recruitment** of new people to the organisation. Since recruitment of good individuals can be a lengthy process it is important that business plans are clear about the number and type of individuals which will be needed and also the **timing** of the recruitment (see Chapter 5).

Normally these issues will need to be addressed in a **combined** way to ensure that there are the proper numbers of capable and motivated people to carry out the organisation's plans.

EXERCISE 6.4

Read Illustration 6.3, Peak Engineering. Divide into two groups. One group should prepare arguments for keeping George Spencer at Peak Engineering; the other should be prepared to argue that he must go. Remember to consider the implications for company morale and efficiency.

Table 6.1 summarises the issues discussed in this section about gaining co-operation with business plans.

6.2 Choosing rewards and incentives

Some of the very best business plans can come unstuck because people are not given the right incentive or rewards to carry out the plans. This is not to suggest that people are only motivated by a selfish desire to improve their own income or position within the company. However, such considerations are important to the degree of commitment individuals are likely to give to the various aspects of their job.

EXERCISE 6.5

Read Illustration 6.4, Reward systems (p. 193). Choose an organisation with which you are familiar and write a briefing paper for the Personnel Manager explaining the advantages and disadvantages of different types of reward systems.

ILLUSTRATION 6.3   Peak Engineering: re-deployment and staff morale

In 1985 Peak Engineering was a medium-sized company in Chesterfield which had just emerged from a lean period but had full order books. This turn-around mainly resulted from the considerable steps which had been taken to increase productivity and cut costs. There had been some redundancies of hourly-paid workers. The amalgamation of the production planning and purchasing departments meant that there was a surplus of five middle managers. The head of the old purchasing department was promoted, two moved to other departments and one retired.

The fifth was George Spencer, aged 58, married with three grown-up children and few interests outside his family and garden. He joined Peak Engineering in 1966 as a clerk and was appointed deputy manager of the purchasing department in 1969. He was regarded as a useful man to the department because he carried in his head so many details about components and suppliers, and was good at sorting out problems with suppliers. However, since a microcomputer was introduced, Spencer's real contribution had been no greater than that of the clerks in the department.

The problem

George Spencer's old job had disappeared, but what should the company do with him? The Managing Director realised that this was a test case as Spencer was the first salaried person to be in this position. His handling of the situation would affect attitudes and morale in the rest of the company. There were several possibilities:

1. Allow him to stay in the new production planning department in virtually a sinecure position.
2. Offer him early retirement.
3. Offer him a less responsible post in the other factory in Birmingham.
4. Offer him a role in training.

These options had been discussed with Spencer, and the main points to emerge were:

1. Spencer felt that he was being used as a scapegoat. He considered that he was now being discarded because he had not pushed for promotion earlier.
2. He argued that his knowledge of the company and suppliers was vital.
3. He was unwilling to consider moving to another plant.
4. He considered early retirement as tantamount to a premature death.

Source: Adapted from case written by Dr George Igler, Oxford Polytechnic and the European Business School (with permission).

TABLE 6.1   Gaining co-operation with business plans

Action	Reason
1. Involvement	People may be more committed if they are party to the plans
2. Education	People may be unaware of the problems faced by the organisation
3. Reassurance	People are worried about the consequences of the plan
4. Step-by-step implementation	People need to try out new approaches before supporting wholesale change
5. Postponement	Resistance is too great until circumstances become more pressing
6. Reassess people's roles	New plans may require new roles
7. Retraining, redundancy, recruitment	People's skills may not fit the new plans

Note: Some or all of these actions may be necessary.

6.2.1 Difficulties

Changing reward systems can run into difficulties for a variety of reasons:

ILLUSTRATION 6.4   Reward systems

Pay on merit

In 1985 the Incomes Data Service reported a trend away from fixed incremental pay scales, where employees are paid according to length of service, to pay awards based on individual performance. However, they also commented that it was difficult to measure quality of output for certain types of workers.

Special discounts

Banks and Building societies have traditionally given mortgages on low rates of interest for their employees. Retail organizations such as the John Lewis partnership have given their staff discounts off the purchase price or priority on purchasing reduced goods.

Profit sharing

In 1983 the Horizon travel company were seeking to promote staff efficiency through profit sharing and preferential share purchase schemes. Employees with the company for more than six years in 1983 earned a bonus of up to 27% on top of basic salary based on company profits.

Promotion ladder

In 1983 the Eagle Star Insurance Company in common with other financial institutions, had a promotion ladder/pay scale of 15 grades. Competent employees could expect to progress, step by step up the scale and thus look forward to an annual increase in pay and status. However, this system would prove difficult to maintain where the firm was contracting or if labour turnover was low.

● A well-established pattern of rewards and incentives already exists. For example, perhaps the production workers are paid on a bonus system related to output, the management may be involved in a profit-sharing arrangement whilst the administrative staff are part of a complex graded-pay structure depending on age, qualifications and job-role. This means that business plans must pay attention to these vested interests. People are unlikely to support a plan if it results in a worsening of pay or promotion prospects. The business plan needs to assess the extent to which the **current** rewards and incentives are likely to facilitate the implementation of new plans.

● It should also be remembered that changing reward/incentive schemes could be a very lengthy process requiring negotiations with several trade unions and other groups.

● A new plan may require the company's efforts to be concentrated onto new aspects of the business. The incentive scheme in existence may make this difficult. This is very often the case when a company needs to pay more attention to **quality** of its products or services whilst operating an **output**-related incentive scheme. There can be difficulties because the increased emphasis on quality will invariably reduce output levels and hence the potential earnings of employees. Clearly, such a plan is likely to come unstuck unless the incentive scheme is adjusted to reward quality or at the very least not to penalise employees for the reduced rate of output.

● Some plans require an increase in the level of **co-operation** between groups and individuals than has been traditionally the case. For example, many computer companies had relied on a sales-force who just sold hardware to customers and had a sales-related bonus system. The customer support services, such as software, maintenance, etc., were operated quite separately and were often paid on a straight salary basis. However, the changing pressures in the market-place required the creation of teams of sales/software/support who were together able to meet customers prior to purchase. In other words customers were becoming more interested in the 'complete package' than simply in the hardware itself. In these circumstances it can be very difficult to continue an incentive scheme for sales-force alone – other staff need to be included and incentives need to be shared on a **group** rather than individual basis.

● Business plans also need to pay attention to the incentives which may be needed by people **outside the company**. For example, without proper incentives for agents and distributors the plans of manufacturers may fail. Many companies rely heavily on self-employed individuals (such as radio and television presenters, designers, authors, etc.). A proper assessment of the incentives needed to motivate these outsiders can be critically important to the business plan. Catalogue mail order companies (for example,

TABLE 6.2   How rewards and incentives might need to change

Change needed	Reason	Example
Aspect being rewarded needs changing	Business plan focuses on new issues	Quality more important than output
Need to change to group rewards	Plan requires greater cooperation and team work	Many service organisations
Rewards to suppliers/distributors need attention	Poor performance of distributors	Mail-order agents
Promotion ladder needs change	New skills become important and need rewarding	Many professional organisations need marketing skills data processing skills

Littlewoods) rely heavily on several thousand part-time self-employed agents many of whom are selling for 'pin-money'. The performance of these agents can be strongly influenced by special incentives such as 'Win a Holiday'.

Table 6.2 summarises some of the ways in which rewards and incentives might need to change.

EXERCISE 6.6

Read Illustration 6.5 Jaguar.

1. Which of the reasons in Table 6.2 best explains why Jaguar introduced quality circles?
2. Why did they run into difficulties in linking payment (bonus) systems to the quality circles?
3. How would you improve matters?
4. Research another company which has used 'quality circles' (for instance, Wedgwood Pottery).

6.2.2 Non-financial incentives

Whilst not everyone may agree with Herzberg that money is not a motivator it is clear that money alone is not a sufficient motivator to get the best out of people. Many organisations have introduced schemes (such as subsidised canteens, etc.) not only to improve conditions in

ILLUSTRATION 6.5   Jaguar: quality circles

The introduction of quality circles at the Jaguar car plant in the 1980s resulted in the number of traditional quality inspectors being reduced by half.

In the 1970s Jaguar was faced with a mounting problem of manufacturing faults. In some cases this was because of faulty components, but mostly it was caused by poor workmanship. Senior management visited Japan and West Germany to investigate their quality-control techniques, and returned with the idea of 'quality circles'. The idea was that men on the shop floor were responsible, *as part of their job*, for building in and monitoring quality. This approach to quality control (and the underlying issue of motivation) proved far superior to the old-fashioned quality inspection.

In 1984 Jaguar had sixty circles, each with around a dozen members, (10 per cent of the work-force) in areas ranging from cylinder-block and cylinder-head production to engine assembly and reconditioning. Following the introduction of the circles in 1980 the number of quality inspectors dropped from 677 to 360. The scheme evolved so that circles addressed themselves to operational problems. They took it on themselves, say, to chase up a supplier and this involvement with, and responsibility for, the whole production process increased employees' commitment to the company.

The ideas that the circles came up with were many and not necessarily earth-shattering, but added up to large savings. On one occasion a circle found that brake discs were being damaged during transfer within the plant, and so designed a new rack for transporting the discs. In 1983, 8,000 proposals were put forward under the suggestions scheme. The worker-representatives were selected democratically, not by elections but through workers putting themselves and each other forward on grounds of experience or special qualifications. The company aimed to extend the scheme so that all 8,000 workers could participate.

Inevitably, though, there was some conflict. Several of the quality circles broke up, because shop stewards took out their men. The unions claimed that people in the quality circles were in a better position to contribute to the suggestion scheme and make money than the rest of the work-force. Management

ILLUSTRATION 6.5   *continued*

argued that people in quality circles were worse off because they had to share their financial rewards.

Source: Abridged from *Management Today*, April 1984.

terms of the working environment but made more fundamental changes in terms of status and working hours, and also schemes to make work more enjoyable. Some examples are shown in Illustration 6.6, Non-financial incentives.

EXERCISE 6.7

1. From the list of workers below, select those for whom it is possible to operate a system of payment by merit, and outline a system:
   - sales staff
   - research worker
   - journalist
   - assembly-line worker
   - personnel assistant
   - marketing director
2. Present a constructive critique of a payment system of which you or a close friend or relative have experience.
3. Group discussion. Divide into two groups. One side is to argue that all incentive schemes must involve money to be successful, and the other group argue in favour of non-financial incentives.

This section has argued that the successful implementation of business plans is dependent on the right climate for acceptance of the plans. The choice of incentive/reward schemes can be an important contributor to producing such a climate.

6.3 Measuring and controlling performance

Although the primary focus of this book is business planning it is impossible to separate planning from the related issues of the measurement and control of performance. However, in discussing these latter issues it is not intended to give a comprehensive treatment of the topics but rather to concentrate on how the approach to, and design of, control

ILLUSTRATION 6.6   Non-financial incentives

Flexible working

In 1984 a Greater London Council group organisation reported an increase in flexible working arrangements at all levels in the public and private sector. This involved not only daily flexitime where workers have to attend for stipulated core hours, like 11a.m.–3p.m., but also contractual arrangements for the flexible working year. These arrangements were considered advantageous for both men and women.

Single status employees

Japanese companies like Sony have introduced this system into the UK but it has been slow to spread. The main features were that all employees have the same status, they all have to start and finish work at the same time, share the same washroom, canteen and fringe benefits, like cars and expense accounts. This greater equality could be regarded as a reward for some and a control for others.

Job enrichment

Work on a car-assembly line has been regarded as one of the most repetitive and alienating of jobs because the worker does not feel he is part of the finished product, and is forced to work at the pace of the moving production line. The concept of quality circles tried to re-establish the workers' interest and pride in the product. In the Jaguar example, quality circles are a form of control via job enrichment, and one that has been successfully used by firms such as Phillips Electrical and Wedgwood Pottery.

systems within an organisation need to be part of the business planning process. It is therefore necessary to discuss:

- Types of control within organisations.
- How the success of a business plan can be affected by the control systems of the organisation. ·
- Some important measures of control.

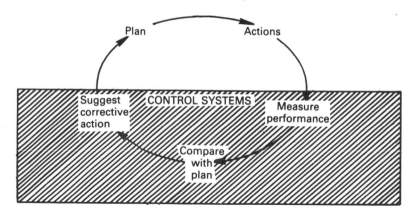

FIGURE 6.2   A simple control system

6.3.1 Types of control

Control is concerned with ensuring that plans and actions remain in line with each other. This will normally require a number of separate tasks to be undertaken as illustrated in Figure 6.2, which represents a very simple control system. First, the **performance** of the company will need to be measured – for example its output and profitability may be assessed. Second, this performance needs to be **compared** with the business plan, and third, **corrective action** may need to be taken to ensure that plans and actions do remain in line with each other. It should be noted that this last task may require a change in the plan – it should not be assumed that the plan is unchangeable and, hence, that control is only concerned with moving actual performance nearer to the plan. There are many situations where good control will be used to modify a plan to be more in tune with the realities of the organisation's situation.

Another common misconception is that control is only exerted through **formal** quantified control systems – for example, by using the information produced by the management accountants in the company, or the clocking-in and -out of employees. In reality control of a company's performace tends to be exerted in two different ways as shown in Figure 6.3.

Formal controls are a feature of large organisations where people are governed by written rules and codes of conduct. Discretion and accountability are carefully defined. For example, branch managers in banks fix their charges in accordance with rules laid down by Head Office.

In addition to the formal control systems, a substantial amount of control of performance is actually exerted informally. **Social control** is a

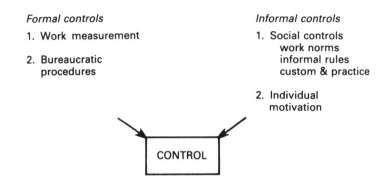

FIGURE 6.3   Two types of control within organisations

very powerful force in all organisations and is best thought of as 'norms of behaviour' which might dictate the speed at which people work, their attitudes towards achieving formal targets, the level of 'pride' in such things as quality. Equally powerful is **individual motivation** which has already been discussed in Section 6.1.

The old craft industries such as leather-work, pottery or silversmithing are characterised by high degrees of informal control. Dependence on detailed formal control systems may not be necessary and, in some cases, it may be counter-productive. This is particularly so in organisations who employ a lot of very creative people such as research workers, designers or actors. Such people are often highly motivated and too many formal controls can be a very de-motivating force. This is not meant to suggest that formal control systems will not be necessary in such organisations but rather that they will need to be used with care and sensitivity.

6.3.2 Influence of control systems on business plans

In the previous discussion of reward/incentive systems (Section 6.2.) it was mentioned that difficulties often arise because new plans are implemented in situations where elaborate incentive schemes already exist. The same problem applies to control systems. Some examples will illustrate the difficulties which may have to be overcome and these are summarised in Table 6.3.

● Major difficulties can arise when a new plan seeks to emphasise **new aspects** of the organisation's activities. It can prove impossible to change the performance of people if the control systems are not changed. So, for example, a sales-force are unlikely to spend much

TABLE 6.3   How control systems help or hinder business plans

Aspect of control system	Care needs to be taken to:
Choice of factors to control	Control the important aspects of the plan (e.g. quality?)
Diversity of activities	Avoid controlling everything in the same way
Frequency of reporting	Use a sensible time period between reports
Performance measures	Avoid misleading measures where quantification is difficult (e.g. Public Services)
Assigning accountability	Avoid holding people accountable where they cannot influence plans
Division of control	Avoid triggering off friction

of their time opening up new accounts if their performance continues to be measured on number of calls and orders received. New accounts can take some time to 'warm up' with resultant decline in performance. If the company's plans are dependent on opening new accounts the control systems must be amended or relaxed to encourage the sales-force to open up these accounts. For example, perhaps a new account is given a 'double-weighting' when measuring the salesman's activity level in order to encourage more visiting of new accounts.

● The problem of an inappropriate control system creating difficulties when implementing new plans is very common in organisations which plan to become **more diverse** in their activities. They overlook the fact that new activities may need to be measured and controlled in different ways. As a result these new ventures are subjected to the established control systems often with disastrous results. For example, a company such as Associated Dairies Group who had diversified from their original base into groceries (Asda), carpets (Allied Carpets), and furniture (MFI) would have considerable difficulty if they tried to apply the same stock control, credit control, or profit margins uniformly across the group. The various businesses are different enough to require different performance measures. Although this point may seem rather obvious there are many occasions within business planning where such self-evident truths are not acted upon, making the implementation of the plan very difficult.

● Often the reason for not acting is the difficulty of cutting across the **vested interests** of certain groups of people. For example, some parts of an organisation might be ear-marked for growth and are, therefore, not expected to generate the same cash surpluses as other parts which are operating in more mature markets. As mentioned in Chapter 3 product portfolio analysis would help to identify these various activities. The problem comes when the employees and managers in the Cash Cow parts of the business start to resent the fact that 'their' earnings are being swallowed up by other parts of the business (Question Marks).

● Difficulties can arise if performance is being **measured too frequently** or too infrequently (this relates to the discussions in Chapter 5). So, for example, it would be unrealistic to expect the benefits from a major advertising campaign to materialise within one week. The success or failure of the campaign would need to be assessed over a longer period of time. In the other direction, measuring weekly-attendance figures at a cinema would hide the very uneven attendances through the week (Mondays and Tuesdays being particularly thin).

● Some organisations, particularly in service industries, find difficulty in devising quantitative measures of their performance. As a result they tend to rely on measuring those things which **are** measurable and hoping that they will provide a guide to the success or otherwise of their plans. Such indirect measures can be very misleading or even dangerous. For example, it is tempting to measure the performance of a dentist's practice by the number of people s/he treats each year. However, there could be an argument that really successful dental care would actually diminish the need for people to have dental work undertaken. The control system could be failing to measure a key aspect of the practice's plan namely, **prevention** rather than cure.

● Since control systems are regarded as an essential part of making business plans work in practice it is also necessary to consider **whose** performance it is that is to be measured and controlled. It is a common pitfall to make people **accountable** for aspects of a plan over which (in reality) they have little control. The managers of retail outlets are often in this situation where the sales of many items is much more dictated by national advertising campaigns than any of the in-store promotional activity controlled by the store management themselves.

● Because performance measurement and control can be such a complicated issue, particularly in large organisations, it is very often felt necessary to subdivide the organisation for the purposes of planning and control as mentioned in Chapter 2. As a result a whole new set of difficulties and rivalries can arise which can affect the ability to implement business plans successfully. For example, there can be disputes about how the **overheads** of the organisation (for example, Head Office expenses) should be allocated to the various departments or divisions when assessing their performance. Sometimes different parts of the company **share resources** (for instance, perhaps, a common sales-force is selling the output of two or more divisions) which can cause friction about the 'fair' allocation of that resource. Sometimes one part of the company supplies another part with materials or components. There can then be arguments about the price at which these goods should be **transferred** since it affects the performance (profitability) of each part of the company.

These examples have been provided to illustrate how important it is during business planning to assess whether the control systems are likely to help or hinder the implementation of the plan. It may be necessary to amend certain control systems as a prerequisite to introducing new plans.

EXERCISE 6.8

Read Illustration 6.7, Alchester Polytechnic Library.

1. Describe the various control systems operating in the library in terms of Figure 6.3.
2. The role of the library is changing – how should the control systems change to adapt to that new role?
3. Why do more formal controls not *necessarily* improve the quality of service?

6.3.3 Some important control measures

In the preceding discussions there have been a number of references to the fact that performance measurement and control needs to be geared towards the monitoring of the critically important aspects of any business plan rather than seeking to measure every last detail of the plan. In order to help readers relate this to specific measurements that might need to be undertaken, Table 6.4 gives some examples of how various aspects of a business plan might be measured. It is likely that much of this information exists within companies but is not necessarily used to best effect.

ILLUSTRATION 6.7 Alchester Polytechnic Library: control system

In 1980 Alchester Polytechnic provided a wide range of full-and part-time courses for its 8,000 students, ranging from technology to humanities, social sciences and management. The library was on three sites, with a total stock of books of 150,000, a staff of 35 and an annual budget of £400,000. The buildings and facilities were up to date. The Head Librarian Alan Rowe had four senior librarians in charge of the following areas: purchasing, classification, counter services, and staff.

In 1980 the Principal of the Polytechnic received a report from the Business Education Council which confirmed his suspicions about the inadequacy of the library service. The report said that the library provision needed immediate changes to provide a considerably higher standard of service to both staff and students. The level of usage of library facilities appeared to be very low. Many academic staff had resorted to keeping their own stock of books, journals and videos for loan to students.

The publication of this report was a great shock to Alan Rowe. It was particularly worrying since he had always prided himself on operating a 'tight ship' and was surprised at the inference that he ran a 'sloppy' system. In his reply to the Principal he explained the ways in which he might increase control over the library.

> The key to running a good library system is having the books in the correct places on the shelves. I've done something about this by reducing the loan period to 14 days – perhaps I should reduce it further? We could transfer staff from the information counter to shelving books. I also think we should increase the fines, but will need your support to get that through Academic Board. Students complain that we don't have the books on their reading lists but this is the fault of academic staff who don't order on time. I also feel that departmentally-based book collections should be housed in the library where they can be properly controlled.

Alan also wanted to introduce a new book security and scanning system, and to prevent outsiders using the library, but senior management had been consistently unsympathetic to the introduction of these controls. 'I really don't understand it' he thought, 'how can I be expected to improve the service without better control over those who abuse the system. This library would be a marvellous place without its users!'

TABLE 6.4 Some important control measures

Aspect of the business plan	Performance measured by:
Human resources	
Productivity	Work/output measurement
Stability of labour force	Labour turnover
Sales	
Competitive position	Sales targets
	Market-share analysis
Sales profitability	Sales budget
Quality of service	Customer satisfaction
Physical resources	
Utilisation of equipment	Capacity fill
Materials utilisation	Yield/waste
Quality	Inspection
Financial	
Cash flow	Cash budgets
Profitability	Ratio analysis
Costs	Variance analysis
Investment	Capital budgets

The really important skill is deciding to which of these measures to pay most attention at any one time, knowing that the relative importance of these factors will shift over time. So, for example, in growing markets **capacity fill** could be the key issue alongside **market share**. However, once the market growth eases off these factors may become less important whereas **quality**, **productivity** and **sales margins** may become the most important aspects to control. Very often companies fail to see this need to shift the emphasis and continue controlling in the same old way with unfortunate consequences. The continued emphasis on capacity fill could lead a company to use lower prices as the primary method of maintaining sales output in the face of increases in competition. This could create a significant squeeze on profit margins and a rapid decline in company performance. A recognition that cost control and quality were more important could secure the company's performance level.

In public service organisations these issues are equally important. So, for example, the establishment of a comprehensive medical service in a new town may be monitored by the doctor/patient ratio as the town grows – taking due account of the demographic make-up of the population (particularly age-structure which affects the demand on medical services). This is the equivalent of 'capacity fill' in the manufacturing sector. When the population growth has ended, more emphasis is then placed on quality of service and the efficiency with which the service is run. For example, there may be pressure to move towards more group practices and health centres to ensure a more efficient use of both doctors' ancillary services (opticians, chiropodists, etc.) and specialist equipment.

EXERCISE 6.9

Read Illustration 6.8, British Steel and Table 6.4.

1. How many of the performance measures in Table 6.4 were being used by British Steel?
2. Why had these factors been chosen?
3. What other factors do **you** feel should be measured and controlled?
4. What performance indicators would you consider to be appropriate for a service organisation?

6.4 Information systems and business planning

Information technology is the obsession of the business world in the 1980s and it is therefore important to reflect on how the information systems of an organisation affect its ability to put business plans into action. Whereas information technology might be regarded as 'new', the importance of information in business planning has always been recognised as long as businesses have operated. The discussions in this section will attempt to show how information systems and technology contribute to business planning particularly in relation to the implementation of plans. It is important to distinguish between different types of organisation in this respect:

- In some service organisations **information** is a **key part of** the company's **product**. An extreme example is an international currency dealer where up-to-date information on exchange rates is essential to the success of the business. In such organisations the exploitation of modern information systems and technology is an absolutely essential ingredient of all the company's business plans.
- Other companies are now facing markets where consumers expect them to provide fast and reliable information. Whereas this is not essential to the running of the business a failure to provide

ILLUSTRATION 6.8   British Steel: key performance statistics and indicators

Financial performance (£m)

	1983/4	1982/3	1981/2
1. Turnover	3,358	3,231	3,443
2. Losses			
Actual	(176)	(383)	(327)
Objective (as fixed by government plan)	(181)	(80)	(318)
3. External financing limit			
Actual	318	569	694
Objective (as fixed by government plan)	321	575	730
4. Net assets employed at year end	2,268	2,190	2,476

Production and deliveries (m. tonnes)

1. Liquid steel production	13.4	11.7	14.1
2. Steel deliveries (in product tonnes)			
Home	7.5	6.8	8.0
Export	2.9	2.5	2.7
Total	10.4	9.3	10.7

Manpower (000s)

1. Number of BSC employees in UK at year end	71.1	81.1	103.7

Performance indicators

1. Ironmaking			
Utilisation of furnace capacity in blast (as %)	93	81	93
Fuel rate (kg of coke and oil consumed per tonne of iron prod.)	553	565	579

2. Steelmaking			
Utilisation of actual manned steelmaking capacity (as %)	91	83	92
Liquid steel production by process - oxygen (as %)	83	80	78
- electric (as %)	17	20	22
Steel production continuously cast (as %)	46	38	29
3. Energy			
Energy consumed per tonne of liquid steel (GJ)	20.9	22.2	22.4
4. Labour in Iron and Steel (ECSC) activities			
Man-hours worked per tonne of liquid steel	7.1	9.3	9.4
Total employment cost (£)			
per tonne of liquid steel	47	55	51
per employee	12,000	10,450	10,050
5. Total Corporation employment costs as % of value added	102	124	112

Source: Annual report.

such a service is likely to diminish the competitive position of the company in the future. Banking and similar services are good examples of this type of organisation.

● Other companies are developing plans which allow them to 'tie' customers into their systems of information and hence gain competitive advantage by making it more difficult for customers to switch to another supplier. A good example here is the increased use of automatic cash-transfer from bank accounts in places like supermarkets rather than paying by cash, cheque or credit-card. Building societies may choose to deal only with solicitors who have information technology compatible with their own, so that funds and documents can be easily transferred when completing a mortgage on a house.

● The most publicised impact of information technology is that on **costs and jobs**. This is a particularly important issue in many service industries. Much of the work of clerical staff in industries like insurance, banking and many public services lends itself to automation – improving the quality of information available whilst reducing costs and also jobs. A careful scrutiny will show that even highly paid professionals such as solicitors and accountants spend much time on relatively mundane tasks. In other words the key source of information has been professional judgement some of which can be replaced by a good computer system. The valuation of houses is a good example. Whereas professional estate agents will use their 'feel' for the market to assess the value of any individual house – this process can be considerably improved by an extensive computer file of all property transactions in the area. The professional judgement is still needed – but the professional's time can be used more efficiently, hence reducing the real cost of the service.

● The last issue to be considered is the **wider availability** of information to people both inside and outside organisations. This means that business plans have to be implemented bearing in mind a much more knowledgeable environment. This can have several implications. For example, the ability to maintain price differentials between competitors is much reduced in many industries and particularly so in the retail trade. Consumers are far better informed about the variety of goods on offer.

A more educated and knowledgeable work-force increases the pressure on management to be more consultative in their business planning (or face resistance to their plans). To many British managers this has come as something of a shock. Traditionally UK companies (particularly in the manufacturing sector) have been noted for their obsession with secrecy. Already legislation has opened up the need for organisations to reveal certain information to shareholders and employees and it seems quite likely that this general trend will continue.

EXERCISE 6.10

Read Illustration 6.9, Stewart Warner, and refer to Table 6.5.

1. Which of the issues outlined in Table 6.5 best explain the reasons why Stewart Warner decided to use new information technology?
2. Brief the Managing Director on how the firm might take further advantage of new IT?

ILLUSTRATION 6.9   Stewart Warner: using information technology

In 1984 a Newcastle engineering business won a prize for the effective use of information technology. Stewart Warner manufactured a range of pneumatic power tools and pumps; 700 individual models, with 20,000 product structures and over 13,000 parts. The company had a policy of keeping spares for each product for seven years. Not surprisingly, the stock manual numbered 600 pages. The company employed 200 highly skilled workers but rejected the option of complete automation as 'neither affordable or desirable'. However what they were looking for was a production control system which would provide the necessary information to 'break down the traditional barriers between departments and bring the whole company together'. After initial difficulties in finding the appropriate software a computer was installed in 1982 at a cost of £200,000. In that year the company achieved a 30 per cent increase in productivity and a 20 per cent reduction in stock, with a total saving of £500,000. The manager had 'all the information I needed about the products, the work centre they were being made in, and where they were going':

- Customer information could provide a list of contacts to help sales personnel, or past orders to help in building up discounting structures or demand forecasts.
- An order for a particular product gave access to a list of the parts needed and a production plan. (This replaced trekking round the factory to see if the parts were available).
- A production simulation could be summoned to pinpoint any shortages.
- Customers' order changes could be fed instantly into the common database so that other orders could be rescheduled and lead-times improved.
- Details of the timing of necessary purchases was also instantly available.
- Standard costing information, with both current and previous prices helped to guard against over-pricing.
- Without moving from his desk the manager could identify bottlenecks in the payment systems.

ILLUSTRATION 6.9   *continued*

Before the installation of the computer all this information would have been dutifully noted down, filed away and forgotten. Now the information was available to all. In addition the computer could instantly perform time-consuming tasks such as conversion of measurements and currencies. The system's major achievement at Stewart Warner had been a reduction in the inventory. The company had become leaner and fitter, not through cutting back the work-force, but by cutting down surplus stock.

Source: *Management Today*, April 1984.

TABLE 6.5   The influence of information systems on business plans

Information may be	Example
A key part of the product	Foreign exchange dealers
Expected by customers	Banks
A means of tying customers/suppliers to your system	Electronic cash-transfer
Produced more quickly reliably and cheaply by new technology	Many service organisations (for example, Insurance, public services)
Used to challenge the validity of plans and/or improve communication	Trade unions better informed

Overall it is clearly essential for companies to be aware of the importance of information to the success of their plans. The successful exploitation of information and information technology is likely to remain a key ingredient of many business plans over the coming decade.

6.5 Summary

This chapter has been concerned with how plans can be made to work in practice. It has been seen that the biggest pitfall in implementing business plans is that people will not be willing or able to make the plans work. This can occur for a number of reasons. First, people might resist the changes which the business plans require, perhaps through a genuine fear of the consequences or even outright stubbornness or complacency. Second, people may not be capable of performing the tasks which the plan requires – they may need to be replaced or retrained. Third, reward and incentive schemes may prove to be a barrier to implementing plans since they discourage people from changing the way they are operating. A similar problem can occur with the systems for measuring and controlling performance within the organisation. Finally, the availability and use of information within the company can be critically important to the success of its business plans.

Recommended key readings

Ray Wild, *Production and Operations Management: Principles and Techniques* (Holt, Rinehart & Winston, 1984) 3rd edn. Chapters 18 to 21 provide a very comprehensive treatment of control systems in operating systems. Chapter 21 is particularly useful for the coverage of performance measures.

Thomas Peters and Robert Waterman, *In Search of Excellence* (Harper & Row, 1982). Chapters 2 and 3 are helpful in understanding the role that people play in organisational change.

John Grieve-Smith, *Business Strategy* (Blackwell, 1985). Chapter 11 is concerned with the impact of change on people.

Ian Winfield, *People in Business* (Heinemann, 1984), is a good general text about the role of people in business.

John Child, *Organization: A Guide to Problems and Practice* (Harper & Row, 1977). Chapter 6 and the Appendix (1st edn only) are useful in relation to issues of control.

John Dunstone, 'Keeping Control of Manufacture' (*Management Today*, April 1986), looks at problems of controlling business plans.

David Hussey, *Corporate Planning: Theory and Practice* (Pergamon, 1982) 2nd edn. Chapter 22 looks at some reasons why planning can fail. Also *Corporate Planning: the Human Factor* by the same author (Pergamon, 1979) extends the same theme.

CHAPTER 7

Planning in practice
– a case study

The previous chapters of the book have looked in some depth at the different planning tasks which were identified in Chapter 1 (Figure 1.3). Whereas the separate discussion of these planning tasks can help in understanding each task more fully there are some dangers that readers will forget that the tasks need to **fit together** within any organisation. For this reason this final chapter will be devoted to an in-depth look at one particular real world organisation and the way in which it approaches business planning. It is hoped to show how the various planning tasks are undertaken and some of the reasons for approaching planning in that way. Equally importantly the example will seek to illustrate some of the very real difficulties of making plans work out in practice and how the company's circumstances affect the choice of planning 'techniques'.

It is not the purpose of the example to suggest that any one particular approach to planning could be regarded as a blueprint for other organisations. Indeed it is hoped that by this stage readers will be aware that the search for such a blueprint is ill-advised. Rather, the example seeks to provide readers with a chance to see how choices on planning are made within one organisation, to reflect on the applicability of the approach to other organisations, and to consolidate their own understanding of business planning in practice.

The organisation chosen as the example is Radio Hallam, the commercial radio station for South Yorkshire and the North Midlands which operates from Sheffield. The reason for using this particular company is that it has several features which are quite interesting in relation to business planning:

● Although the company is privately owned and operated it does so within a framework of public accountability (through the IBA) and is committed to the provision of a public service.

- The recent history of the organisation covers the period of **establishing** the company as well as **operating** in an established market. This provides a rich variety of examples of planning problems.
- Although the organisation is located in Sheffield it is very similar to many of the other forty-seven commercial radio stations throughout the UK with which readers are undoubtedly familiar.

EXERCISE 7.1

1. Read Illustration 7.1, Radio Hallam, and ensure that you have a basic understanding of how a commercial radio station operates.
2. Tune to your local commercial station (if possible) and become familiar with the type and format of programming.
3. Look in your local newspapers (if possible) to see the programme plans for each day.

7.1 People involved in planning

Like most organisations the management team in Radio Hallam was centrally involved in the business planning. Table 7.1 shows the directors and senior management in 1985. However, there was a quite deliberate attempt to involve a whole range of other people – particularly in the process of strategic planning.

To a large extent the history of commercial radio dictated that this wide involvement should exist. For example, Table 7.2. shows the shareholders of Radio Hallam. Because of the initial concerns that local radio would damage the local newspapers the latter were given a right to purchase share capital in the radio stations. It is interesting to see how the other Radio Hallam shareholders were largely 'local' interests but represented a variety of stakeholder groups. The Company Secretary explained the importance of this:

Whereas in any truly commercial company the prime concern of most shareholders is financial return on their investment this is not true with Radio Hallam. Some shareholders simply want to foster local radio; others want to see more competition in local advertising and so on. As a private company responsible to a public authority (IBA) the possibilities for earning and distributing unlimited profits are removed, for example through the secondary rental system.

ILLUSTRATION 7.1   Radio Hallam: all aspects of planning in a local radio station

In 1984 Radio Hallam, the commercial radio station for South Yorkshire and the North Midlands celebrated its tenth birthday. The station, based in Sheffield, had been one of the first 'wave' of nineteen stations to be set up following the Independent Broadcasting Act of 1973. Hitherto the British Broadcasting Company (BBC) had a monopoly on radio broadcasting in the UK. Independent radio stations, like Radio Hallam, were independent companies operating under a franchise (renewable every eight years) from the Independent Broadcasting Authority (IBA) who were responsible for the maintenance of *standards* in the programming, laid down strict guidelines about the duration and style of advertising and transmitted all programmes from IBA transmitters. By 1985 there were forty-eight stations in the UK.

Radio Hallam was primarily a music and information station broadcasting a mixture of pop records, middle-of-the-road music and news (including sport). Its output was quite similar to BBC Radio 2. The station broadcast for 24 hours per day. From October 1985 the company extended its broadcast area by taking on the franchise for Doncaster and Barnsley supported by new IBA transmitters.

The company's revenue came almost entirely from the sale of advertising time to both local and national companies. By 1985 the company employed fifty staff and a number of freelance broadcasters. Fifteen staff were employed selling advertising time, writing and making commercials, or promoting and publicising the radio station; seventeen staff and the freelancers were in programming output and news; six were engineers engaged in maintenance or equipment design and construction. The remaining staff were in the secretarial pool, clerical services, maintenance, reception, administration and management. With the station operating 24 hours a day, weekend and weekday shifts had to be arranged to provide staffing around the clock.

Radio Hallam broadcast area covered an adult population of some 1.63 million. The size of the broadcast area was determined by the IBA through its choice of transmitter power and location. Radio Hallam agreed with the IBA the geographical extent of its editorial and advertising coverage. By 1985 some 45 per cent of the local population were listening to Radio Hallam with average listening time of 13.3 hours per week. This compared with BBC radio 1's 46 per cent and 10.7 hours, BBC Radio 2's 27 per cent and 8.4 hours and BBC Radio Sheffield's 26 per cent and 9.4 hours.[1] Radio Hallam was particularly popular with the under-35-year olds but less so with the middle-class population. Peak listening occurred at breakfast time during the week and on Saturday and Sunday mornings. Evening listening was appreciably lower.

Company sales of advertising had reached £1.4m by 1985. The IBA restricted the advertising time to 9 minutes per hour. Unlike television the company prepared many of the advertisements in its own studios. The volume of advertising varied through the year – for example, in September 1984 almost 70 per cent of 'available' time (i.e. 9 minutes per hour for 24 hours) was sold compared with less than 40 per cent in February 1985. Breakfast and tea-time were the two most popular times of day for advertising as these were the peak listening times. The company's 'rate-card' (price-list) reflected this – off-peak advertising rates were considerably lower than peak-rates.

The IBA operated a system of 'secondary rentals' which was effectively a levy on the profits of the successful (usually larger) stations as a means of supporting the smaller stations. As a result, stations like Radio Hallam were unable to pursue a policy of maximising profits to distribute to shareholders. Increased profits would result in increased secondary rental payments.

Note: 1. Audience statistics were prepared annually by an independent body called the *Joint Industry Council for Radio Audience Research* (JICRAR).

EXERCISE 7.2

1. What is the prime interest of each of the shareholder groups shown in Table 7.2.
2. How might the planning of the management group be influenced by this mix of shareholders?

TABLE 7.1   Radio Hallam: directors and senior executives, 1985

Company Directors	Age (June 1985)	Occupation
Mrs Dawn de Bartolomé	61	None
Michael Mallett (Chairman)	53	Consultant
Frank Benson	64	Professor
Keith Skues	46	Programme Director
Lord Fred Mulley	66	Member of House of Lords
Herbert Whitham	64	Retired retailing executive
Tom Watson	59	Deputy Chief Executive
Bill MacDonald	58	Managing Director
John Jewitt	61	Managing Director

Senior Executives' Position		Length of service	Age	Formerly
Bill MacDonald	Managing Director	11 years	58	Trident Television, Evening newspaper advertising bureau, and American commercial radio
Keith Skues	Programme Director	11 years	46	BBC, Pirate stations, British Forces Broadcasting
Graham Blincow	Company Secretary	11 years	47	Woodhead Components Limited, Sheffield Newspapers Limited.
Derrick Connolly	Chief Engineer	11 years	37	Capital Radio, IBA (Television)
Mrs Audrey Adams	Sales Manager	11 years		Sheffield Newspapers Limited, Gestetner Limited
Jim Greensmith	News Editor	11 years	38	Sheffield Cablevision Limited, Sheffield Newspapers Limited.

7.2 Influences on planning systems

All organisations need to develop planning systems which suit their particular circumstances. Bill MacDonald, the Managing Director, explained how he saw this issue in Radio Hallam:

> Hallam has several features which I think make us plan the business the way that we do. The facts that we are small and in the service industry are

TABLE 7.2   Radio Hallam: shareholders, June 1985

	% of total equity (all figures rounded)
Local press	
Sheffield Newspapers	13.0
Worksop Guardian	4.5
Derbyshire Times	3.7
Rotherham Advertiser	0.9
South Yorkshire Times	0.9
	23.0
Other media	
Trident Television Limited (Leeds)	9.0
Hallamshire Industrial Securities Limited (now owned by Local News of London Limited)	2.3
Unions	
General and Municipal	4.5
USDAW (Distributors)	4.5
Local companies (7)	22.8
Company directors (9)	7.4
Other company employees (31) (or ex-employees)	3.6
Individual shareholders (11)	8.5
Finance houses and banks (2)	6.7
Others	
Sheffield University	4.5
Sheffield Chambers of Commerce	0.5
Automobile Association	2.7

very important if you compare us with, let's say, BP or Ford. You should also remember that we are primarily a one-product company – over 90 per cent of our revenue comes from selling advertising time. We also have a very strange mixture of highly creative tasks – in both programming and selling – together with some pretty basic routine tasks such as sales administration, and many of the administrative jobs supporting programming. Of course we must not lose sight of our position as a franchise holder to a public authority (IBA) – public accountability certainly influences the way that you plan. These are what I would see as the most important influences on our approach to business planning.

EXERCISE 7.3

1. Consider the various influences on the planning systems needed in Radio Hallam and mentioned by Bill MacDonald. Rank them in what you consider to be their order of importance.
2. Explain, briefly, how each of these factors might affect the approach to any aspect of business planning.

7.3 Dividing responsibility for planning

Although the term 'responsibility centre' was not used as such in Radio Hallam, responsibilities and accountability were clearly defined. Figure 7.1 shows the company structure in 1985. The company as a whole was held responsible for profit performance by its shareholders and also overseen by the IBA. Capital investment would require the approval of the Board, who regarded the control of profit to be 'revenue-led', that is, the forecast of sales revenue dictated the spending levels which each section was allowed. Consequently the sales department was held responsible for *revenue* and its performance was controlled through detailed monthly revenue targets. All other parts of the company were measured by the quality of their output of service within their agreed budget. Clearly this involved a considerable element of judgement regarding the 'quality' of a section's output. In the area of programming the annual audience-survey figures from JICRAR gave an indication of the popularity of the station and its major competitors (see Table 7.3), and were used to judge the performance of the programme production team.

One or two new ventures had been made profit-responsible – for example, the *Hallam Road Show* (touring programme unit), merchandising activities, commercial production, leasing of studio facilities and contract engineering (which provided an engineering consultancy service to other – usually newer or smaller – stations). In 1984 contract engineering had generated about £100,000 revenue.

EXERCISE 7.3

1. Identify the types of responsibility centres present in Radio Hallam. (refer to Table 2.2).
2. Why is the company organised this way?
3. Would you make any changes?

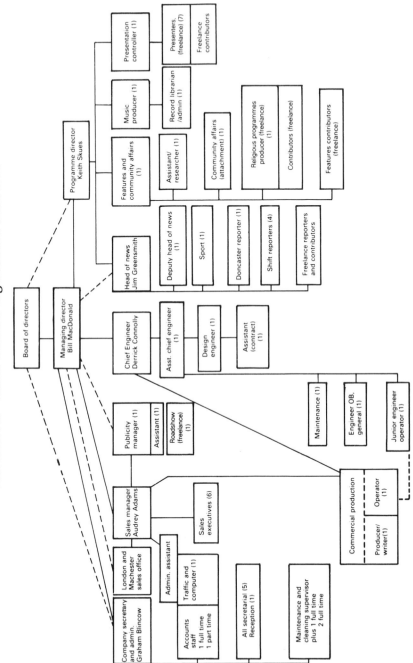

FIGURE 7.1   Radio Hallam: organisation chart 1985

TABLE 7.3   Audience profile for broadcast area: Spring 1985

Spring 1985 Radio Network Survey – Radio Hallam
Cumulative weekly audience (Reach), total and average hours

	Radio Hallam	BBC Radio 1	BBC Radio 2	BBC Radio 3	BBC Radio 4	BBC local Radio	Radio Luxem- bourg	Any other station
Unw. sample	313	313	313	313	313	313	313	313
Estimated population	1060	1060	1060	1060	1060	1060	1060	1060
Monday–Sunday weekly reach	473	488	290	38	152	275	35	84
	45%	46%	27%	4%	14%	26%	3%	8%
Total hours	6287	5229	2421	118	1930	2573	116	281
Average hours	13.3	10.7	8.4	3.1	12.7	9.4	3.4	3.4

	All adults 15+	Adults in home	Sex		Age		All house-wives	Social class		Child-ren 5-14
			Men	Women	15-34	35+		ABC1	C2DE	
Unw. sample	313	313	161	152	97	216	141	95	218	69
Estimated population	1060	1060	513	547	397	663	474	317	743	197
Radio Hallam										
Monday-Sunday weekly reach	473	388	232	241	196	277	205	123	349	68
	45%	37%	45%	44%	49%	42%	43%	39%	47%	35%
Total hours	6287	4952	2998	3290	2282	4006	2918	1208	5080	397
Average hours	13.3	12.8	12.9	13.7	11.7	14.5	14.2	9.8	14.5	5.8
All stations										
Monday-Sunday weekly reach	926	878	457	468	370	555	396	294	632	146
	87%	83%	89%	86%	93%	84%	84%	93%	85%	74%
Total hours	18956	14672	9473	9483	7043	11913	8800	5348	13608	1081
Average hours	20.5	16.7	20.7	20.2	19.0	21.5	22.2	18.2	21.5	7.4

Source: Joint Industry Council for Radio Audience Research (JICRAR)

** Populations and audiences are in 000s

7.4 Co-ordinating planning efforts

Most senior executives within organisations are all too familiar with the problems and frustrations of keeping the various planning efforts of the company properly co-ordinated. Bill MacDonald was no exception and explained some of these difficulties and how Radio Hallam tried to overcome them:

> You must remember that our board members are all non-executive directors except Keith Skues (Programme Director) and me (see Table 7.1). This, together with the fact that we are relatively small, makes **our** position quite crucial in terms of translating the general policy directives of the board into the operational activities of the company.
>
> Co-ordination between different sections is also made somewhat easier by being small. Our weekly executive meetings help considerably in keeping people up-to-date on what's going on elsewhere in the company. Quite regularly I find that special activities or events need to be co-ordinated by an individual – not normally a senior manager – in order to make sure that everything clicks into place. Most of our promotional activities need to be organised this way. A good example of this is the planning that went into the launch of our new broadcast area from October 1985. Here it was crucial that I had one person who was responsible for ensuring that the launch promotion was properly tied-in with the push the sales team was making with potential new customers, etc. Without someone overlooking this job I would have been very worried about a serious 'misfire' of a very important event for the station.

EXERCISE 7.4

The Managing Director talks about three major ways of co-ordinating planning – Executive Directors, meetings, and assigning special co-ordinating roles to individuals:

1. Are these concerned with vertical or horizontal co-ordination (see Figure 2.5)
2. How useful are these methods in larger organisations?
3. What other methods might be useful?

7.5 Company objectives

Shortly after the launch of Radio Hallam the station was subjected to some adverse criticism in the local press by the labour leader of the

South Yorkshire County Council – on the grounds that its prime motive was the collection of revenue from advertising. Bill MacDonald's reply was interesting:

> This is totally untrue. Radio Hallam's reason for existence is to provide a broadcast service under the terms of the Independent Broadcasting Act 1973 . . . The cost of providing this service has, by law, to be met by sale of advertising time, and therefore, in contrast with other broadcasting services, Radio Hallam provides its services to the community without any charge in the form of rates, taxes or licence fees.

Although this might be regarded as a relatively straightforward statement of the company's **mission** there were some inevitable problems in translating this broad statement of intent into objectives for the company as a whole and for its various operational sections. For example, this mission statement says nothing about the target audience which should be served, the type of programming that should be provided, the expected financial performance of the company etc. Like most statements of mission it allows for a wide variety of objectives to be pursued 'legitimately'. It is for this reason that the IBA would regularly review the **actual** programming of each of the independent radio stations and often make suggestions or even requirements on how the programming should be changed.

The objectives of any organisation are best understood by observing what the organisation **does** rather than by looking at its formal statements of intent. In the case of Radio Hallam it is clear that the objectives being pursued were the result of a series of **pressures** all of which needed to be addressed:

- The IBA had a prime responsibility for overseeing **standards** and ensuring that the station's programming had some degree of **balance** within it. As the supervisor of franchise holders the IBA clearly had significant power to influence the company's policies as already mentioned.
- Since the company needed to be self-sufficient financially, its programming had to provide the opportunity to sell advertising-time at attractive rates. Clearly this could create friction within the company concerning the balance between minority-interest programmes and more-popular programmes. The former were unlikely to attract sufficient audiences to interest many advertisers whereas the later might be regarded as ignoring the interests of a significant section of the local community.
- As previously mentioned the IBA operated a system of 'secondary rentals' which were effectively a levy on the profits of the

successful (usually larger) stations as a means of supporting the smaller stations. As a result stations like Radio Hallam were unable to pursue a policy of maximising profits to distribute to shareholders. Increased profits would result in increased secondary rental payments.

The company explained its programming policy as follows:

Majority tastes served over the main part of the day. Minority tastes catered for at times when it gives the real fan a chance to sit down and appreciate his or her favourite show in comfort and with the attention it deserves. That is Hallam's policy.

EXERCISE 7.5

1. Why had Radio Hallam chosen such a policy on programming?
2. Could any other policy be pursued bearing in mind the possible conflicting interests mentioned above?

7.6 The business environment

Radio Hallam needed to be conscious of two separate business environments:

1. The environment relating to **broadcasting**.
2. The environment for the **advertising part of the business**, which was concerned with selling advertising time to both local and national companies.

The relationship between these two environments was a very important issue in the business planning within Radio Hallam. When buying advertising-time customers would wish to see details of the audience size and profile for the radio station. These statistics were prepared annually by a specialist media research company under the auspices of, and to specifications laid down by, an independent body called the Joint Industry Council for Radio Audience Research (JICRAR). Table 7.3 shows the kind of details which were available on the audience profile. Clearly, the audience being attracted by the station was determined by the style of programming.

About 60 per cent of the company's advertising revenue came from local companies – the major part of this being retail organisations. The

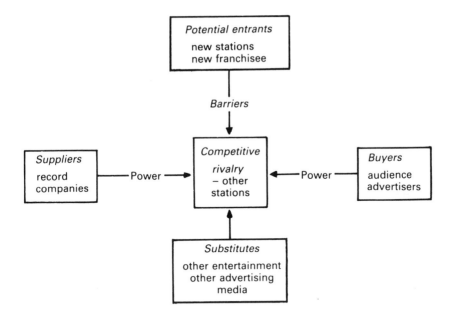

FIGURE 7.2   Radio Hallam: its competitive position

national advertising revenue tended to be from manufacturers of goods such as electrical appliances, food and drink, records, cosmetics. A London-based company called Broadcast Marketing Services (BMS) sold 'National' advertising as an agent for a number of the commercial stations mostly in the north and east of the country including Radio Hallam. Figure 7.2 shows some of the key aspects of the company's competitive environment as discussed in Chapter 3.

EXERCISE 7.6

1. Explain the way in which Radio Hallam's competitive position was likely to be influenced by the various organisations shown in Figure 7.2.
2. How do you suggest they should cope with these influences?

Both broadcasting and advertising are 'fast-moving' businesses in the sense that the products are relatively flexible and can be amended at fairly short notice. This had a significant influence on the way in which the company undertook its forecasting as Bill MacDonald, the Managing Director, explained:

I play a key role in the forecasting of advertising revenues utilising the forecast of national trends from our London sales company (BMS) and the careful assessments of local sales potential by our sales manager in Sheffield. Despite all the uncertainties surrounding the company I am a great believer in formalised forecasting. I use our computer spread-sheet package to produce monthly forecasts of revenue stretching six months ahead. These are done in April and October. The forecasts rise and fall in a seasonal manner which is common to all media. A further adjustment to the individual monthly projections compared with corresponding months of previous years in then made in the light of observed general economic trends and local conditions. There may be a desire to raise these projections by, for example, a cost-of-living factor such as the Retail Price Index, but this will not necessarily apply during periods of reduced economic activity (recession) whether of a general or a local nature. The previous year's figures may also be misleading if they were subject to unusual influences either of depression (for example, during the miners' strike of 1984–5 when retailing activity in the South Yorkshire area was considerably depressed) or inflated (for example, when major competitive media are not available to advertisers for a prolonged period, as happened when ITV was off the air for several weeks). Other seasonal adjustments must allow for the varying date of Easter, for example, or the introduction of new holidays, such as the two in May. Unlike some other radio stations the forward planning at Hallam is **revenue-led**. By this I mean that the forecasts of sales revenue **dictate** the spending levels that each area of the company is allowed. This may seem like a fairly obvious thing to say but all too often companies seem reluctant to tailor their spending to what is practically obtainable. They go chasing revenue that does not exist to cover their excessive costs. Within our forecasting and budgeting system I always have areas of cost which I know I can switch-off quickly if sales are below forecast – outside broadcasts would be a good example. This built-in flexibility is an essential addition to our forecasting efforts.

EXERCISE 7.7

1. What kind of forecasting methods are being used at Radio Hallam? (Refer to Section 3.3.3)
2. Referring to Table 7.4, which are the most difficult items to forecast when projecting future profits?
3. By plotting the data in Table 7.4 on a graph make your best estimates of sales and profits for the period April to September 1984.

TABLE 7.4 Radio Hallam: Trading summary and budget April 1983

Account	April	May	June	July	August	September	1st half[1]	2nd half
Final summary								
Revenue	131383	143883	117383	126383	107383	106383	721950	732798
Rev. rltd ded.[2]	−15600	−17100	−13920	−17500	−14840	−14700	−86040	−93660
Operational Revenue	115783	126783	103463	108883	92543	91683	635910	639138
Music and general	8358	8308	8308	8408	8258	8308	51540	49948
Talk	3747	3747	3747	3747	3747	3747	22542	22482
News	16074	16429	15877	15905	16285	15905	98100	96475
Engineering	9323	9323	9323	9523	9523	9523	57650	56538
Sales	14911	14853	14207	10873	10753	10873	91118	76470
Publicity	4849	3049	4799	2859	2859	4809	12078	23224
Administration and management	22444	22444	22444	23644	22444	22444	132126	135864
Establishment	21280	21280	21280	21280	21280	21280	126204	127680
Operational costs	100986	99433	99985	96239	95149	96889	591358	588681
Profit/loss	14797	27350	3478	12644	−2606	−5206	44552	50457

Notes:
1. 1st half refers to actual performance October 1982 to March 1983. Figures for April to September 1983 are budget figures.
2. Revenue-related deductions are payments for royalties and performance rights which, under the terms of the franchise, are based upon sales revenue earned.

7.7 Capabilities

Like many service organisations the capability and performance of Radio Hallam was dominated by the **people** within the company who were its major resource. The image and reputation of the station was built on the performance of the **presenters** and the way in which they were supported by the programming staff. This had been a key-factor in deciding to bring in well-known presenters like Keith Skues, Roger Moffatt and Johnny Moran when the station was launched in 1974, and proved crucial to the success of the station in those early days. However, locally-recruited presenters were also introduced into the station to ensure that the local image was maintained since this was considered to be essential to the long-term success of Radio Hallam.

Bill MacDonald commented on the capabilities of the organisation as he saw it:

In all companies, but particularly service organisations like Radio Hallam, you are only as good as your people. We are very fortunate in having a very able team of senior staff most of whom have been with us since we started, which is almost unique in independent local radio, given the rapid expansion (and job opportunities) which there has been over the past ten years.

However, behind a good team there have to be some other key-resources. Money is clearly central to the success of any business. On the whole we have had a very conservative attitude to our funding which some people have criticised. From the start it was a key objective to pay off our indebtedness within three years – which we did – and to fund all further developments from our trading profits – which we have done. We opted to keep out capital base low – for example, by leasing rather than buying premises. When I look at some of the stations which have suffered financial difficulties (including liquidation) I am convinced we took the right path. Perhaps it is easy to say this in hindsight when we look at the phenomenal rates of interest needed to service loans but, as I said, this was a quite deliberate policy on our part.

Physical resources is a difficult area to pass judgement on. Managers and those with special responsibilities feel squeezed and they argue that they could provide a better service if they had more or better facilities. For example, we currently have good satellite studios in Chesterfield and Rotherham but only a shared studio in Barnsley and none at all in Doncaster. If we spent lots of money on improving these facilities we would then have considerably higher fixed costs to cover and more pressure to find extra revenue. Although additions to the sales team could undoubtedly generate more sales it is our judgement that the marginal nature of such revenue would represent a great drop in sales productivity and would be unlikely to cover all these additional costs.

A comparison with the BBC is interesting. Clearly we can not touch them on programming areas which are labour-intensive and organisationally extensive – documentaries and drama in particular. As a national organisation they can pay better wages and attract more big-name presenters and producers. However, the price they pay for their size is **inertia** – we can move quickly here, after all there are only fifty of us.

Within my general philosophy regarding company resources is a reluctance to remove areas of weakness – which we all know about – unless the benefits clearly outweigh the costs of sorting the problem out. It is the easiest thing in the world to try to spend your way out of problems – but then you have to live with the consequences.

EXERCISE 7.8

1. Present your assessment of the strengths and weaknesses of Radio Hallam.
2. How might future business plans be influenced by this analysis?

7.8 Range of company activities

Over the company's history there had been different emphases in the business plan and this was foreseen at the outset. The initial strategy was one of **market penetration** in both programming and advertising largely at the expense of the BBC stations and other advertising media respectively. This was then followed by a period of **consolidation** where the distinctive character of the station became more important. On the advertising side **market development** then became an important part of the business plan. Whereas originally the plan had been to sell the concept of radio to those companies who already advertised using other media this was supplemented by convincing 'non-advertisers' to advertise – particularly in the small company sector. In this respect the development of new products or services was seen as important and the reason for offering a specially discounted advertising rate to this sector.

EXERCISE 7.9

1. What development opportunities would you see for a company like Radio Hallam? (refer to Table 3.7)
2. Which would you regard as the most sensible? Why?

7.9 Coping with uncertainty

It has previously been mentioned that both broadcasting and advertising are relatively fast-moving businesses. As a result business plans were often having to be made against a background of considerable uncertainty. Bill MacDonald commented on how this affected the planning in the company:

> When you stop and think about the number of things happening that could have a significant impact on our business it can be quite frightening. For example, at the moment we could list: breakfast television; cable and satellite TV; video-viewing; car-radio cassettes; proposals for community radio stations; the BBC going commercial, etc. I expect one approach might be to ignore all these possible developments on the grounds that it is far from clear how and when they are likely to affect our business. However, at Hallam we do take these matters seriously – in such a volatile market we need to be aware of these developments and have plans to deal with them. Much of the time of Radio Hallam's Board of Directors is spent considering likely future changes and how we might respond. Equally important are the steps we are prepared to take to influence the direction of some of these developments. Hallam on its own can only do so much, so we place great reliance on collective action with our sister independent radio stations in Yorkshire and the North East. Through our trade association, the Association of Independent Radio Contractors, we are lobbying the IBA, government and various other bodies who have a controlling influence over the conditions under which we trade so that in meeting new competitors we are given an equal and fair opportunity to compete.
>
> Within the management team we tend to use 'scenarios' and contingency planning as an important way of thinking about how we would respond to many of these developments. Most of our contingencies will not be needed (we hope) but at least it raises people's awareness of the issues and gets us psychologically ready to respond quickly.

7.10 Leads and lags

One of the ways in which local radio stations managed to penetrate the advertising market was by offering advertisers a reduced lead-time than had been traditionally the case in other media particularly television. The Sales Manager commented on this as follows:

> One of the competitive advantages we hold over newspapers – and, in particular, television – is the speed with which clients can get advertise-

ments on air. We can produce and broadcast an advertisement within 45 minutes and, in some cases, advertisers can broadcast 'live'. The equivalent time for newspapers and television is three days and six weeks respectively.

The ability to maintain this competitive edge clearly required a plan to ensure that the company had sufficient capacity in all its resources to respond quickly. It also depended on the fact that very few advertisers, in reality, would need to take advantage of these short lead-times on a regular basis, but welcomed the opportunity to do so from time to time.

EXERCISE 7.9

1. What planning problems do you think the short lead time presents to Radio Hallam?
2. How would you overcome them? (Refer to Figure 5.2).
3. What differences would you find in a manufacturing company which would make this planning easier or more difficult?

7.11 Sequencing and scheduling

Sequencing and scheduling were extremely important issues in the business planning at Radio Hallam:

- In 1974 there was a whole series of tasks which had to be undertaken to ensure a successful launch, on time. The initial work in the formation of a radio station to serve Sheffield and its catchment area came from the two major media in the area; United Newspapers (the parent company of Sheffield newspapers) and Trident Television (the then parent company of Yorkshire Television). Both had appointed radio executives to handle the company's policies with regard to the incipient commercial radio forecast by the Government's White Paper of 1970 and subsequent Sound Broadcasting Act of 1972. The two companies decided to work closely in respect of their mutual interests in Sheffield and Rotherham, although in other areas they pursued their interests separately. The companies saw that a successful launch in the Sheffield area would require the following tasks:

    Formation of a consortium (company)
    Bidding for the IBA franchise

Market research (audience and advertisers)
Hiring executives, presenters and other staff
Finding premises
Purchasing and commissioning equipment
Drawing up plans for premises and equipment
Obtaining funds
Establishing regular advertisers
Establishing an audience
Financial feasibility plan
Investigating legal matters and IBA contract conditions
Assessing competitive bids for the franchise

EXERCISE 7.10

1. Draw a network analysis showing the sequence in which the above tasks should have been undertaken.
2. Why do some tasks precede others? (Refer to Figure 5.4).

● Day-to-day programmes were planned from a weekly *play-list* of records made up of top singles, new releases, LPs and 'oldies'. The format of any one programme was built up from the play-list in a predetermined sequence. For example, immediately following the news a top-ten record would be played, followed by a new release, etc. The tempo of the programme could be varied within this broad plan by the selection of specific records.

The scheduling of certain items, such as news bulletins, was critically important to the programme plan and other items (mainly music) had to be worked around these fixed items.

Equally important was the correct scheduling of customer advertisements. Since the cost of advertising was determined by the time-slot in the day it was essential that customer advertisements appeared within those time-slots. Scheduling also had to take account of the IBA limitation of 9 minutes per hour advertising and the desire not to disrupt programme continuity too much (programme quality). In some cases customers would require that their package of advertisements be properly **sequenced** – particularly when they had bought a mixture of both long-and short-time slots – they would pay a premium for this. The company had developed a computer programme for scheduling advertisements into programmes. This had been so successful that they had sold the 'system' to other radio stations.

EXERCISE 7.11

1. Take the role of a programme planner and build up a two-hour programme consisting of:
   - Current top-forty records (duration 2–4 minutes).
   - News bulletins on the hour (5 minutes).
   - Advertising 9 minutes per hour (16 × 15 seconds, 6 × 30 seconds, 8 × 45 seconds, 5 × 60 seconds).
   - Linking time (chat) 10 minutes per hour.
2. Explain your sequencing and scheduling decisions. (Refer to Figure 5.4.)

7.12 Motivating people

In 1978 Bill MacDonald, looked back over the first four years of operation of the company and commented as follows:

> In the early days people were very motivated by the excitement of being involved in something new and wanting to make it a success. When that success came it opened up a new challenge for me. How could I now keep people interested and involved once this original goal had been met? I was aware of the dangers of organisations like radio, television and newspapers where there can be a big cultural difference between the two sides of the business. In many newspapers the editor is God and the advertising side of the company is tolerated as a necessary evil. I am determined to avoid this in Hallam at all costs. I feel we are small enough for most people to see us as **one** business and not two. The real challenge is to provide people with a challenge – not to relive the early days of the company but to keep the best of the spirit which existed at that time.

As a new company Radio Hallam had been able to select people with the capabilities to undertake the jobs as they were seen at that time. Later the business-planning problem changed from one of finding the skills through **recruitment** to the need for **retraining** as new skills were needed.

Bill MacDonald commented on the general issue of managing the changes which new business plans inevitably brought:

> This is a fascinating part of any manager's job. Generally I think people are very suspicious of change and tend to fear the worst – particularly if they feel our current performance is good – as it is. In programming we also have the horror stories of listeners ringing in and complaining about

programme changes – they are quite conservative too. With the news-staff change can often be seen as questioning their professionalism. Last year when we wanted to change the format of the news slots there were one or two delicate discussions. In fact we ended up giving them an extra slot in the late afternoon – I expect you might call that a bit of healthy 'horse trading'. On the whole I feel that being a small organisation helps a great deal – there is less empire building and it is far easier for me to communicate the overall company angle behind any changes.

7.13 Rewards and incentives

Radio Hallam had some interesting factors to consider in deciding on its policies towards rewards and incentives:

- The big-name presenters would require to earn significantly greater money than the company would be prepared to pay for a staff-member whose job would be restricted to Radio Hallam work. Therefore the practice elsewhere in broadcasting of working as a freelance, and being allowed to work in any related (though not competitive) field gave the big-name presenter the opportunities he wanted, while giving Radio Hallam the obligation of paying only part of the presenters' expectations. Nearly all Hallam presenters were therefore self-employed on individually-negotiated contracts.
- Despite the difficulties facing new presenters there was no shortage of people applying for the job. Prior to launch there were 600 applications from prospective presenters. One of the reasons for this was the glamour of the job and also presenters were usually in demand for night-club appearances, opening shops, etc.
- The fact that incentive payments are quite common in sales-related jobs but not in programming-type jobs. The sales team had a low basic salary but could earn commission based on both individual and group performance. In addition there were regular special incentives based on specific campaigns aimed at particular customer groups. These latter typically took the form of holiday vouchers, free restaurant meals, etc. Audrey Adams, the Sales Manager, commented on the company's incentives:

Although it is only my team who are commission-based it does **not** cause much friction within the company. Generally people accept that sales people tend to be paid this way. In addition I think it is fair to say that most Hallam employees know where the bread comes from. Certainly when we do particularly well everyone will join in the celebrations.

● When the company was founded provision was made for a profit-sharing scheme for employees. Indeed Bill MacDonald claimed that he would have been unhappy to take the job as Managing Director had this not been agreed. All staff with more than two years service were included in the scheme and payments were based on length of service and salary. A small group of employees met to advise the Managing Director on how available money should be distributed between individuals. Payments had varied from zero to 20 per cent of an individual's annual salary depending on the company performance in the year.

● The company also had a policy of employee share-holding despite some administrative difficulties in arranging the scheme. By 1985 more than thirty employees or ex-employees held shares in the company. Bill MacDonald believed this made identity with the company stronger, encouraged productivity and economy, while also allowing employees a direct say, through the Annual General Meeting, in the affairs of the company in a manner preferable to confrontation through union representation.

EXERCISE 7.12

1. How important are these rewards and incentives as part of the business plan?
2. Are they applicable to other types of organisation?

7.14 Control systems

Bill MacDonald explained his attitude towards control as part of making business plans successful:

> Let me first talk about our relationship with the IBA which has changed somewhat over the years. We now have the situation where we hold a franchise for eight years and we have our overall company performance formally monitored mid-term – for us that will next occur in 1989. However, we do report regularly to the IBA on the separate aspects of our business, programming, finance, engineering etc. Generally we are able to report in whatever may **we** feel best except in the financial area where information is required in a standard format. This arrangement seems to work well – although I gather that some stations are often required to supply additional information when their reporting is regarded as inadequate.

Internally we tend to work a mixture of formal and informal reporting. The key meeting for me is the weekly executive meeting where each senior manager reports on his/her section and takes questions from the others and myself. Each month a wider group meets – including the section managers. In turn I report to the board quarterly. However, as you would expect, many planning matters get worked out informally between individuals and in those circumstances the formal meetings may simply be used to give approval to new ventures or to share information more widely. I also have on-line access to the current state of sales through my computer terminal which I find absolutely invaluable. I am also able to do some of my own cash-flow projections using the spread-sheet packages.

EXERCISE 7.13

1. Given the attitude expressed above by the Managing Director what *reports* do you think he should receive:
   (a) each day;
   (b) each week;
   (c) each month.
2. How should he use these reports to ensure that the company remains successful?

7.15 Conclusions

In summarising some of the most important lessons about business planning it is useful to return to the issues raised in Chapter 1 as a reminder of the role that business planning plays within organisations (see Table 7.5):

- Planning is concerned with the **future** health of an organisation. However, it should be clear from the discussions that a careful reflection on the organisation's past performance and current circumstances will be an essential part of understanding how the company best prepares itself for the future. Often difficulties experienced in the past provide useful lessons for the future and there are many examples of this within business planning.
- Business planning is a major activity in **all** organisations irrespective of whether or not they have 'glossy books' called business plans. Indeed the majority of business planning is rarely committed to paper yet proves to be quite effective as the example of Radio Hallam would suggest.

TABLE 7.5   Some important lessons about business planning

1. Although planning is about the future, **past experience** can be a valuable guide
2. Business planning does not necessarily require the preparation of **glossy books** of plans
3. Business planning is not just the sum total of separate functional plans (production, marketing plans etc.)
4. **Many** different people are involved in business planning
5. Planning is necessary at different **levels** and these need to be properly co-ordinated
6. There are many different **approaches** to planning – the key is to choose an approach which fits the circumstances
7. Planning is **difficult** because of the wide variety of planning **tasks**. People need to be sensitive to the difficulty of planning
8. Planning is not an end in itself – it is a means to an end

- There are considerable dangers in assuming that an organisation's business planning can be regarded as the sum total of all the separate 'functional' planning (marketing, financial, etc.). It is very likely that these functional plans will be inconsistent with each other unless there is some **overall** view of how the various plans of the organisation should fit together. There have been many examples of such dangers within the book. Marketing departments trying to woo customers on the basis of quick delivery and a wide variety of products/services whilst simultaneously the production departments are attempting to minimise costs through longer runs requiring larger orders, less variety and longer lead-times.
- Although running a successful business involves many other activities besides business planning it is also true to say that **many** people within an organisation will be involved in planning in one form or another. Business planning is not the preserve of a few specialist planners. For example, at Radio Hallam the presenters use their experience and discretion in building up the final content of a programme **within an agreed framework**. Each presenter stamps his/her own style on the programme.
- Planning occurs at different **levels** within any organisation – creating many difficulties in ensuring that the day-to-day (operational) planning is actually consistent with the broader (strategic) direction in which the organisation is supposed to be moving. Of course, this is a two-way process – strategic plans must pay proper

attention to the realities of making plans work out in practice, whereas operational planning must not be so rigid and bureaucratic that it provides an insurmountable barrier to achieving any changes within the organisation. This latter problem is one of the greatest areas of difficulty in planning within large public-service organisations.

- There is no single 'correct' approach to business planning. It is clear that different organisations have a wide variety of approaches ranging from the highly formalised to the very-unstructured entrepreneurial approach. There are many factors which determine the way in which organisations approach business planning from the type of products and technology through to the personality of the dominant people in the company and the general culture of the organisation. Readers should not expect to find a planning system which could be transferred from one organisation to another but should seek to understand what planning approaches are most likely to prove successful within their own particular organisation's circumstances. This is a very pragmatic view of business planning which argues that it is better to approach planning in a way which people are likely to accept and be influenced by rather than use theoretically 'neat' planning methods which are neither comprehended nor accepted by other people within the organisation. The temptation to allow planning to become an 'ivory tower' activity is considerable but should be avoided at all costs.

  The practical implications of this view are often quite simple to implement. For example, the presentation of quantitative analyses in graphical rather than a mathematical/algebraic format has immense impact on the way in which planning is **understood** within an organisation.

- Business planning consists of many different tasks, which have formed the framework for this book. The real challenge of planning is making sure that these tasks are undertaken in a way which makes **sense as a whole**. Whereas in a book it is useful to discuss these various tasks separately in reality they are **not** separate. Indeed they are usually all being undertaken simultaneously as was seen in the case of Radio Hallam. This, of course, makes planning in real life very much more difficult than might be expected from reading a book on planning. This comment is meant to encourage readers to be sensitive to the very real difficulties of making planning work out in organisations. These difficulties are often underestimated by people working within one business function, such as finance, who may fail to see that what might make sense to them is not necessarily in the **overall** best interests of the organisation.

● The concluding thought in this book is that business planning should be a key part of all successful orgnisations but is **not the purpose** of those organisations. Business planning is not an end in itself but the means to an end – namely, the maintenance or improvement of an organisation's performance in whatever particular field they are involved.

Index